PLACE IN RETURN BOX to remove this checkout from your record.
TO AVOID FINES return on or before date due.
MAY BE RECALLED with earlier due date if requested.

DATE DUE	DATE DUE	DATE DUE
OCT 1 7 2005 0 5 0 4 0 7		JUL 01 7 9 1 2011
DEC 0 5 2005		
MAY 14 2006		
0 4 2 6 0 6		
APR 1 4 2007		
MAY 0 5 2008 8		
APR 2 2 2014		
0 4 2 2 1 4		
NOV 0 9 2015		

6/01 c:/CIRC/DateDue.p65-p.15

D1366835

Smashing Barriers

PLA⌐

⌐ckout from your record.
fore date d'
if

Smashing Barriers

Race and Sport in the New Millennium

Richard E. Lapchick

MADISON BOOKS
Lanham • New York • Oxford

This Madison Books paperback edition of Smashing Barriers *is an unabridged, retitled republication of* Five Minutes to Midnight: Race and Sport in the 1990s, *first published by Madison Books in 1991, and here updated with a new introduction and a new part 5. I is reprinted by arrangement with the author.*

Copyright © 1991 by Richard E. Lapchick
Updated edition copyright © 2001 by Richard E. Lapchick

All rights reserved.
No part of this book may be reproduced in any form or by any electronic or mechanical means, including information storage and retrieval systems, without written permission from the publisher, except by a reviewer who may quote passages in a review.

Published by Madison Books
4720 Boston Way
Lanham, Maryland 20706

12 Hid's Copse Road
Cumnor Hill, Oxford OX2 9JJ, England

Distributed by National Book Network

GV
706.32
. L36
2001
C. 2

Library of Congress Cataloging-in-Publication Data
Lapchick, Richard Edward.
    Smashing barriers : race and sport in the new millenium / Richard E. Lapchick.—
Updated ed.
      p. cm.
    Originally published under the title: Five minutes to midnight, c1991. With a new
introduction and new pt. 5.
    ISBN 1-56833-177-0 (pbk. :alk. paper)
      1. Discrimination in sports— United States— History. 2. United States— Race relations.
I. Lapchick, Richard Edward. Five minutes to midnight. II. Title.

GV706.32 .L36 2001
305.8'96073— dc21   2001031216

⊖™ *The paper used in this publication meets the minimum requirements of*
American National Standard for Information Sciences— Permanence of
Paper for Printed Library Materials, ANSI/NISO Z39.48–1992.
Manufactured in the United States of America.

I dedicate this book to two people.

The first is my mother, **Elizabeth Lapchick**, who instilled in me the values that have become so important in my life.

The second is **Winifred "Peggy" Pasnak**, my mother-in-law, who gave me the gift of my beautiful bride, Ann, and imbued her with all the values that have made her such a strong person.

Contents

Acknowledgments

It is with a profound sense of appreciation that I acknowledge the people who have been central to the publication of *Smashing Barriers*.

First, I have to express appreciation to my family, who gave me the time to complete this book, and in particular to my wife, Ann, who offered constructive criticism of various sections of the book.

I would like to thank Alyssa Theodore and Matt Loughran at Madison Books for their help in giving birth to the book. A special thanks goes to my executive assistant, Philomena Pirolo, for her tireless efforts and support.

Muhammad Ali made me so proud with his willingness to write the foreword for this book. Ali is one of the great heroes of my life. He has done so much to make this a better world and to have him as part of this project makes me feel especially proud.

I owe profound appreciation to the editors of *The Sports Business Journal* and *The Sporting News* for giving me the joy of writing for them and drawing on that work in *Smashing Barriers*.

I must also thank everyone associated with Northeastern University's Center for the Study of Sport in Society and the National Consortium for Academics and Sports. The people in both places make me think everyday about the issues that I have discussed in this book. Also appreciation to Irving Louis Horovitz and *Society Magazine* for their support with "The New Racial Stereotypes."

Finally, I would like to thank Robin Roberts and Donna Lopiano for their support of this book.

Foreword

This book gets to the heart of the matter, the spirit of sport.

For all that sports are and claim to be—entertaining, brawny, commercial, tough, competitive, fulfilling—they are still a catalyst for human interaction Whenever humans get together in mass situations, such as in teams, they divide or unite. Sports, more so than any other popular medium, have the ability to divide or unite based on ability, talent, skill, and even ethnicity.

Richard Lapchick, in chronicling his personal experiences within the sports world, has provided us with a rich and hopeful vision for the new millenium. He recalls past and current attitudes toward athletics, from New York to South Africa, and shows how discrimination and politics have configured racial barriers in sports.

We must reclaim, he say, the true spirit of sport, deconstructing these barriers and ensuring they will never rise again. By doing so, we can enjoy for once the actual design of sports: to rise, and flal, and rise again together, all cultures, all nations, all races.

Muhammad Ali

Introduction

My third book, *Broken Promises: Racism in American Sports,* appeared in 1984, thirty-seven years after Jackie Robinson broke the color barrier in professional baseball. Numerous black athletes were paid more than $100,000 per year to play baseball, basketball, and football. The majority of thoughtful, intelligent Americans believed that this was a sign of society's progress. Many young men and women, black and white alike, believed that sport was a great racial equalizer.

A virtually unknown man named Al Campanis shattered these illusions of equality through sport in April 1987 when he said on Ted Koppel's *Nightline* that blacks might not have "the necessities" to be head coaches or general managers. More than a decade later, Atlanta Braves pitcher John Rocker's verbal assault on virtually every racial and ethnic group reinforced the nation's shortcomings in a dramatic way. The sports press, which until then had rarely surfaced stories on racial problems in sport, was finally forced to take a penetrating look at how far American sport had to go.

At the beginning of the twenty-first century, the American public watches even more black athletes earn not $100,000 but literally millions of dollars each year. However, images of highly paid professional black athletes can be overshadowed by racist remarks, such as those of Campanis and Rocker, or segregated conditions such as those revealed by the 1990 Shoal Creek golf course controversy.

Tiger Woods was heavily criticized for speaking out against restrictive golf courses as part of his first commercial endorsement with NIKE. In spite of racist remarks and negative criticism, athletes of color such as Woods and Venus and Serena Williams continue to smash barriers to the participation of people of color in sport.

As part of a white, middle-class family with a sports celebrity for a father, I was lulled into a false sense of sport being the great equalizer. Born just before the Jackie Robinson era, I was so oblivious to the reality of inequality in sports that I was unconscious even of my own father's role as a quiet pioneer in bringing about racial change in American basketball. As the country's star pro center in the 1920s and 1930s, my father's Original Celtics team was among the first to play against the Rens, the nation's first great black team. During a thirty-year career as one of America's most successful coaches, he brought Nat "Sweetwater" Clifton to the New York Knick's in 1950 to help break the color barrier in the NBA. His actions earned him the epithet "nigger lover." Five decades later, I have also been called a "nigger lover" for my own efforts to end racism in sport.

This book is the story of what it was like to grow up with a famous father who cared about more than just basketball as a game, as well as my determination to continue my father's legacy, not as an athlete on the basketball court, but as an activist for racial equality in sports. I have remained involved in this struggle in spite of several life-threatening incidents that took place in 1978 and in 1981.

The first eleven chapters, taken from *Broken Promises* and *Five Minutes to Midnight,* retell my story, a story which remains relevant in these times of turbulent and traumatic racial relations. Chapters 12 to 14 from *Five Minutes to Midnight* examine the early days of blacks versus whites in sports as traced through the rivalry between the Celtics and the Rens. The powerful rivalry between the two teams reinforced for me the positive potential for playing with and against players from different racial groups. Writing those three chapters in *Five Minutes to Midnight* also reinforced my own limited experiences and made me believe that sport could really be a model for better human relations.

The last chapters are all new and show both how much and how little has changed since Jackie Robinson took that courageous first step. *Five Minutes to Midnight* is more optimistic. Perhaps my views were influenced by the lessons of the Celtics and the Rens or by the faithful and fearless smiles of Emily, our young daughter, who was then a toddler, as she learned about love. *Five Minutes to Midnight* brought hope that in the ensuing years since *Broken Promises* was published that sport had become more open for players of color. *Smashing Barriers* brings even more good news while carefully measuring America's distance from the final goal of racial equality. Sport may yet show every American a better way.

America has made many promises to its people that it has not fulfilled. The promise of racial equality in sports is one that has been broken time and time again. A decade ago, some commentators said that time was running out, that it was five minutes to midnight.

I saw the other side of midnight in 1978. It was an ugly place that I hope my children's children never see. After the Civil Rights marches of the 1960s, the 1970s lulled many Americans into thinking that racial violence was a thing of the past, yet I was attacked in 1978.. Throughout the 1990s the news media reported such attacks regularly. In 1999 alone, a gay man was crucified in Wyoming; twelve high-school students and a teacher were slaughtered on Hitler's birthday in Colorado; eleven African-Americans, Jews, and Asian-Americans were shot by a white segregationist in Chicago; and a neo-Nazi armed with a machine gun attacked a Jewish day care center in Los Angeles.

The rise of neo-Nazism as the ideological core of many hate groups today is a frightening reality. Each Memorial Day we celebrate those who gave up their lives for our nation. Nazism, with its torrent of hate and death, was once our great enemy. It was even denounced by the KKK and other American hate groups whose members fought inWorld War II. Now, neo-Nazism has become the central philosophical tenet of the white supremacist movement. The Internet, which brings somuch useful information, has become the nation's number onedistribution method for hate literature.

I work for a university, the supposed bastion of our democratic ideals. According to the Southern Poverty Law Center, there has been a horrible increase in hate crimes on college campuses. At the State University of New York Maritime College in the Bronx, twenty-one Arab students fled after a series of assaults and incidents of racial harassment. At Brown University in Rhode Island, a black senior was beaten by three white students who told her she was a "quota" who didn't belong. At the State University of New York at Binghamton, three students were charged in a racially motivated assault that left an Asian-American student with a fractured skull. One Harvard resident tutor quit after being subjected to homophobic vandalism. E-mail threats and slurs were sent to 30,000 students and faculty at Stanford University, along with others at many other schools.

In the fall of 1999, two pipe bombs went off in men's rooms at historically black Florida A&M University in Tallahassee, the first such incidents in years. After the first attack, an anonymous caller told a local television station that he wanted to "get rid of some of them niggers." After the second attack, a caller to the same station said that blacks "got no business having a college where there ain't nobody . . . smart enough to get a degree." A local white man was ultimately charged and convicted.

These were several of the estimated 250 reported hate crimes on campus in 1999. Experts agree that 250 is a fraction of the actual number since most incidents are not reported. Even so, campuses are the third most common venue for hate crimes. "Bias incidents"—events that do not rise to the level of prosecutable offenses but that may nevertheless poison the atmosphere at a college and lead to more serious trouble—are rampant on campuses. One academic journal, *The Review of Higher Education*, estimated recently that a total of 1 million bias incidents occur every year on American campuses.

What happened in Colorado, Wyoming, Los Angeles, and on the campuses of American colleges and universities, shook many people to their foundations. What these horrors do, however, is reinforce the message that I want to give the readers of *Smashing Barriers* through analysis of racial bias in sport. I hope to challenge readers to do their part in reshaping the racial history of our nation. Part five concludes with stories of the transformation of peoples' attitudes on race.

We should never doubt that we can make a difference. We may not change the world but if we change one heart, just think of what a ripple that may have throughout humanity. We have the power to bring change, to give hope. It is never too late. The more we communicate that value to our children, the quicker America will heal.

I originally wrote *Broken Promises* to ensure that my children would never have to live in fear. Eighteen years later, the entire nation seems to live in fear. We must smash the barriers in sports and in life once and for all.

**Part One
The Attack in Virginia**

Chapter 1

No Defense

―――――――――――――

" 'Nigger,' they carved 'nigger' on his stomach!" As I heard one of my students say this to his friends while pointing to me, I realized with horror that my life might never be the same again. Still dazed, I tried to reconstruct the night. Within a week I would have to try to reconstruct my life.

It was Valentine's Day, 1978. Early that day, I told my wife Sandy (we were divorced several years later) that I couldn't go out to dinner since I had to work late in my college office to prepare for the next day. There had been little time for dinners in recent years; the pace of our lives had accelerated too fast. My belief that I "had to work" usually prevailed.

We had both reached a stage where we felt comfortable with our individual lives. Sandy, who had retreated from a career as a commercial artist after achieving early success, was now re-emerging into the art world. I had somehow learned to balance my life as an academic teaching political science at Virginia Wesleyan College in Norfolk, Virginia, as an activist on civil rights and anti-apartheid issues, and as a father. Being a husband was getting less attention. So on this particular Valentine's Day, neither of us worried about missing time together.

Several of my students tried to persuade me to go to the basketball game at the college that night. It was hard to say no to them. This was partially because I would do almost anything to enrich the relationships I had with my students. However, on this night I especially wanted to prove to that small part of the world that cared about these things that I was not anti-sport. I was a critic of racism in sport, both in South Africa and in America, and I had heard myself accused of being anti-sport more frequently during the preceding weekend than ever before. How could I be anti-sport? How could the son of Joe Lapchick, a legendary figure in basketball, be anti-sport? When my father criticized basketball for not being integrated, did his contemporaries think he was anti-sport? That was a question I would reflect on frequently after this night.

But now it was my time to be judged. As National Chairperson of ACCESS (American Coordinating Committee for Equality in Sport and Society), I had been campaigning to end all sports contacts between the United States and teams from South Africa as long as sport and society there were segregated. I had spent two years writing a book on the subject, *The Politics of Race and International Sport: The Case of South Africa,* which was published in 1975, and had already been involved with the issue for eight years. However, at this time, there was a new intensity over this issue in the United States.

The tone of South Africa's press coverage in America and Europe had significantly changed. Images of the slaughter of children in Soweto in June 1976 were still fresh. The South African police were trying to explain how Steve Biko, the founder of the Black Consciousness Movement and one of the most important contemporary black men in the country, had died in their custody as a result of a crushed skull in September 1977. The Western press could hardly ignore the October 1977 bannings of most of the other important voices of dissent in that country. News items were beginning to appear about the scandal in the Ministry of Information—a scandal that would eventually bring down Minister of Information Connie Mulder and Prime Minister Vorster with him when it was revealed that huge sums of money were spent to buy favorable foreign opinion.

With its image tarnished, South Africa felt it was even more crucial to successfully stage its Davis Cup tennis match with the United States. Having an integrated team play the matches at

Vanderbilt University in Nashville, Tennessee, before thousands of spectators and possibly millions of television viewers might do for South Africa what a ping-pong match did for U.S.–China relations in 1972. If investment dollars, bank loans, and trade, which had been reduced due to anti-apartheid criticism, were to resume on a grand scale, the South African government knew it would have to win this battle in its propaganda war.

Therefore, my visit to Nashville from the tenth through the thirteenth of February was not warmly welcomed by either South Africa or its supporters in the United States. The earlier announcement that the National Association for the Advancement of Colored People (NAACP) would make the Davis Cup a focus of its efforts guaranteed the high level of attention we wanted on what apartheid meant for black South Africans. My visit generated a great deal of attention in Nashville as to why we wanted the matches canceled.

The Nashville sports media wanted to raise the accusation that I was anti-sport. However, the news media and the people of Nashville concentrated on what apartheid was about and the oppression it created in South Africa. By the time I spoke at Vanderbilt on October 13, I could feel the momentum shifting. This was confirmed when the news came, during my speech, that the financial backers of the tournament had pulled out. When I flew home to Norfolk that night, I sensed that, possibly for the first time in all my years as an activist in the 1960s and 1970s, I had made a real contribution. Although I was tempted to go to the basketball game that night, I told my students that I needed to work and couldn't go out.

My office was situated on a balcony that circled the main reading room of Wesleyan's library. At about 9:30 P.M. there was a commotion in the library, which had begun to temporarily fill up with students after the game. When I looked out I saw Lambuth Clarke, the president of the college. I liked Lambuth and had always gone out of my way to greet him. However, I gave him a special greeting that night because I wanted him to know I was working late in my office. Although I had no classes to teach on Friday and Monday, I felt slightly guilty that I had been in Nashville and not on campus. We exchanged pleasantries and I went back to my office to work.

At approximately 10:25 P.M. I went to the water fountain for a drink. The two librarians still there were about to leave. I told them I would be working late and said good night. I returned to my office and began typing a quiz that I would give to my urban studies class the next day.

There was a knock at my door at 10:45 P.M. I assumed it was campus security police routinely checking the library.

Although I could not clearly see who or what stood outside when I opened the door, my life began to change with one rough shove across the room. My shoulder was slightly cut as I landed on one of the railroad spikes that comprised a steel sculpture. As I stared up at the two men attacking me I realized that they were both wearing stocking masks.

I was terrified and confused all at once. Was this a robbery? If so, why would they choose a college professor in his office? Were these Cuban exiles coming after me because of favorable remarks my students and I had made after returning from two weeks in Cuba in January? I knew that the Cuban exile community of Norfolk was extremely upset, but could they be doing this to me now?

My confusion grew along with my fear as they tied me up in my chair and stuffed one of my thick winter gloves into my mouth. I felt like I was gagging and losing my breath. The first man, speaking without an accent, said, "Will you continue doing what you have been doing now?" Had my trip to Nashville provoked this?

The second man, also speaking without an accent, said, "Nigger–lover, Nigger–lover." The first man then said, "You know you have no business in South Africa." The confusion about why they were there was over.

All the time the attackers were saying these things, they used the top two drawers of my file cabinet as battering rams on my chest and face. I did not believe they were trying to kill me; they could have been hitting me with much greater force. Also, they were turning my head from side to side so the blows never hit me squarely and were cushioned by the glove in my mouth. No, it was to frighten me. And they succeeded.

They untied me and one held me up with a hammerlock so I could not move. The hooded hunters were both behind me as I faced the file cabinet. Unable to see them, I listened carefully to their voices. Were they Klansmen? South Africans? All they said were the three phrases, repeated as if they had been rehearsed. They were definitely American although I could not tell where they came from in the United States. Of course, I later realized that if South Africa was behind the attack, the last thing they would do was send nationals with South African accents.

After the file cabinet beating was finished, I could examine at least the one man who was not holding me. Beyond the impenetrable stocking, I could tell he was white, about six feet tall, and well built. He reached for the steel sculpture.

The spikes were set in a four-by-four-inch wooden base. The attacker wielded it like a bludgeon, working his way up the backs of my legs to my back and my arms while the man holding me asked, "Will you continue doing what you have been doing now?" His friend said, "Nigger–lover, nigger–lover," and then he repeated, "You know you have no business in South Africa." It seemed so orchestrated, so set, but their fury was genuine. He pummeled my stomach; the ferocity of the bludgeoning made me wonder if they were still only trying to scare me. I passed out as the pain and horror became too much.

When I came to, both men were kneeling over me. My shirt had been ripped open and one of the men was using what appeared to be my office scissors on my stomach. I was scared, not knowing what they were going to do. The pain was intense; my terror grew.

I thought I heard a noise from the library. The men pulled me up as if they had also heard something. The one who had been holding me said, "Let's get out of here." That was the only deviation from their script. He was slightly taller with broader shoulders than his partner. He was also white. He opened my door and was gone. The other pushed me to the floor and, as a farewell gesture, knocked a bookcase on top of me. It hit me in the head and I passed out again.

When I regained consciousness I was in great pain and my head was ringing. The office was dark and quiet. The door was closed. I had only one thought—to get out of there. I could not stand and had to use whatever I could to prop myself up. I half-staggered, half-crawled along the balcony of the library to the stairs, where I began to make my way down until I lost control and rolled down the last eight or ten steps.

Finally I made it to the library desk, where I reached for the phone. I noticed the clock on the wall—it was 11:40 P.M. What seemed like an eternity of torture had begun and ended within an hour. I dialed campus security but, amazingly, there was no answer. I called Sandy.

I told her what had happened but that I was not badly hurt, and asked her to call the police and rescue squad. It was obvious that she was worried, but at the same time she was remarkably calm. When we were finished I called campus security again—this time they responded and said they would be right there.

I fell back and rested on the stacks of newspapers that lined the inside of the library desk. It seemed forever before anyone came. At first I was afraid that the attackers were still somewhere in the building. Worse yet, I worried that they or their associates might go to my home. Our house was always open to students and people from the community, even at late hours. It was too vulnerable.

I thought of my mother, who was living in an apartment that adjoined the house. She had been through this before with my father, who had paid an emotional price for his commitment to racial equality in sport, and with my sister Barbara's second husband, who had been a political prisoner in Uganda.

At that point two members of the campus security force entered the library. I did not have the strength to yell to them and they seemed to walk around endlessly. Finally, the older man found me. He ordered his assistant, a young black man, to go up to check the balcony. I don't remember him saying anything to me as he scurried around the library desk. I guess he wanted to make sure that no one was around; maybe he was embarrassed that this could have happened while he was on duty.

"It's a wreck up here," the black guard shouted, but the older man seemed to ignore him. The library suddenly came alive with men from the rescue squad and with students. As I was being examined by the rescue squad, Mike Mizell, a student whom I did not know well at that time, took a long look at my abdomen, which had been exposed during the examination. Although I was quite dazed, I will always remember the expression on his face, which changed from simple concern to horror. He got up, walked over to his friends, and said, " 'Nigger,' they carved 'nigger' on his stomach!" I had forgotten about the scissors but suddenly realized that this was what the attackers must have done with them.

"Nigger–lover, nigger–lover" began to ring through my head. Images of my children flashed in my mind. Chamy, a soft three-year-old with a golden Afro, would be sound asleep and was surely too young to be affected. Joey, an intense, high-energy five-year-old, might not be able to escape being traumatized by the repercussions of the attack. Only one week before, he had come to me in my study and asked, "Daddy, are you a 'nigger–lover'?" I was stunned until I recalled my own experience when I was his age.

My father, as coach of the New York Knickerbockers, had just integrated the team by signing Nat "Sweetwater" Clifton, who had been playing for the Harlem Globetrotters. We lived in Yonkers in an old three-story house. Like other children, I loved to answer the phone. I had picked up the phone upstairs when my father picked it up on the first floor; it was one of a number of "nigger–lover, nigger–lover" calls. At five, I didn't know what a "nigger" was, but it certainly sounded wrong to love one. The callers obviously hated my father. I could not understand this because to me he was such a sweet, gentle man—the center of my universe. Why did he love a "nigger" if it was such a bad thing to do? It hurt to hold it in, but it was half a lifetime before I had the courage to ask him.

I had asked Joey, "What do you think a 'nigger–lover' is?" He replied, "I don't know. But some mean man on the phone just told me that you were one." I was enraged that people would still play on the minds of children to get to their parents. I didn't want Joey to carry images of doubt about his father around with him as I had done, so I tried to explain to him what I was doing that would provoke racists to call me "nigger–lover." Why did a five-year-old have to understand such ugly things? He would have to know soon enough.

I was brought to Bayside Hospital in Virginia Beach and underwent a number of tests. The doctor in the emergency room was Dr. Martin Lorenz. He was very sympathetic to my injuries and became even more so after he heard about the attack.

Sandy arrived and I regained a sense of reality when she said, "Did you know that they carved 'nigger' in your stomach?" When I said I did, she responded, "Did you know they misspelled it: *n-i-g-e-r*?" We both laughed. The injuries didn't seem so bad now and I hoped I could go home. I wanted to teach a class the next day. After the tests were over, Lambuth Clarke, the president, Bill Wilson, the dean, and Alan Stowers, the college information officer, came into the emergency room. Lambuth said, "They misspelled 'nigger.' At least we know it wasn't one of our students." I told him it was obvious he hadn't read any student papers recently.

Sandy told me that Dennis Brutus, one of the founders of the movement to end racism in sports in South Africa in the 1950s and still one of the leading voices in exile, had been trying to reach me. Two police detectives entered the emergency room and began questioning me. Sandy excused herself to call Dennis and tell him what had happened. I knew he would empathize; he had been banned, imprisoned, and shot in the stomach by police for his work in South Africa. I thought that at least here the police would be on my side and would try to help.

They were pleasant enough and my trusting nature did not lead me to read anything into their questions at the time. I recounted what had happened. They told me they knew nothing of my "political" background and asked a great many questions about it, about my trip to Nashville, about my local involvement with race relations and migrant workers, and about my recent trip to Cuba. At the time, all their questions seemed directed at finding out who might have attacked me. Later, I began to wonder.

Dr. Lorenz returned to tell me that there was evidence of kidney damage since they had found blood in my urine. I also had a concussion and was forced to stay in the hospital for other tests. I began to realize there may have been more damage than I had thought.

One of the detectives stepped out at this point while the other remained to ask me to write out a description of the attack. The one who left approached Sandy and said, "When we heard who he was, we expected to find a screaming, shouting radical. We were surprised to see that your husband is so soft-spoken and gentle." She laughed and took it as a compliment, but it clearly indicated the attitude of the police toward political activists.

The officer returned to the emergency room as I was finishing my written account of the attack. I could not understand why they wanted a written statement from me since I was exhausted at that point and had already given a detailed oral account.

I was told, "We don't want this to get into the newspapers. Do not talk to the press under any circumstances." I was surprised at this request. I said, "It's hard for me to imagine how you could keep this quiet even if you wanted to. And why would you want to keep it out of the papers?" I was informed that "We don't want to spoil our chances of catching these men." "If they know what we are doing it would be more difficult," one of the policemen explained. I said I would try to go along with their wishes but considering the national and international implications of the attack, it would be almost impossible.

I was then told, "Okay, if the story does break don't, under any circumstances, say they used scissors, or refer to the statue or the misspelled 'nigger.' We must keep these clues to ourselves." This made some sense and I agreed.

"I just called Dennis Brutus and told him all of those details," Sandy interrupted. She was asked by the detectives to call him back and tell him not to say anything.

It was now 4:00 A.M. Just as the police were about to leave, a hospital orderly came in and asked Sandy to take my clothes home. "Don't you want the clothes for evidence?" Sandy asked the police. Much to our astonishment, they did not.

When Sandy finally reached Dennis at 6:00 A.M. he had already informed the protest organizers in Nashville. Sandy immediately called Yolanda Huet-Vaughn, a local organizer in Nashville, only to be told that they had already issued a statement to the *Nashville Banner* condemning the attack. Sandy asked her to call the paper and ask that they not mention that "nigger" was misspelled. Yolanda said she would try. Like so many other seemingly small details, this turned out to be important in the weeks to come.

For now I only wondered if the police would catch the attackers. I was still in a state of shock and could not think about the meaning of their behavior: the lengthy questions about my involvements, their surprise at my demeanor, the request for a written account of the attack at such a late hour, the plea to keep the story out of the press, the lack of interest in the clothes I was wearing. I didn't add these things up at the time. All I could think about was getting my attackers off the streets so I could be safe, so my family could be safe.

By the time I was left alone it was about 5:00 A.M. Exhausted, I finally dozed off. An efficient nurse woke me with the stark reality of an enema slightly after 6:00 A.M.

I called Sandy to tell her I was tired but okay and to find out what had happened when she called Dennis. Joey and Chamy were still asleep and unaware of what had gone on that night. The same was true of my mother.

The phone rang soon after I hung up. It was a Nashville radio station. I was amazed that the hospital switchboard had let the call through at that hour.

"Dr. Lapchick, all of Nashville is appalled to learn of this attack on you," the interviewer said. "You are being called a hero by your admirers here." I told her I was no hero and that I had merely followed my conscience. The Paul Robesons, the Malcolm Xs, and the Martin Luther Kings were heroes. They had been long-distance runners whose steel wills and compassionate hearts had been constantly tested by society.

This led to the inevitable question: "Will you continue your work now that this happened to you?" Although it was the obvious question, it stunned me. While she meant it sympathetically, it brought to mind the vision of the hooded hunters eight hours before. I lost control and began to cry. I was not sure whether the interviewer heard me. "How does your family feel about this?" she asked. "Do they want you to continue?"

I remembered my terror as a child when I would fantasize that those anonymous callers would hurt my father. I wanted to protect him. Now my own son would not only fantasize such fears but would have to cope with the reality of the attack.

What did it all mean? Was it worth it? Had the integration in American sports that took place in the 1950s, 1960s, and 1970s really made life any better for all but the minute fraction of blacks who had made it to the professional ranks? If my work, along with that of others in the movement, did result in the integration of all sports in South Africa, would it really change the lives of people there? Would it lead to the eradication of the heinous apartheid system? Do sports serve as a vanguard for change in our culture? Would I continue now? Who should be asking me this? Certainly not the attackers or the press. I was quite shaken now—more so than at any time since the knock on my door.

I replied, "Of course I'll continue. This has only strengthened my resolve to remain in the struggle. It proves that our efforts have been successful enough to provoke an attempt to destroy us. I'll go back to Nashville next week as planned." While I knew I would do all of this, I also knew I would have to ask myself all the hard questions I had thought about that morning. I knew I would have to confront my values. I would have to come face to face with all the assumptions I had made while growing up, with all that my father had taught me, and finally with what I had learned the night before.

Chapter 2

Offensive Attack

The scabs from the carving of "*n-i-g-e-r*" on my abdomen began to come off within a few days after the attack. But the physical scars were there, as were the mental ones that kept me awake at night. Calls of "nigger–lover, nigger–lover" played over and over in my dreams and wrenched me out of bed. First, my father with the Knicks; now me with South Africa. I knew I had to go back to Nashville to continue the fight over the Davis Cup. It was as reassuring to receive support from people all around the world as it was to hear from friends around the country. I was told that the attack had resulted in growing support for canceling the matches. That helped ease the pain. The strategy of the attackers was backfiring.

Trying to educate the American people about the reality of apartheid in South Africa had increasingly become my life's work and I was sure that our successes had led to the attack. Sport had become the vehicle for the message. But it is a reasonable question to ask why, with all the racism rampant in America and even in sport in America, I chose to work on the South African sports issue.

Part of the answer is fate. My meeting with Dennis Brutus while writing my doctoral dissertation on the subject and the publication of my book led me to confront the enormity of the oppression in South Africa and the role played by the United States in propping up the apartheid regime.

Part of the answer is analytical. I realized that many of the same institutional forces perpetuating racism in America were operating in South Africa. The same corporations that grow rich from the pool of cheap, unskilled, largely black labor in the United States, grow even richer from their operations in South Africa. American corporate exploitation of South African laborers, who work for extremely low wages, makes the position of black American laborers even more tenuous as they become increasingly expendable.

In the process, American dollars, through investments and loans, have helped South Africa remain "stable." "Stable" in South Africa means two things. First, that economic dislocations do not become too severe. Second, that part of the nation's wealth can be diverted to build its aggressive military machine, which in turn attacks its black neighbors to destabilize them.

With only 13 percent of its population white, and being surrounded by independent black African countries free from minority rule, the future of South Africa is clear. The forces of history dictate that it is not a question of whether black South Africans will be free. The question is when and how.

The situation inside South Africa had come under intense scrutiny by the American press after more than six hundred people were killed by the police in Soweto in June 1976. Most of those killed were schoolchildren. The murder of Black Consciousness leader Steve Biko in September 1977, followed by a series of bannings of remaining opposition figures in October, left South Africa's image badly tarnished as the scheduled Davis Cup tennis matches approached. Even the spending of $72 million for propaganda in the previous four years could not overcome the negative publicity. The Davis Cup was a potential propaganda coup desperately needed by the apartheid regime.

But the time was not right for South Africa. Nashville, Tennessee, the scheduled site of the Davis Cup, had many college campuses. And the campuses nationwide seemed to be coming alive on the anti-apartheid issue. The media was predicting—inaccurately as it turned out—that the protest against apartheid would rival that against American involvement in Vietnam. It was in this context that I had gone to Nashville on February 10.

The Davis Cup matches, in particular, and tennis in general, were the only areas left where South Africans were partially welcome. Successfully staged, the Davis Cup could reopen the flow of investments and loans. Better still, it could soften the image of apartheid and put a damper on the growing anti-apartheid movement in America. There was a great deal at stake for the Pretoria regime.

However, anti-apartheid groups in the United States were well aware of this and prepared a counteroffensive. Franklin Williams, who was president of the Phelps-Stokes Fund and the former U.S. ambassador to Ghana, took the lead with the civil rights groups. He organized the Coalition for Human Rights in South Africa, which included the NAACP and the Urban League. Franklin and I had spoken several times shortly after South Africa had defeated Colombia in Johannesburg in December 1977, "earning" itself a trip to Nashville. We exchanged ideas and materials and Franklin agreed to have the Coalition join ACCESS, the group of which I was chair, to plan the strategy to protest the matches. We both felt that the participation of the NAACP would assure a large demonstration in Nashville.

The creation of the Coalition was a major development. The traditional civil rights groups had historically been less involved in the anti-apartheid movement than predominantly white groups. Their priorities were, justifiably, at home where racism was on the rise. But Soweto, Biko's death, and the bannings helped make the connections. Black unemployment in the United States was steadily increasing as corporate dollars went to places like South Africa to exploit black labor there. The same banks that were "redlining" predominantly black and minority neighborhoods by denying them loans were making loans to South Africa. The same conservative politicians that opposed busing and the extension of the Voting Rights Act were supporting legislation that favored white minority regimes in Rhodesia (now Zimbabwe) and South Africa. The same men who fought as mercenaries were Klansmen with expert paramilitary training.

ACCESS had the information on the issue and kept it before

the public whenever sports contacts with South Africa came up. We were a coalition of thirty national civil rights, religious, political, and sports groups formed in 1976 to oppose sports contacts with South Africa until apartheid was eliminated.

Our main focus had been on tennis since it was the only remaining team sport in which South Africa competed for the world championship. The U.S. Tennis Association (USTA) had long been a supporter of South Africa's membership in the International Lawn Tennis Federation (ILTF), the tennis world's governing body. But South Africa was becoming more and more of a problem. Many countries refused to compete with them in the Davis Cup (men's) and Federation Cup (women's) championships. South Africa had won the Davis Cup in 1974 when India had refused to play against them in the championship round. As European, especially Eastern European, countries withdrew, the event became more of a farce.

For this reason South Africa was moved from the European to the North American Zone to compete. Most teams in this zone also withdrew except Colombia and the United States. The government of Colombia refused to allow the opening round with South Africa to be played in Bogota so it was moved to Johannesburg.

Thus, the confrontation was set up. We all felt that Vanderbilt University, under the leadership of its chancellor, Alexander Heard, would be the most likely to agree to cancel the matches. We were unfamiliar with the NLT Corporation, which agreed to back the event financially. We had been meeting with the USTA for two years. It had already announced it would press for South Africa's expulsion in 1979, but our concern was 1978. Therefore, ACCESS joined local Nashville groups in putting maximum pressure on Chancellor Heard. He agreed to meet me at the university.

I began the trip that would turn my life inside out on Friday, February 10, arriving in Nashville in the morning. The issue was catching fire and the exposure I received that weekend was amazing. I spoke on four university campuses, including Fisk and Tennessee State, the two major black schools. I appeared on two television shows, and did lengthy interviews with the *Nashville*

Banner and the *Tennessean*. We held press conferences on Friday, Saturday, and Monday. All three received top news coverage. I spoke at a black church on Sunday morning. We met with local organizers to plan strategy several times.

The only disappointment of the weekend was the meeting with Chancellor Heard and Vanderbilt President Emmett Fields. It was obvious that they were not going to change their decision to allow the matches to take place. On the one hand they said sports and politics don't mix; on the other they said that this was an "open forum" or free speech issue. I had been told by Vanderbilt's black students that the university's liberal reputation was a false one. My meeting with Heard and Fields accomplished nothing.

Other than this, everything else felt positive during these four days. You could feel the momentum of the city shifting toward cancellation of the matches. Local organizers had set up an excellent itinerary to maximize the impact of my stay.

On arriving Friday, I perceived the nature of the debate. Opponents of the matches felt that "South Africa is an evil country and we shouldn't play tennis with them," without having a deep knowledge of what apartheid meant on a daily basis for black South Africans. Proponents felt that "Tennis is a wonderful sport so let's see good competition and keep politics out of it." This was an issue I knew very well. The combination of being able to bring the information to Nashville, coming from a famous and respected sports background, and having the academic credentials enabled me to effectively deliver my message that weekend.

South Africa saw the momentum shifting and tried to change it by naming Peter Lamb to its Davis Cup team. Lamb was a "colored" (mixed ancestry) South African who was a student at Vanderbilt. He was a good player, but at eighteen was hardly of Davis Cup caliber. Announced on Sunday, February 12, the decision backfired immediately as the press perceived it as tokenism on South Africa's part. I knew that Lamb would soon find himself in an agonizing position—reviled by black Americans and by black South Africans for being unwittingly used by South Africa.

The element that I didn't recognize at the time was how much white South Africans resented my whiteness. I was later told that it was one thing to have a Franklin Williams or Benjamin Hooks do anti-apartheid work. It was, after all, blacks who bore the brunt of the oppression. More hated and less understood were whites like George Houser, then the executive director of the American Committee on Africa, or me. The same was true for white racists in America. It was "nigger–lover" time all over again.

By Monday afternoon, as I was about to address students at Vanderbilt, I knew that a great deal had been accomplished. There was an air of excitement, of anticipation. All three local television stations were there. One technician had a remote system back to the studio. Just as I was about to begin my speech, he told me that the NLT Corporation had announced that it had withdrawn its financial support for the Davis Cup.

I relayed the decision. The hundreds of students and faculty in the audience burst into a sustained applause. They were on their feet cheering several minutes. I told them, "The victory is yours. It is only the first." We were on our way to cancellation.

As I began the speech, the NLT decision made even the "Your father is a nigger–lover" call to Joey the week before seem slightly less painful. I told the audience about the incident. Usually a self-assured speaker, my eyes welled up with tears. I had to pause and drink some water. I had never said anything so deeply personal in a speech before. I caught my breath and went on with the speech. It was more passionate, more alive than the others that weekend.

I was feeling euphoric as I was rushed to the airport. We had the South Africans on the run. A Piedmont Airlines attendant at the gate said, "Well, Doctor, I guess there won't be tennis in March."

Sleep did not come easily that night after I got home.

I left at 7:45 A.M. for my 8:30 class on Tuesday. I had three one-and-a-half-hour classes on Tuesdays and Thursdays and usually was fatigued by the end of the day. But on this day I was flying, for it was the day after the NLT Corporation pulled out.

The only damper on the day was the word that Norfolk's

Cuban exile community was extremely upset about my "biased" reporting of what I had seen with my students in January. Peter Galuszka, a reporter from Norfolk's *Virginian Pilot*, was writing both sides of the story and called me for information. We went out for an hour or so to have a sandwich before I returned to my office to continue catching up on class work. I respected Peter as a journalist and watched how he tried to study the Cuban issue from all sides. Moreover, I liked him as a person and felt a friendship developing.

I opened up to him that night and told him about the call to Joey and about a series of calls I had received late in 1977. They began after a feature story on my anti-apartheid work appeared in a regional magazine.

I was called three times by the same person. At first I was told I had three weeks to live, followed by the tapping of a metal object—presumably a gun—on the phone. Exactly one week later the caller said I had two weeks to live. He again tapped the object. Another week had passed when the message that I had only a week left came through. The tapping was harder and louder. I slammed down the receiver, realizing that this could be serious.

I told Peter that I had gone to Bernard Barrow, a neighbor and friend. Barrow was a member of the Virginia House of Delegates. I had totally trusted his judgment when he told me to hold off calling the police until I returned from a one-week lecture trip. When I told Peter that the series of calls had stopped, I could see relief in his face. Yes, we could easily be good friends. As I ate the sandwich I could never have imagined the emotional wringer that Peter and I were about to be thrown into together.

Three hours after I left him, the attack began, lasting less than one hour. As it turned out, it only set the stage for the ensuing nightmare.

Part Two
The Aftermath of the Attack

Chapter 3

Riding Momentum

There was a sense of total unreality for a minute or two after I was awakened by the nurse. I could see I was in the hospital room. There was a nurse and a bed; I was in an antiseptic, nondescript room. Yes, it was a hospital.

Slightly dazed, I assumed I must be a visitor. After all, I had not been hospitalized in the twenty-five years since my brief bout with polio. There were remnants of my jock mentality left. A jock is invulnerable. My body was now a highly developed, muscular one hundred seventy pounds after years of consistent workouts three days a week at a gym.

My mind swirled. I thought of my three most recent visits to the hospital. I had come to watch and assist in the births of Joey and Chamy. I had come moments after the death of my father. The nurse did, at least, shake me back to reality. It was I who was in the hospital.

I thought of both ends of my family's life-cycle—Joey and Chamy, and my mother. I thought of last night—of masked men and of the police.

My body literally shook as "nigger–lover" rang through my head. But the image was of Joey asking me if I was a "nigger–lover" and not of the hooded hunters of the previous night. Were they the ones who had called Joey? Who had called me?

I called home. Everyone else at home was asleep. Sandy and I talked briefly about last night, about Dennis Brutus, and about the Nashville press release condemning the attack. Since a press release would obviously bring out the story, I asked her to call friends to tell them I was fine. Included in the long list was Peter Galuszka, the reporter from the *Virginian Pilot* whom I had been with shortly before the attack.

A few minutes later that Nashville radio station phoned and the circus began. Peter Loomis of the *Ledger Star,* Norfolk's afternoon newspaper, called to request an interview. He came by and I went over some details of the attack, deleting the parts the police asked me to leave out. Then I told him and he wrote that I was "beaten with a blunt instrument until he [I] lost consciousness." He reported that "nigger" (not "*n-i-g-e-r*") had been carved into my stomach "with a sharp instrument" and not with my scissors. He also wrote that I had cuts on my face, chest, and stomach. All he saw, of course, was my face. I wondered if deliberately withholding such details could really help the police to apprehend the men who had beat me. I wondered if the detectives were on the case. I realized they were probably asleep after their own long night.

Loomis was followed by Peter Galuszka. His was a welcome face, a face that told of his concern for me. We joked for a while, and then he told me he had been assigned to write the story for the *Pilot*. We talked about the details. He was puzzled when I repeated blunt object, sharp instrument, and "nigger." Peter assured me that the specific details were in the wire services stories already. He knew it was a steel sculpture, scissors, and "*n-i-g-e-r*." I abruptly realized that the Nashville people must have been unable to change their press release.

So I told him the whole story of the attack. By the end of the day I had told and retold the story more than a dozen times. The three local television stations sent crews. The networks, both television and radio, did phone interviews as did the wire services and the Nashville papers. Over and over I said I would go back to Nashville, that "As long as I'm able to get out of bed, I'm going to intensify my activities. This has strengthened my resolve." However, seeing the fear in my mother's face that afternoon when she came to visit made me question my bravado, sincere though it was.

I decided not to tell the children what had happened. When Joey called, I told him I was sick. He said that he had heard that "Bank robbers got you and cut out your heart and put it in your stomach." I was very upset, more so because I had no time to think. When I wasn't being interviewed I was being examined. Could I really go back to Nashville? Should I take the same risks? Time, I needed time to think.

A Sri Lankan physician, Dr. D. C. Amarasinghe, entered my room and announced that he would be in charge of my case. He gave me a thorough exam and ordered a battery of tests and X-rays. When he began to examine me for a hernia I protested, saying that I was sure there wasn't one since no one had hit me in that area.

Dr. Amarasinghe patiently explained that such a beating on the abdominal wall could easily cause one. Sure enough, when he said "cough" the bulge popped out. I was impressed by his competence and professionalism but distressed when I learned that I would eventually need surgery. The next day he told me that a liver scan showed that there were indications of minor damage to that organ. Dr. Lorenz had told me of blood in the urine indicating kidney damage the night before.

Wednesday afternoon was filled with friends. My adrenalin was pumping. Homicide Sergeant William Hayden, who was heading up the investigation, came by to talk. I could tell he was frustrated by having so many people going in and out of the room. When Hayden asked if he could come to my house when I got home to talk without interruptions, I agreed.

Then he asked if he could send the police doctor to examine me "to make sure you are okay." He had been talking about the massive press coverage the case was receiving and I assumed that he simply wanted another doctor to examine me to be sure I wasn't more seriously injured. I even thought that it was possible that he was concerned that Dr. Amarasinghe was not white and, therefore, somehow less qualified to provide adequate care. I had no objection to being examined again and agreed. I was, however, surprised that Hayden had not talked to either Dr. Lorenz or Dr.

Amarasinghe. I had no idea how significant all of this would become in the next few days.

Howard Cosell sent a film crew from New York to do a segment for ABC's *Good Morning America*. They arrived late in the afternoon. Much to my amazement, the hospital arranged at that moment for a series of lab tests that lasted an hour. It seemed to create a certain amount of tension among the crew. (I wondered if the black skin of some crew members and the fast pace of the "Yankees" prompted the hospital to insist on the tests at that moment.)

The interviewer was much more intense and insistent than the seemingly more sensitive local reporters. He said he wanted to film the scars on my stomach. I thought he was kidding but he was very serious. I told him I thought this might upset the police so I called Hayden, but he was out. The reporter assured me he would talk to the police before using it. I became really uncomfortable when they filmed the scars of "*n-i-g-e-r*"—it seemed too private.

It turned out that Bob Lipsyte, then a columnist for the *New York Post,* had called Cosell about doing the interview. Bob and I had a long conversation earlier in the day. I had respected him as a writer ever since he wrote the "Sports of the Times" column for *The New York Times.* One of the nicest things that happened to me was that I had become close friends with Bob. He was the most honest and forthright person I knew. His sense of humor was devastating. He began the call with "You'll do anything to publicize the cause." Bob and I both assume phone tapping is a widespread practice; we later wondered if his joke had given the police an idea.

One who had many insights was Mike Heaney. Mike was a graduate of Virginia Wesleyan who had joined the Norfolk police and was quickly moving up in the ranks. He came to visit me that evening because, he said, he was upset about the attack. But he was even more upset about the attitude of some of the local police. I had gathered from my conversation with Sergeant Hayden that the police were bothered by the media coverage. I asked Mike if that was it. No, what disturbed him was that some police were saying "he got what he deserved." I was so stunned that I asked him to repeat it. He did, adding that many policemen generally believed that anyone working for black rights deserved to be beaten up.

I remembered the first time I met Mike. He enrolled in the first class I taught on Black Politics in the spring of 1971. By then I had the reputation of being an activist in race relations. Students in the class I taught suggested to me that Mike was a racist. He seemed very uneasy in the class and the few times we met outside it. My first impression was that he was trying to be defiant, to show me I was wrong. I soon learned one of my first lessons as a professor. Mike had joined the class because he really wanted to shed the stereotypes that are the result of being raised in a racist society. Like others, he only needed to be exposed to the roots and consequences of racism to begin to change.

Mike mostly listened that semester, but you could see confusion, uncertainly, and anxiety melt away. The integrity and the sincerity were always there. In my eight years at Wesleyan, Mike probably grew more than any other student I taught. I don't mean he became radicalized. He became open. He came to look at all situations with an unbiased mind.

Mike was apprehensive one afternoon when he dropped by my office during his last semester. I sensed that something was wrong. Suddenly he blurted out, "Rich, I'm going to join the Norfolk Police." I said, "That's great, Mike." His jaw, rigid with tension, noticeably relaxed. "Great?" he asked, "I thought you would be angry." He knew I was critical of the police in many areas. But I was genuinely pleased to think of Mike—honest, caring, intelligent Mike—on the police force.

It hurt me to see Mike so tormented by the hatred of his colleagues for me. But I was also grateful that he was there. He gave me a feel for what was going on.

I had had dozens of moving, memorable moments at Wesleyan. That night I remembered what was probably the most memorable. In spring 1976 I taught a senior-level seminar on international race relations that compared racial questions in different areas of the world. The seminar gathered the best students I ever had together in one class.

One was Charlie Hatcher. A charismatic man, Charlie had

been among those who had integrated Norfolk's public schools, and in the process became an all-star basketball player. Although he had a satchel full of scholarship offers, Charlie entered the army. He was too burned out by the integration experience to do anything else.

Four years later he enrolled at Wesleyan as a twenty-three-year-old man. He quickly became the star of the basketball team. The other students, black and white, admired and respected him. If there was a cohesive force on campus, it was Charlie Hatcher. With two children to support, he eventually had to quit basketball and took a job working with juvenile offenders. I knew he would be late on this particular afternoon because he was to be a character witness in court for two black youths.

Leading the class that day was Leon Donald. Leon was from Milwaukee. Tall and thin, he was another ballplayer. But Leon was more into the black movement than basketball. He had shared with me some touching poetry that he had written about George Jackson, Malcolm X, Franz Fanon, and other important black American and Third World leaders. Intellectually, he was the brightest student in the class. That day he was giving a presentation on Jamaica's Rastafarians.

Listening and absorbing, as always, was Jack Schull. Jack was frail and almost never talked in class. But I knew he was sharp and quick from his writings and from discussions outside class. His shyness prevented others from seeing that he was sensitive and intelligent.

Charlie arrived an hour into Leon's presentation and, uncharacteristically, said nothing for the next thirty minutes.

During the break we took a walk. I was certain that something was wrong. Suddenly he stopped and turned to me. I could see that his eyes were filling with tears. His voice was cracking. This was a different Charlie Hatcher, a man losing control of his emotions. "Damn it," he said, "the judge gave both kids the maximum. Seven years for Bobby and six for Johnny. They're only teenagers. I was sure they would be put on probation. That judge was just another racist seeing two black objects in his court. And I was beginning to believe. It's all the same." He put his arms around me and I held him in turn. His feelings were so intense, so powerful, I could practically feel them through his body.

Charlie insisted on going back to the seminar. He sat quietly, listening to what was a good, academic analysis. Suddenly Charlie stood up. "I can't listen to this anymore. I have to go now. I appreciate that we can all talk so logically and even care about such problems. But the whites in this room, no matter how much they care, can never know what it is like to be black. Never!"

No one else knew what had happened in court. The class was stunned. No one moved. No one spoke. As Charlie moved toward the door, Jack Schull shouted, "Hold it, Charlie!" Like everybody else, I was amazed.

Jack said, "I appreciate what you said. I even agree with it. I only wish I could know so I could understand better. But you, Charlie, you will never know what it's like to know that my grandfather would have been likely to shoot you dead for being bold. My grandfather. A sweet old man who hated blacks. I have to live with that. I have to overcome that. You can never know what that is like."

The other thirteen students were frozen like statues. Charlie stared at Jack, then glanced toward me. Jack was shaking, tears in his eyes. Charlie went over to him, gave him his hand, and nearly crushed his slight frame with a hug.

Almost everyone was in tears. It was the most electrifying moment of my teaching life. We had always talked about understanding and about trying to understand. But at that moment Jack and Charlie understood, perhaps for the first time.

I thought about this moment early that evening. The beating I had absorbed and the misspelled "*n-i-g-e-r*" on my stomach had given me something that I thought no one else could ever fully understand. Yet I hoped that my going through it would serve to reiterate that some white people do care about blacks and vice versa. Then this otherwise senseless beating would have been given some meaning.

My thoughts were broken by Leon Donald, calling from Milwaukee. He had just heard about the attack on the CBS Evening News. I hadn't heard from Leon since 1977. When the phone rang again, it was Charlie Hatcher, calling from Chicago. He was flying in to see me the next morning. Ten minutes later Jack Schull phoned to ask if he could visit the following day. It had been a night of remarkable coincidences—proof of the sympathy that like souls have for each other.

I fell into an exhausted sleep at about 10:30 P.M. My last thoughts were of Mike, and the cops saying "he got what he deserved"; about Charlie's agonized "it's all the same," about Charlie embracing Jack.

I woke up early the next morning and began reading the morning paper. I read Peter's story titled "Masked Men Beat Rights Chief." When he came to visit I teased him about two errors, never thinking them to be important. The first was that I had gone to Nashville "as part of ACCESS's opposition against the inclusion of Peter Lamb . . . on South Africa's Davis Cup team." I told him we were simply against the team playing in the United States, no matter who was on it.

The second error was his reporting of the sequence of events in my office "according to Lapchick and Homicide Sergeant William Hayden." He wrote that the attackers first beat me with the steel sculpture and then beat me with the drawers from the file cabinet, at which point I passed out. Neither of us thought anything of this at the time.

Of all my visitors, the one that came as the biggest surprise was my brother, Joe. We had never quite seen eye to eye on politics, but this time he was on my side. That night he addressed a gathering of some two hundred fifty Wesleyan students. He began by saying, "The only one who can beat up my kid brother is me." My big brother. I felt secure with him around. We never had to say much to communicate. The Lapchick family bond was still a unifying force.

Ibrahim Noor, a Somali who was the assistant secretary of the United Nations Special Committee Against Apartheid, called to tell me that the U.N. would be issuing a statement condemning the attack. I was still in awe of the U.N. so this meant a great deal to me. I knew it would also help in Nashville. I received a call from Saundra Ivey (who was covering the story for the *Tennessean*) shortly after talking to Mr. Noor. She reported that the paper was moving toward calling for the cancellation of the matches. An editorial that day (February 16) had come close:

> There can be no doubt that this community would have been better off had it never heard of the Davis Cup matches. Dr. Lapchick's painful experiences should serve as a stark reminder that the mere debate of racism still has the potential for violence. At this point, that must be the real concern of every sane person in Nashville.

Saundra told me that one of the Nashville student leaders had received harassing phone calls, including a "warning call" on the night of the beating. This student was the same person who had taken me around Nashville for the weekend.

I tried to get permission to make a surprise appearance at the service held for me at Wesleyan although I knew what the answer would be. Instead, Dennis Govoni, the first faculty member to visit, arrived. His stay was interrupted by Faruk Presswalla, who identified himself as the doctor sent by the police. My initial theory that he might have been sent because my doctor was not white was instantly disproved. Dr. Presswalla was Indian.

When Dennis asked if he could stay, I eagerly agreed. It was nearly a month later that Dennis reminded me of it. How fortunate for me that he was there!

The other part of my theory about why the police would send their own doctor also evaporated during the course of Dr. Presswalla's visit. The examination he gave me lasted no more than a few minutes and was extremely superficial. He obviously wasn't there to make sure I was in good health.

However, I didn't make much of this at the time because we had a good one-hour discussion about politics. He told me of his involvement in a group called Indians for Democracy. I discussed my anti-apartheid work. Then I went over the details of the attack. Dennis listened with interest. I was surprised that Dr. Presswalla didn't take any notes, but not as surprised as I was about how cursory the examination was.

When he asked if I had ever thought that the attackers would kill me, I pointed out that they did not use much force with the file cabinet drawers and that they kept turning my head so I was never hit squarely in the face. I suggested that when they beat me in the abdomen prior to my passing out they might have gotten carried away.

After he left, I thought that, while I liked Presswalla, I wouldn't want to have him as my personal physician. I slept well that night with the good news that I was going home in the morning.

Chapter 4

Hidden Ball

I was feeling great on Friday morning—I was going home. Life would be normal again. When I arrived home, I felt compelled to prove to myself how well I was. But after taking a few steps in the front yard, I began to ache.

The day was again a full one with friends, students, and neighbors coming to visit. Sergeant Hayden dropped by in the midst of it all to try to talk. Frustrated but apparently understanding, Hayden asked me if I could come to the police station Saturday afternoon to "quietly discuss" where the case was going.

The best part of the day was being with my family. Although my brother Joe had left, my sister Barbara and her daughter Tayu had arrived from New York. But the stars of the day were Joey and Chamy. Their presence made life good again.

I called Lambuth Clarke, Wesleyan's president, and asked him if I could meet with the whole student body on Monday rather than trying to explain how I was to everyone individually. He agreed that this was a good idea and we set it up for 11:15 A.M., which wouldn't conflict with classes.

Father Joe, the priest from the church I attended, called to say that he was offering masses for me. He said he was proud that I went to his parish as I was an example of what he preached regarding social commitments. I told him I attended his church because he was so human and so inspirational. Not many priests had inspired me before and I rarely went to church in Virginia prior to discovering him.

On Saturday, however, my wounds began to ache and my adrenalin decreased. I called Hayden to tell him I had to take a nap and he said I could come down about 6:00 P.M.

When I awoke, the house was filled. Barbara had gone to the bus terminal to pick up a package from Nashville. I had a fleeting thought it might be a letter bomb, but it turned out to be news clippings sent from Nashville. Barbara read them and brought me one from the *Nashville Banner*. She was very disturbed.

It was the first article written on the attack and appeared on February 15. Although we had not yet met, Sergeant Hayden was quoted extensively.

The story began: "Authorities said Dr. Richard E. Lapchick . . . was beaten with a wooden statue and the letters N-I-G-E-R were scratched on his stomach with a pair of scissors." I found this quite perplexing since the only "authorities" I met in the hospital had emphatically asked me not to reveal any details. As I've said, I took this request so seriously that I was initially withholding such information.

The *Banner* explained that point awkwardly: "Huet-Vaughn's wife, during a telephone call this morning to the *Nashville Banner,* requested an editor change the letters scratched on Lapchick's abdomen to read N-I-G-G-E-R, instead of N-I-G-E-R, which actually was carved on the victim's abdomen." The article made no mention of why the request was made or that it was the police who had asked that the request be made.

As disconcerting as these inaccuracies were, they were nothing compared to the quotes attributed to Sergeant Hayden. First some misinformation—perhaps innocent: "Hayden said Lapchick apparently was assaulted as he walked back toward his office located in the same building as the Virginia school's library. He had gone outside his office to get a drink of water at a fountain and as he returned, he said he was accosted by two men wearing stocking masks." The attack, of course, took place entirely inside my office.

Then the article directly attributed the hold-at-all-cost details to Hayden. "The detective said Lapchick, thirty-two, suffered cuts and bruises when struck about the head and body with the wooden statue and cut on the abdomen with the scissors."

It proved to be only the beginning. "Most of his injuries were not tremendously serious at all," said Sergeant Hayden. But the two detectives had known of the kidney damage and concussion before Hayden said this. What is more, Hayden had not talked to Dr. Lorenz, the only one who had examined me, prior to talking to the *Banner*. When confronted with this later, Hayden responded, "The quote is true. Most of your injuries were not serious. I didn't say all weren't serious."

Then came the clincher. "Hayden . . . said he 'finds it rather interesting' that Lapchick's associates released a press statement before police had an opportunity to hardly start an investigation into the case." The Norfolk police knew exactly how the Nashville people learned of the attack.

I was outraged when I read the story. Nancy Lowe, a neighbor, said that her husband Fred, an attorney, would go with me to the police station to lodge a formal complaint.

We arrived and showed Hayden the article. He excused himself to "make a copy." Since he didn't return for twenty minutes, we assumed he was asking his superiors for advice.

When Hayden returned he apologized and said he could understand why we were concerned. I chose that moment to tell him that I had been told by a reliable source that one of the two detectives on the case was considered to be a racist. We were assured that he was no longer assigned to the case.

Then Hayden asked me to come with him to discuss the details of the attack, telling Fred to stay behind. I went through everything. At the end I pointed out that Peter Galuszka's article had reversed the order of the events, attributing his account to me and to Hayden. I said that considering what he had told the *Banner*, I assumed that he was the source of the confusion. However, I still saw no significance in this.

Sergeant Hayden had been very attentive. When I was finished he simply said, "You know, Richard, we have no suspects and leads in this case. I have faith in you, but you should know that it has been raised as a possibility that you staged the attack."

I might have been calm on the outside, but inside I was stunned and seething. "I want to prove this to be untrue so we can get on with the investigation," he went on. "I want to offer you the opportunity to take a polygraph. It just so happens that our polygraph expert is here tonight and has agreed to administer the test if you accept."

It was an interesting choice of words. He was "offering" me an "opportunity" to prove myself innocent of a crime that had been committed against me! I had a sudden flash of insight into how thousands of American women feel who had been subjected to a lie-detector test to prove they had been raped. For the victim to have to prove she was victimized in such a dehumanizing way is wrong.

If Hayden had looked into my background he could have easily surmised that I would refuse. I quickly realized that this would be an easy way for him to dismiss the case or to discredit me. I told him I would think about it but was almost totally sure that I would not subject myself to such a test. I suggested it was time for Fred to join us. When he did, I asked Hayden who it was that was raising the possibility of a staging. His response was unambiguous. "The local press."

"You mean Peter Galuszka and Peter Loomis?" I asked. Hayden said that he could not name individuals.

Fred asked what would happen now. Sergeant Hayden replied no one would know of the "offer" until I responded. If the press asked, he would then have to tell them if I said no. He requested me to sign over the hospital records to the police, and I complied.

We left the police station shaken and disturbed. I told Fred that I was likely to refuse the test because I was the victim and the police were making me the suspect. He said he agreed but warned me that many people would interpret any refusal as a sign of guilt. I kept thinking of all those rape victims.

Fred and I arrived home late. There were friends over for dinner, but I was not very good company. I felt I was being set up. But for what?

My physical strength was being eroded. Lack of sleep wasn't helping. My weight at the time of the attack was one hundred seventy. On Saturday I weighed one hundred sixty. Within a week it would be one hundred fifty.

I called trusted friends on Sunday morning. Franklin Williams promised to call other civil rights leaders. Bob Lipsyte said to refuse the request. Without exception, everyone agreed. Franklin called back and reminded me of the attacks on King and Malcolm X followed by police allegations of "staging." Franklin said, "We need to keep you alive."

I also called Peter Galuszka. I didn't believe Hayden when he said the press had raised the doubts. Peter said he had heard nothing like this. I was glad it wasn't Peter. However, he called back later to say that police had been leaking it everywhere that I had been asked to take a polygraph. They would have to write the story, he said, and suggested he call me later for a statement.

Fred and I got together to prepare it. I called Hayden. He denied that he was leaking the story and said he would try to stop the leaks. I believed him, just as I believed him when he said I wasn't being "set up."

The front-page story of Monday's *Virginian Pilot* was headlined, "Prof Suspected in His Attack." "Sources" claimed I may have staged the attack, but Hayden wouldn't say I was a suspect. He said I was being very cooperative with the police investigators.

The paper printed only two paragraphs of my statement. Curiously, the story did not say the police had requested the polygraph. Here is my statement in full:

> My initial reaction upon being asked to do this was one of shock, dismay, and anger. I asked myself, "Why aren't they out looking for the men who made the brutal attack on me instead of questioning the victim's truthfulness?"
>
> Since Sergeant Hayden has been most cooperative with me on a personal basis, I can only feel that this request made of me arises out of the traditional trend displayed by law-enforcement authorities in doubting those who are willing to take a stand on civil rights issues. More than a few people have suggested to me that the TV broadcast of the life of Dr. King last week may have created a climate for the police to attempt to discredit me as they had done to Dr. King prior to and after his assassination.

It is my firm belief that police procedures should not include placing the victim of a crime, regardless of its nature, in the position of having to submit to this type of humiliation. To do so only weakens the entire system of justice and threatens the ability of all people to feel secure with the protection that the police in our society should offer. We are paying the police to catch people who commit crimes.

After consulting all day yesterday with friends, family, and national civil rights leaders, I have decided not to succumb to the police request for a polygraph. There are several reasons for this: First, police have uncontroverted evidence of the seriousness of the injuries. Second, the two examining doctors have stated that due to internal bleeding, kidney damage, and a hernia, it is virtually impossible for the wounds to be self-inflicted. Third, there was absolutely no evidence to contradict my statements. But most important, to succumb would be to perpetuate the police use of this type of negative approach in the cases of civil rights assaults and other assaults such as rape.

As long as people agree to have their veracity challenged in this way, this process and practice will continue. I have decided that in this case it will stop.

As noted, the story quoted only two of the paragraphs. But it did cite Dr. Amarasinghe's doubts that the wound could have been self-inflicted and quoted Dr. Lorenz as saying that "the only wounds that could have been self-inflicted were the scratches on his stomach."

The *Nashville Banner* story was even more heinous. It quoted at length a "Virginia Beach detective official who asked not to be identified" as saying, "This whole thing just did not ring completely true." He added that my refusal to take the polygraph made me the focus of the investigation to see if I "was in on it."

The *Banner* quoted part of my response, then went for the jugular. "Lapchick, who recently returned from a trip to Cuba and has also visited Russia and Red China. . . ." No matter that I had never been to Russia. The truth was receding rapidly into police leaks.

Enter Sergeant Hayden again. "Dr. Lapchick and I had a conversation the other day and that conversation and what took place during our conversation are really between Dr. Lapchick and I," he told the *Banner*. "If Dr. Lapchick wishes to make comments with regard to our conversation, that's his prerogative. I'm not making any comments." The implication was that it was up to me to announce that I wouldn't take the polygraph test.

Both articles mentioned that I had been seen by the state medical examiner. Reading this was the first time I had thought of Dr. Presswalla since Thursday. Dr. Lorenz was again quoted as to how "the wounds on the professor's stomach could have been self-inflicted."

I was slightly confused by his comments. Saundra Ivey of the *Tennessean* probed him more deeply. "It amazes me that reporters are making so much out of this statement," Lorenz told her. "Obviously, you could inflict almost any wounds, so one could say of almost any assault that the wounds could be self-inflicted. I didn't feel, taking everything into consideration, that the wounds in this case were self-inflicted."

Again, Hayden declined to comment. "The comments you are seeing in the newspaper are not from me, because what I say, I put my name on," he told the *Tennessean*.

All of this had happened by 10:00 A.M. Monday. By the time I got in the car to head toward Wesleyan, I realized that I would have to address the polygraph issue with the students when I met them at 11:15 A.M. I decided to repeat my statement of the previous night.

My mind was filled with images. Security was tight at the entrance. This hadn't been the case last week. Driving into the parking lot reminded me of being put in the ambulance there, of the students swarming around me late at night, of Mike Mizell discovering the word "*n–i–g–e–r*" on my stomach.

The students were gathering outside Pruden Lounge where I was to meet them. Some greeted us in the parking lot, telling us that the lounge was packed with students and press. I wanted the meeting to be for my students alone, but knew it would become a press conference.

I was weak-kneed and couldn't catch my breath. Like a child wanting to please his parents, I wanted to please my students. I had always tried to get them to believe in themselves, to take responsibility for their actions, to stand on their principles, to be proud. They were also my family: Wesleyan had become an extension of my home.

So I worried about how the students would react to the morning headlines. Could I convince them that I was standing on principle by refusing the polygraph? Or that I was using good judgment in taking such responsibility for my actions rather than submitting to the police requests? Could I be proud at that moment? Did I really believe in myself?

I grew weaker and less determined as I wound my way up the stairs. I heard one student shout "Here he comes!" and the building filled with cheers. The students were on their feet, shouting, applauding. The television and newspaper people were everywhere, but all I could see were my students, my friends. I was home.

I began with words suggested to me the night before by Bob Lipsyte. "If you think you might be a murder victim," I told the group, "be sure you cross the city line so the Virginia Beach police don't claim you committed suicide!" The students roared. The ice was broken. I then read my statement. "For the first time, I clearly understood what a woman who has been raped must feel like when asked to take a polygraph." I concluded, "As long as people agree to have their veracity challenged in this way, this process and practice will continue. I have decided that in this case it will stop." The audience rose to its feet and applauded for several minutes.

I felt very good about both what I had chosen to say and the response I had gotten. The press began to ask questions, but I could sense they were not hostile. One reporter, whom I did not know, said, "The police told me this morning that the fact you have not received any threatening phone calls since the attack is very unusual. What's your response?"

More leaks from the police. I told the reporter that the attack was not likely the work of neighborhood kids who then make prank calls, that the business of sports relations with South Africa was a serious one. I didn't expect such calls. I added that I could not tell whether the Virginia Beach police were trying to discredit me or to close a difficult case in which they had no leads.

It clicked in my mind at that moment that there was no way I could get help from the Virginia Beach police. They had refused to give me around-the-clock protection as I had requested, choosing instead to beef up patrols near the house. We had noticed that even the patrols seemed to stop Sunday night, when the polygraph story was breaking.

I decided I had better consult with some legal experts and that I would follow the advice of the civil rights people and seek the help of the Justice Department.

After a friendly meeting with President Clarke, at which I told him I would ask the FBI to intervene, I taught my Urban Studies class and went home.

Andrew Fine, a lawyer who was an old friend from the Beach, had offered to help in any way he could. I called Andrew and he immediately arranged for a meeting the next day with the U.S. Attorney-General in Norfolk.

The local media was giving the statement I made at the college considerable coverage, although the *Pilot* put it on page B-3 after running the "suspect" story on page 1. The national press began to phone me at home. I was too exhausted to speak to many people.

I did speak to Bill Nack of *Newsday*. I felt he and his editor, Sandy Padwe, were two of the best and most serious analysts of the reality of sport as a reflection of society in America. Indeed, he wrote a scathing column on the actions of the police.

Franklin Williams issued a statement on behalf of the Phelps-Stokes Fund, the NAACP, and the Urban League, "deploring the libelous actions of the Virginia Beach police" against me. "Against reason, evidence, or acceptable standards of decency and honor, these authorities have cast doubts on Dr. Lapchick's veracity in the matter of his own brutal attack by racist terrorists. The suggestion that this man of integrity be subjected to a polygraph test says more about the method and morals of the police than it does about Dr. Lapchick, a fact that all who know the man are quick to grasp."

I was receiving calls and telegrams of support for my stand against the polygraph from all over the country. Several were from local women who still carried the scars of mistreatment by police after they had been raped and then forced to take a polygraph.

Andrew Fine and I met with the Norfolk U.S. Attorney-General on Tuesday at 11:30. I told him that I had lost faith in the police and that I felt that my civil rights were being violated. An interview with the FBI was arranged for that afternoon. I told Peter Galuszka about the morning meeting. He was anxious to write the story if the FBI agreed to take the case.

I had some misgivings while we waited for the FBI to arrive. As a child of the civil rights and antiwar movements, my image of the FBI was not of Ephraim Zimbalist, Jr., but of J. Edgar Hoover. The same Hoover who went after Dick Gregory, who tried to get Martin Luther King, who harassed innumerable dissenters and protesters, all the while breaking the laws he was supposed to protect.

I thought, "Times have changed," but then realized I was living proof that one still could not freely speak out without the potential of serious reprisal. I thought of the hate calls to my father and of how he internalized it all. I thought of the modern-day sports critics—Dave Meggyesy, Jack Scott, Tommy Smith, and Phil Shinnick. All were such threats to our society that in this February of 1978 they were all virtually unemployable. Harry Edwards was fighting to keep his job at Berkeley.

So I had no illusions as I saw FBI-Norfolk bureau chief James Healy and his partner drive up to the house. But I had heard good things about Drew Days, the head of the Civil Rights Division of the Justice Department, and knew that whatever help I got from the FBI would be better than what I was getting from the Virginia Beach police.

We talked for an hour. I was pleased by their reactions and they said there appeared to be grounds for the Justice Department to take jurisdiction in the case. As they left I asked how I should handle press inquiries. Healy said I could tell them that "the FBI had begun an inquiry."

I smiled as the agents drove away. It would be the last smile for a long, long time.

Chapter 5

Injury Time-out

The phone rang immediately. It was Peter Galuszka. "I guess you called about the FBI," I said. For the first time, Peter was abrupt.

"No. The state medical examiner has just announced that your wounds were self-inflicted. What is your response?"

I had no response. I just sat there, unable to speak. "Richard, Richard?" Peter kept repeating. Finally, I said, "Peter, I am absolutely astonished. How can he refute the doctors who treated me? Dr. Presswalla's exam was superficial. We spent most of the time discussing politics." Naively I asked, "Are you going to print this story?"

Peter advised me to call Presswalla, saying he had just spoken to him. He gave me his home number. He agreed not to write anything until I had prepared a response.

I just sat there a few minutes in a state of shock. Then I called Presswalla. His wife answered, pausing when I said who was calling. After a few seconds she said he was not there and that she didn't know where he was. I didn't believe her, and practically begged her to put me in touch with him. She could tell from my voice that it was imperative for me to reach me. She said she would try.

I collapsed on the bed, literally speechless. I just couldn't believe that this was happening to me.

I was being accused of a sick act of self-mutilation. What could I say? "I didn't do it." There would always be people now who doubted me no matter how much evidence I put on the table.

I knew I couldn't go ahead with plans to go to Nashville the next day. When I called to cancel, my friends encouraged me to come, but were understanding. Bob Lipsyte called. As usual, Bob was tonic for me. On this night I needed more than tonic, but still he helped.

"Who is this Presswalla? Was he paid off?" Bob asked. "You can't look back. If you don't go to Nashville, then they will have accomplished their aims. You have to go."

I said I didn't see how I could, but that I would reconsider it.

Then that unwanted call from Peter Galuszka came. I told him Presswalla hadn't returned the call and he said he was on a deadline. He was writing the story with Steve Goldberg, who had also coauthored the "Suspect" article.

Peter gave me the details. Dr. Presswalla based his conclusions on the markings on my stomach. He said they showed hesitation, that is, the person inflicting the wound was cautious not to cut too deeply. An attacker would not do that, but a person would do it to himself. In forensic medicine, such cuts are called "hesitation marks."

Presswalla told Peter that his decision to make his opinion public was based partially on the fact that the FBI had entered the case.

After our conversation ended, Peter called back. He said his editor realized I hadn't said whether or not I had self-inflicted the wounds. I said that the answer was obvious. Peter said "Then say it." "I didn't do it," I told him. It was hard to utter those words to Peter.

I was talking to Saundra Ivey at about 11:15 when the operator broke in with an emergency call from Presswalla. The timing was not insignificant; the deadline of the *Virginian Pilot* had long since passed.

My heart began to pound uncontrollably. I asked, "What are you trying to do to me? Do you really believe what you told the press?"

Dr. Presswalla responded that he was sympathetic to me, that as a political activist he knew the importance of publicity for the cause. He added, "What you did is not uncommon in India."

I said that Drs. Amarasinghe and Lorenz had contradicted him, but he quickly pointed to the Lorenz quote saying the cuttings on the stomach *could* be self-inflicted, and said that the doctors had no background in forensic medicine. "In my thirteen years of medical practice, I have never seen an exception to this rule [of hesitation marks]."

He sounded sincere and concerned. I asked, "Couldn't the attackers have made the wounds look self-inflicted?" He said it was conceivable, but the issue now could only be resolved by a polygraph. I should go to another state and be examined by both a polygraph expert and a specialist in forensic pathology, he suggested. After all, he noted, "I didn't say you weren't attacked. You may have been assaulted and carved *n-i-g-e-r* yourself for political effect."

Dr. Presswalla told me he had made his report to the police on Friday, and it was he who had instructed them to give me a polygraph. He said he couldn't understand why Sergeant Hayden hadn't told me this.

The phone rang, jarring me. It was Walter Searcy, a local organizer from the black community in Nashville. He insisted that I come to Nashville as a testimony to my truthfulness. We went around and around on this until I finally gave in to him.

The next day I woke up early to see the damage done by the *Virginian Pilot*. "Lapchick's Wounds Appear Self-Inflicted, Examiner Says," proclaimed the headline of a five-column page-1 story.

The story repeated what Peter had told me the night before—"hesitation marks," Presswalla's reason for "stepping forward now," etc. It ran twenty-eight paragraphs before saying that Dr. Amarasinghe stood by his findings that the wounds could not be self-inflicted.

Presswalla said he was waiting for reports from Drs. Amarasinghe and Lorenz before making a "final statement on the matter." If he was, in fact, still waiting, then the police were taking an exceptionally long time in delivering the hospital report I had released to them five days earlier. I was amazed to read a newspaper report quoting unnamed sources which said Presswalla had found "no evidence of serious internal bleeding, kidney damage, liver damage, or recent hernia," even though to the best of my knowledge he had not seen the report nor talked to my doctors.

Then Goldberg and Galuszka set the tone of the debate when discussing the polygraph: "Lapchick refused and *denounced* police, who he said were harassing the victim instead of pursuing the perpetrators."

Not only did I never publicly denounce the police but I am now embarrassed at how naive and reticent I was about their actions.

Next came more from Presswalla: "I have great personal support for Dr. Lapchick's cause, and I don't want to harm him." This was followed by: "Perhaps there is an extra note of caution [in my report] because I have been in an activist role myself."

According to the story, he had not wanted to perform the examination on me because of his sympathy and, when he did do it, he had hoped to "find a graceful way out of the situation" for me.

If Dr. Presswalla thought such statements wouldn't harm me, I wondered what he thought would. If this was his idea of a graceful way out, I wondered what he would do if he were hard-hitting. The answers to such questions were soon to follow.

I was literally sick to my stomach when I remembered that Leonard Sharzer, a noted local surgeon, had examined me in the hospital. It turned out that Leonard was at a conference in Dallas. The frantic search for Leonard began.

Facing my students in my 10:00 A.M. class that morning was terribly difficult. I tried to concentrate on teaching but instead I became unglued. I just couldn't talk about Tanzanian politics.

Karen Gilbert, a good friend who helped me with several programs I ran in the community, interrupted to say that Leonard Sharzer was on the phone. It was the first time I had ever walked out of a class in progress. I didn't hesitate for a second—I had become obsessed with my plight.

Sharzer said he would definitely inform the press that his conclusions supported Lorenz's and Amarasinghe's. As a courtesy he wanted to speak first to Dr. Presswalla to tell him what he was going to say. I admired Leonard for his integrity and professionalism. Now the score was 3 to 1. Certainly the press would now be forced to change its tone.

I ran back to the class and told them, "There is a god after all. A third doctor has just come forth. The truth will soon be known."

I was driven to the airport. Ironically, I felt somewhat sorry for Dr. Presswalla. He would have to swallow hard now with three doctors opposing him. The compassion came from a nagging belief that he was being sincere, that he really believed what he was saying. I thought that perhaps my assailants were so professional that they had carved the "hesitation marks" to discredit me. After all, Dr. Presswalla was a "liberal."

I still didn't realize how deep the waters were as we drove to the airport. Kathy Kent, a reporter for the local CBS-affiliate, approached us. "Will you take a polygraph now?" she asked. I said that I was continuing to stand on my principles.

We were met at the Nashville airport by a dozen or so well-wishers. A press conference had been set up there. The theme of it was that I was in Nashville to refocus attention on the Davis Cup. I didn't yet realize how out of focus things had become. I expected many of the questions would be on the attack and Presswalla's allegations. I gave a detailed explanation.

Finally, one reporter asked, "Why not just submit to a polygraph test to clear up any doubts?" I reiterted my reasons, adding, "In many ways it would be easier to do it, but it would also be easier not to speak out against apartheid. I have taken what I consider to be a consistent moral stand."

I did a lengthy interview with Wayne King of *The New York Times*. He questioned me on my athletic background, if I had kept in condition, etc. When I asked why, he responded that it would be very unlikely that someone who took care of and cared about his body would inflict injuries on himself. I sensed that we had recaptured the momentum, that we could remount the protest against South Africa.

We drove to Don Beiswinger's house for dinner. Don was a

theology professor at Vanderbilt. I again thought of Presswalla, wondering how he must feel.

Walter Searcy, the Nashville organizer, was at Don's with "J.J.," the armed bodyguard hired to protect me in Nashville. It was almost funny watching J.J. dart around the house, checking windows, seating me in exactly the right chair for safety. Some of the pressure was off; I was okay again.

Don asked if we had seen the Nashville papers that day. When he brought them to me, I was devastated. The *Tennessean*'s headline was:

LAPCHICK'S WOUNDS RULED SELF-INFLICTED

The *Banner*'s read:

LAPCHICK WOUNDED SELF, DOCTOR RULES

A TV was on in the other room. We went to see Walter Cronkite's Davis Cup coverage but he had moved to a related item:

> Last week we had a story about Richard Lapchick, the Virginia Beach political science teacher who had planned to protest South Africa's entry in the Davis Cup Match. Lapchick claimed two masked men had assaulted him and carved a racial slur on his stomach. Now a Virginia State medical examiner has concluded that Lapchick apparently inflicted the stomach wounds on himself. Lapchick denied the allegation, but refused to take a lie-detector test.

Everyone was stunned. This wasn't Steve Goldberg reporting but Walter Cronkite. This was the man whom America believed. Someone tried to break the silence with "What was the news about the Davis Cup?" No one had heard it.

Next we were driven to Vanderbilt for my 7:30 speech. J.J., as they say, cased the joint. The only difference was that it was no longer amusing. The balance had shifted again. I didn't feel up to the speech, but I had to give it. Walter Searcy, Bob Lipsyte—

everyone insisted I had to go no matter how I felt. I would rather have been anywhere else in the world as I walked down the steps of the same auditorium where only ten days before I had triumphantly announced that the NLT Corporation had withdrawn as financial backer of the Davis Cup.

That triumph was a distant memory now as a handful of people in the auditorium hissed when I entered. Ninety-five percent may have applauded; most of them were on their feet. But I heard only the hisses. It was close to being the most humiliating moment of my life. I found it hard to believe that all of this had happened in ten days. I knew then, before I uttered a word, that I would soon have to do something dramatic. *I* was the issue in Nashville, not South Africa.

We were back at Don's by 9:30. When Saundra Ivey arrived, she told me that Presswalla had again gone to the press, saying essentially the same thing but now insisting all the injuries were "consistent with self-infliction." He said there was no evidence that I had been knocked unconscious with the file cabinet drawers as I had "claimed." He added that there were no cuts—save a small one on my lip—on my face and no injuries to my chest. A beating such as I said had taken place would have produced such cuts and injuries. Even though, for all practical purposes, this was the same story as had already appeared, it was again to be page-1 news in Virginia the next day. The story would include the statement of my three doctors, which I had simplistically assumed would be the lead, in the seventeenth paragraph. Presswalla had upstaged Leonard Sharzer by issuing his renewed allegations. I suspected that Leonard's call to Presswalla had provoked him to take action.

Presswalla had told Saundra that clinical physicians such as Sharzer, Lorenz, and Amarasinghe were more concerned with treating patients than with examining injuries in the manner he did and were not adequate judges of whether his conclusions were correct.

Presswalla was absolute in his opinions. There were no more "notes of caution" or "not wanting to harm me." He claimed the wounds were "definitely self-inflicted." He told the *Washington Post* that the hernia "was an antecedent. It was not related to the assault." He said although I claimed resulting internal injuries, there was no evidence of them being caused by the beating. He admitted he still had not talked to Lorenz or Amarasinghe, who had made the diagnosis.

He even implied that he had called me on his own initiative Wednesday night, failing to mention that he was returning my call some five hours after I had made it. He told the *New York Post,* "I'm sure this is going to be ammo for the conservative red-neck types to say liberals are pinkos and liars—which includes me because I am a liberal."

The press loved it. During the six weeks that the case received national attention, I was interviewed regularly, mostly by men. The only women who followed it from start to finish were Saundra Ivey, Athelia Knight of the *Washington Post,* and Ianthe Thomas of the *Village Voice.* Interestingly, it was these women who probed most persistently and deeply.

It was, in fact, Saundra's persistence that first raised my doubts about Presswalla's sincerity. For someone who was so definite in his opinions, he made some curious statements to her.

"I feel sure of what I have said based on my experience but another person may have a different opinion. This is why I have suggested he [Lapchick] consult others in this field and show them photographs of his wounds."

He said he would accept my version of events if I passed a polygraph test "administered by a competent examiner. The only person I knew of who could beat the polygraph is a pathological habitual liar and I'm sure Dr. Lapchick is not a person like that. I have never said he is totally lying, but that I see inconsistencies in the story he has given."

Presswalla told Saundra that it was possible that in an "elaborate plot" assailants could have cut me in such a manner as to duplicate the hesitation marks characteristic of self-inflicted wounds. He reiterated that a polygraph was "the crux of the matter now" if he was to accept my version of what had happened. The *Tennessean* printed all of this.

He had told Athelia Knight, "I'm not saying he wasn't assaulted, but there are some medical inconsistencies."

How could a man of science say I "definitely" did something

but would reverse his opinion if I took a polygraph or if another forensic pathologist offered a different conclusion? Could he really believe that someone could be assaulted and while recovering think of carving "*n-i-g-e-r*" on his abdomen for political effect? Did he honestly believe that I had made up the internal injuries when he had my hospital records in hand? Or that my story of the attack was inconsistent? Did he trust his memory so much that he didn't need to take notes that night in the hospital? Or was he relying on the account mistakenly written by Peter Galuszka in the *Pilot?*

It's true Dr. Presswalla had a great deal of experience—fourteen years. It wasn't until March 21—a month later—that the *Ledger Star* pointed out that in his years in America I was only the second living patient that Dr. Presswalla had examined (he claimed he had seen living patients in India and Europe prior to coming to America) and that the other case had had nothing to do with self-inflicted wounds. Presswalla claimed it made no difference in interpreting wounds whether they were examined on a living body or a dead one, and that he had performed thousands of autopsies.

Furthermore, it was not until that weekend that I learned that the term "hesitation marks" in forensic pathology refers only to suicide attempts where a person first superficially cuts his wrist or throat to see how deeply he will eventually have to cut. It had no application at all to a carving such as the one on my abdomen.

Nor did I know that the Cronkite story just preceding the one about me was this: "South Africa has quietly ended segregation on its tennis courts, a move that's expected to result in an end to thirty years of sports apartheid in that white-ruled country."

There was no comment—the story was just accepted as fact, although such South African statements were as common as real change was rare. More than a decade later, South African sports were still segregated. However, on February 24 the one-two punch hurt. First the announcement that South African sports were integrated, then the story that a man associated in the minds of the public with anti-apartheid activities in sports was discredited. Was it a coincidence that Presswalla's first announcement about self-infliction came out within hours of the announcement made in South Africa? It certainly didn't help the next day when the media asked me what I thought of the changes in South Africa. I was not very believable then.

However, I did not know such things that night as I went to bed. I only knew that I was exhausted and humiliated and that I would have to agree to take a polygraph if I was to get the focus back on South Africa.

I met with John Zeigenthaller, the publisher of the *Tennessean*, for two hours the next morning. He recounted problems he had had with a bogus FBI investigation and assured me the truth would come out in the end, that there was no need for a polygraph. Even while he was saying this, I had decided to take a polygraph and had called Zeke Orlinski, a friend in the Washington area, to try to arrange for the polygraph.

The need to do this was again underlined during a TV interview that took place at the Beiswingers'. It was a good free-flowing session but ended abruptly with "Will you take a polygraph?" I replied, "No," since nothing had been arranged. Thirty minutes later Zeke called to say the test was all set for the next morning.

I had abdominal pain all morning and was taken to see a local doctor. It had been suggested that my symptoms sounded like possible spleen damage. The doctor said it was only remaining muscle damage and tenderness. I was actually disappointed. The obsession with proving that the attack had taken place had grown so great that I had hoped he would discover a new injury that Drs. Lorenz and Amarasinghe might have missed.

The local doctor then sent me to a lab for some tests. When the receptionist called me inside, she said, "I want you to know I believe you." I thanked her, but I realized how awful things had become when a total stranger felt compelled to reassure me. As nice as it was, it furthered the obsession—I couldn't wait for the polygraph.

The anxiety and tension built as I flew to Washington. I felt so nervous and upset that I was afraid my emotions would have a negative impact on the polygraph. I was met at the airport by Zeke and Rebecca Orlinski. My tension was not reduced in spite of many reassurances by Zeke, who was a lawyer and former prosecutor in Baltimore. I later called Ron Ellison, another attorney who had actually arranged the polygraph. I was wound tight as a drum, and wanted to take a sleeping pill but was told that it might affect the test—no pill, no sleep.

At breakfast, Ron Ellison tried to calm me. At 10:00 A.M. I went to the office of Bob Niebuhr, the polygraph expert. Ron had been careful in choosing him, as we didn't want any doubts raised. Niebuhr was president of the Maryland Polygraphers Association and was also licensed in Virginia, which we felt was important. In the course of his career he had administered 20,000 polygraph tests. Most important, Bob Niebuhr was in no way associated with the left or liberal political causes.

We talked at length about the case. Having read many of the newspaper articles, Niebuhr said he wanted a friend named Al to assist him in preparing the questions to be asked and in evaluating the results. He was cautious, he said, because he recognized the importance of the test.

We went over the questions. Did you ever lie before you were twenty-one? Did you ever lie for personal gain? There were several control questions such as name, place of birth, etc. The big questions were:

Did you cut that word on your stomach?

Did you want someone to cut it?

Did you arrange for someone to cut it?

Did you know who cut it?

I felt like I was on trial even though Bob and Al were sympathetic to my state of mind. Taking the polygraph was among the most humiliating and nerve-racking experiences I ever went through.

Niebuhr saw that I was convinced that the machine couldn't compute my frenzied emotions. They ran a control series to prove I was wrong. They said to pick a number from one to seven. I picked five and wrote it down. I was told to say no every time as Niebuhr asked "Was it one?" "Was it two?" etc. He went from one to seven, then from seven to one. Then they showed me the charts with marked differences each time I said "no" on number five. I felt more at ease, and we went through all the questions for the third and last time. When the wires were removed from the various parts of my body, I left in the room.

Ron Ellison, Bob Niebuhr, and the mysterious Al met in the other room. They called me back in and asked me who I thought attacked me. I said I couldn't be sure but felt it was either a Klan member or a South African. With this, Bob Niebuhr glanced at Al and then turned to me. "The test proved you were truthful," he said.

I broke down. The emotional pitch had racked me. Bob Niebuhr said the FBI might ask me to take another polygraph test. If they did I would "feel like an old friend was giving it to me," he assured me. He looked at Al as he said it and I finally realized that he must have been from the FBI. Al was not there officially, so I couldn't reveal this at that time. With a tear in his own eye, Al hugged me and said, "God bless you."

On the way to the Orlinskis', I thought that the agony was over at last. I called Andy Fine in Norfolk. He was, of course, thrilled by the result and said he would drive directly over to tell my mother so I wouldn't have to call her. Even Andy was sure the phone was tapped and we didn't want the police to know about the test. I also called my sister, who insisted that I come to New York City. She said a group had formed there that wanted to help me.

Zeke and Rebecca were the perfect people to be with that night. We had met on a charter flight to London and had instantly become friends. Zeke didn't practice law anymore but had bought the *Columbia Flyer,* a dying newspaper he then successfully rebuilt. Zeke and his wife Rebecca shared a marvelous wit. We gorged ourselves on food and drank a lot of wine. The lives we had led up to February 14 seemed ready to be resumed. Sleep was long and deep that night.

The next day I took the Metroliner to New York. Barbara's apartment was half filled when we arrived. Roy Brown, Barbara's first husband, Sam and Helen Rosen, whom I had known for three years, Jack Geiger of the Medical Commission for Human Rights, and Florence Halperin were all there. All were from the New York medical community.

They had read the Bayside Hospital official report and were outraged by what Presswalla had said. They said that the internal injuries diagnosed in the report proved that the wounds couldn't have been self-inflicted. They were even more sure when they saw the "*n-i-g-e-r*" on my stomach. The consensus among them was that Dr. Presswalla had been used by the police to set me up. They felt that as doctors their profession had been misused.

They decided to form a committee and to hire an attorney to investigate. Everyone agreed that Paul O'Dwyer, the former New York City Council president, was the best choice. He agreed to drive in from his country home that night to meet us.

I sensed I was somehow losing control of the situation. Others, who believed either in me or in civil or human rights in general, had taken command of my destiny. So I was reassured when, much to my surprise, my brother Joe arrived.

Barbara, Joe, and I went to Franklin Williams' apartment. He offered us all the facilities of the Phelps-Stokes Fund—an office to use and any other practical help we might need. We liked the idea of the committee and of retaining Paul O'Dwyer as counsel.

We met Paul as planned at 9:30 P.M. He was an impressive man whom I had admired for several years. As president of the City Council he had helped pass a resolution against South African tennis players competing in New York–area facilities. We gave him all the details and he said he would let me know by Monday afternoon whether he would represent me.

We all went back to Barbara's. Jack and Roy had prepared a statement for the "National Committee to Protect Civil Rights." Both the statement and title seemed too broad. We settled on the "Committee for Justice for Richard Lapchick" with a more tailored statement. Paul O'Dwyer had stressed that the word "Defense" should not be used because it implied a defense was necessary. Barbara, Joe, and I stayed up and talked until 1:30 A.M. They were both great. Barbara had been through this and worse with the arrest of her husband Rajat in Uganda in 1968. Joe, a political conservative, had not only never experienced anything like it but I don't believe he thought it was possible for it to happen in America.

Dr. Bernard Simon, a prominent New York City surgeon, examined me early on Monday. He was more thorough than any doctor who had examined me since the attack. His conclusion was that the wounds could not possibly have been self-inflicted.

Momentum was building. I couldn't wait to get back to Virginia with this mess cleared up. I was beginning to miss my students, and I took it as a positive sign that I was able to think about them again.

Bob Lipsyte drove into the city to meet us. It was the first time I saw him in person after thirteen straight days of encouragement and help on the phone. We discussed strategy. Bob felt strongly that we needed a knockout offensive. He said we should announce a $1-million libel suit against Presswalla and the police. Bob argued that simply saying "I didn't do it" would be a page B-10 story while Presswalla's accusations were all on page 1. My only misgiving was the lingering doubt that Presswalla believed what he said. Others suggested that, if anything, the police might have misled him.

Paul O'Dwyer called and agreed to take the case. That evening I was to see Dr. David Spain, the top forensic pathologist in the country who dealt with civil rights cases. The only bad news was that O'Dwyer couldn't go to Virginia until the following Monday, meaning we could not hold our press conference until Wednesday—nine long days away. I knew we had run this risk when we asked someone as well known and in demand as Paul O'Dwyer. Nonetheless, it was frustrating.

Dr. Spain conducted a lengthy examination, having already seen the hospital report. He was critical of Presswalla, reiterating what others had said about hesitation marks only applying to suicide attempts. He said the marks were obviously made to make the letters stand out.

This ended any sympathy I had for Presswalla. While I never reached a firm conclusion about his motives, all the evidence led most of the committee members to believe the worst about him. As evidence mounted, I agreed more and more with them. I wanted to sue him for libel, to make him pay for the suffering he had inflicted on me and my family.

I was honored to be somehow involved with Dr. Spain. He was the man who had done the second autopsies of the three civil rights workers murdered in Mississippi in 1964. He had also done the second autopsy of Fred Hampton, the Black Panther leader slain by police in Chicago, and those of the prisoners killed in the

Attica revolt. Of all people, David Spain knew how medical examiners had been used in the past to bolster falsified police versions of happenings. He had always courageously stood up for the truth.

We took a taxi back to Barbara's. I realized that all was now in place—the opinion of one of the nation's most renowned forensic pathologists, a positive polygraph, the testimony of the three doctors in Virginia and several others in New York. And yet I knew I couldn't return to Virginia in the nine days prior to the press conference; we had been advised that the climate would be too hostile before we released the information planned for it.

I tried to call Lambuth Clarke that afternoon without success. I did reach Del Carlson, who taught political science with me. He agreed to cover my Urban Studies class. I arranged for Jim Brown, the African History professor at Norfolk State, to teach my African Studies class and for Bill Wycoff, a former Wesleyan history professor, to teach my class in Third World Studies. Del, Bill, and Jim all said the climate surrounding the case in Virginia was terrible.

Everyone advised me to get my mother, Joey, and Chamy out of Virginia to avoid retaliation. Bonnie and Phil, my sister-in-law and brother-in-law, offered to drive to Virginia, pick them up, and drive them to my brother's house in Media, Pennsylvania. Eight students offered to remain in the house to protect it.

After two days of working on the committee at the Phelps-Stokes Fund with Shelby Howatt of the Fund and Helen Rosen, we all converged on my brother's house in Pennsylvania on Wednesday night. The plan was for Sandy to fly the children to Florida to stay with her parents on Thursday morning.

Both the children were surviving the ordeal and looked forward to the plane ride. I was pleased that they would be with my in-laws. Sandy's father was the ultimate practical man, politically far more conservative than I. I had waited for the call from him for days after the police request for the polygraph, for I was sure he would want me to take it. He never did; that cemented our relationship.

My mother and I drove back to New York on Sunday morning so we could meet with Paul O'Dwyer. He was scheduled to fly that afternoon to Baltimore to meet Zeke Orlinski and Bob Niebuhr, the polygrapher. He then planned to fly to Virginia on Monday morning. Unfortunately we crossed signals and missed each other in New York.

Finally, O'Dwyer called me at 12:15 A.M. to tell me that he was very impressed with Bob Niebuhr.

I spent much of Monday trying to reach Jack Dici, who did press work for Paul O'Dwyer. He had been assigned the task of setting up the all-important press conference, now only two days away. We knew how much was riding on the conference—everything from clearing my name to getting me back to work at Wesleyan and on South Africa and the Davis Cup.

The matches now appeared set. Vanderbilt had obtained new financial backing. South Africa was still scoring public relations points. Peter Lamb, their "colored" player, was being mentioned more and more in Nashville.

Also getting considerable publicity was the announcement by Piet Koornhof, the South African minister of sport, that tennis and all other sports would be integrated inside South Africa. No one would care—or remember—that almost four years later, the new minister responsible for sport, Mr. Gerrett Viljoen, would make the same announcement to cover for South Africa's first major sports tour since 1978—the Springbok rugby tour of New Zealand and the United States.

With the matches set, the dark, unseen forces I had warned against when I was in Nashville began to materialize. Ads started running in the *Tennessean:*

WELCOME BRAVE CHAMPIONS OF WEST CHRISTIAN CIVILIZATION,
PRO SMALL BUSINESS, AND ANTI-COMMUNIST SOUTH AFRICA

Don Henson, grand dragon of the Nashville chapter of the Ku Klux Klan, announced that the Klan would protect spectators from demonstrators by having between 300 and 500 members present during the demonstrations. When the Nashville police chief said he didn't need their help, a Klan spokesman said it didn't matter since so many Klansmen were on the Nashville police force.

Unknown to me at the time, an officer of the South African Ministry of Information gave a briefing in New York City prior to our press conference. As stated before, news of the so-called Muldergate or Ministry of Information Scandal was just beginning to break in the Western press. In March 1978, we didn't know how bad it would get. But we did know it was bad. By this time I was convinced that the attack and all subsequent events either were engineered by South Africa itself or by their sympathizers in America. To me nothing else could make sense.

The representative of the ministry was asked at this briefing whether or not the Ministry of Information would continue to operate. First, there was Biko's death, the October bannings, and now a major government scandal centering on his own ministry. What good could the ministry do in this climate? The representative said, "South Africa's image is getting better and better. We have already had a number of successes this year." The questioning then went off in a different direction. After it was all over, Richard Walker, the U.N. correspondent of the *Rand Daily Mail*, asked, "What do you consider to be the successes for South Africa this year?" The second success listed was "the destruction of Richard Lapchick."

Richard Walker told me this in late May. I couldn't understand why he hadn't informed me at the time. He explained that it was just so obvious that my "destruction" would be a gain for South Africa that it wasn't worth mentioning.

Yes, these were big stakes. International sports had become South Africa's Achilles' heel. It was clear that these stakes made our press conference on Wednesday increasingly important.

In Virginia Beach, O'Dwyer had met with Dr. Lorenz, Captain Buzzy of the police department, Presswalla, and Wesleyan Vice-President Jim Bergdoll. I was about to call him to find out the results when Helen Rosen informed me that Paul's sister had died in Ireland. Paul would have to fly directly to Dublin from Virginia Beach. When I told Paul the sad news, he asked me to call Jack Dici, his press liaison, to postpone the press conference, which was scheduled to take place within some forty hours at the United Nations Church Center in New York.

When I reached Dici, he replied that the postponement was a

good thing since he hadn't had a chance to call anyone yet! We decided to get additional help in organizing the press conference. A press conference without the press would not do much to get us back on the Davis Cup track.

On Monday night we let Saundra Ivey know about both the formation of the committee and about the press conference, now rescheduled for Friday to allow for O'Dwyer's return. Andy Fine suggested that we also tell Peter Galuszka so he wouldn't feel left out. Sandy called him on Tuesday and read him the release that listed ten of the most prominent committee members. Peter asked if there were any more. Sandy read him some from the master list. Unfortunately, she included Anthony Lewis, the columnist for *The New York Times*. His name had been penciled in for later confirmation.

Lewis had been at a meeting of the Freedom to Publish Committee, convened by Win Knowlton, president of Harper & Row. Of the twelve well-known writers and publishers present, eleven had joined the committee. Anthony Lewis was the only person who did not.

We received a call from him on Wednesday afternoon explaining that he understood why people might have thought he was on the list. He said, however, that his position as a writer for the *Times* meant he had to stay off such committees even if he sympathized with their purpose. Lewis said he had told Peter Galuszka this when Peter called him.

I immediately called Peter to explain. Peter was extremely hostile. "Off the record," I said, "I wanted to tell you what happened with Anthony Lewis." "I'm not talking to you off the record anymore!" he replied emphatically. It was the first time I had talked to Peter since I left Virginia for Nashville fourteen days earlier.

Those two weeks, lengthened by O'Dwyer's circumstances, were the closest I have ever been to "disappearing." We carefully avoided talking to anyone in the media because we did not want the polygraph story to leak out and be lost. We had been told by half a dozen friends that someone called Buzzy Bissinger of the *Ledger Star* had been calling them in reference to a "sympa-

thetic'' profile on me that he was writing. As much as I wanted
some sympathy, I was not returning his calls—or anyone else's.

That is why I was both hurt and angered by Peter. I envisioned
the next day's headline as "Lapchick Committee a Fraud."
Instead, the *Ledger Star* ran "Pro-Lapchick Organizer Charges
'Witch Hunt.' " In Virginia, that was just as bad. Bob Lipsyte
was quoted as suggesting two theories. "One, that the police
can't solve this case so they're trying to close it; two, that the
police are somehow implicated. I'm not saying either is the case,
but that's what jumps to mind. It could be that the sixties are
back again, and what's scary about it is that people are a lot
smarter this time around. This time it won't be a lot of sweet
college kids.''

The only good news was the resolution passed by the Wesleyan
faculty. It said, "The Faculty Association of Virginia Wesleyan
College wishes to express its outrage at the attack on our colleague and to affirm categorically its faith in his integrity and
truthfulness.''

However, one *Virginian Pilot* story was careful to note that
three of the thirty-one faculty members who voted did not favor
the resolution. Furthermore, it stated that "Lapchick asked the
association to issue a statement on his behalf." In fact, Joe
Harkey, an English professor who headed the FA, had called to
ask what could be done to help.

There were rumors that I would be arrested if I went back to
Virginia. Many members of the committee warned me not to
return until the day of the press conference. They said that if I
were in jail the police could do *anything* to me. In other words if
the public believed I was crazy enough to self-inflict internal
injuries in the confines of my own office, they could be led to
believe that I would do much worse to myself when distraught
and humiliated in a jail cell. Andy Fine assured me that I would
not be arrested, but the whole situation had become so perverted
that I just didn't know what to think.

There were also rumors of the convening of a grand jury to
investigate. Presumably such an investigation would be into my
account of what had happened on February 14. When O'Dwyer
was in Virginia Beach he informed Presswalla and the police that

I had taken a polygraph and that other doctors had examined me. This seemed to squash the grand jury idea. The police began to leak the information about the polygraph.

Suddenly, the Wednesday issue of the *Pilot* quoted deputy assistant commonwealth attorney Scortino as saying, "We considered the special grand jury, but we decided against it because, frankly, there's not that much to investigate." Alluding to the positive results of the polygraph, Scortino said, "You're not supposed to present evidence to a grand jury that you couldn't present at a trial." Was Scortino preparing the public to discount the results of the polygraph that his local police had asked me to take?

He added that any evidence from other doctors—presumably meaning other than Presswalla—would be improper evidence. "You'd get into a conflict of opinions and not hard facts." It sounded as if he had already discounted the further medical evidence that Presswalla had requested. I wondered how the network that seemed to be setting me up was tied together. Did they act in concert? The police, medical examiner, press, now the commonwealth attorney's office. Or was it all coincidence?

That afternoon I had lunch with Pete Axthelm of *Newsweek*. He was the first person from the press to whom I had talked since Nashville. It was good to talk with someone who was somewhat removed from the event and could look at it with more objectivity.

In fact, the whole atmosphere in New York was much different from Virginia, where many people who had been casual friends for five or more years suddenly pulled away from us. Our neighbor who occasionally wrote for the *Beacon,* a local newspaper supplement, told me that it was "assumed" by the editors that I was a communist. After all, I had gone to Cuba and China. What more proof was needed?

In New York, people rallied to our support. This was true of friends and strangers. Many of them had lived through the McCarthy era. We met most through Sam and Helen Rosen, who had virtually adopted us. It was much easier to put our fate in some perspective in New York. We had felt our world was collapsing and there was not much time left; yet by March 9 we had been in our nightmare only three weeks since the attack on February 14. Some of the people we met had suffered far more than we, and had for years. Knowing they had been able to pick up the pieces of their lives helped us to realize that we could as well.

We finally neared the long-awaited press conference. The pressure was building; the press regularly called my sister's apartment where we were staying. The police had seemingly once again leaked the information that I had taken a polygraph. We were asked over and over again by the press if it were true. All I could say was that all would be revealed on Friday.

Bob Lipsyte, with whom I spent Thursday, decided it would be best if we all left the apartment. We started by taping a fifteen-minute interview for National Public Radio's "All Things Considered." Bob and I then cohosted Howard Cosell's class on Sport and Society at New York University, talking about South Africa and how it uses sport for propaganda purposes. Bob mentioned the press conference since these were primarily journalism students. Five actually showed up for it the next day.

Our friendship grew as we spent more time together. Bob challenged me as no one else had. His integrity and sincerity, combined with his sharp wit, always kept me alert. He would often criticize what I said, but I never felt put down. He let me be myself but made me a better person all at the same time. I was glad I was with him on this day.

Paul O'Dwyer returned from Ireland and went directly to his office to meet us at 6:00 P.M. The strain of his sister's death was obvious. Exhaustion had slowed his step.

He said we had three choices for tomorrow. First, we could attack the police and Dr. Presswalla. Second, we could announce a major libel suit against them. Or finally, we could simply present the evidence and let it speak for itself.

Paul said his first inclination had been either of the first two choices. He hated to see authorities get away with abusing the rights of individuals. But he added that his trip to Virginia had caused him to change his mind. If we chose to attack or sue, he warned us, we would be subject to incredible harassment and predicted the climate would be so hostile that we wouldn't be able to continue to live in Virginia. Even after all that had happened, Virginia Beach was home. I knew I wasn't ready to move the family.

Paul added that if we attacked or filed a suit it would mean prolonged agony for our family. I flashed on UPI's Tom Ferraro asking my mother if she thought I had cut myself. I knew that Sandy and I could get through this no matter what. But I also knew that at age seventy-four my mother had already had several years taken off her life. Could I put her through any more?

Finally, Paul said that an attack or the suit could continue to divert the focus away from South Africa and keep it on me.

My conscience was retreating from the direction I had been sure we would choose when we convened that night. For two weeks, we had discussed nothing but an offensive. At 6:00 P.M. there was no doubt in my mind about what I wanted to do. At 7:30 I asked Paul what he would do. "Present the evidence, return as a hero, and carry on the battle." Bob and Sandy agreed. At the time the decision seemed right. Within days, I think we all had misgivings.

As I lay in bed that night I thought of my father's forced departure from St. John's because of mandatory retirement and how he had left with dignity. I had wanted him to fight to stay, but he had chosen to win the victory on the basketball court. In some ways I saw my situation as a parallel—I was choosing to win my point by helping to build the best possible anti-apartheid demonstration in Nashville. None of us doubted that Presswalla would abide by his word and recant after the evidence we would present at the press conference. We were convinced that this ugly episode would be forever behind us.

Chapter 6

Blocked Shot

Friday dawned bright and crisp. Snow was still piled up in the street, the remnants of a terrible winter storm. We drove to the Church Center for the United Nations where the press conference was to be held. It was a familiar place; ACCESS had been housed there during the tennis protests at Forest Hills in 1977. I was still in awe of the glass tower across the street that housed the United Nations, its flags fluttering in the wind.

I met Buzzy Bissinger who had requested some details before the press conference so he could beat the noon deadline for the *Ledger Star*. His aggressive style turned me off. He kept assuring me of his sympathy, and how a few words from me to my friends could help him write his feature story. I decided to have as little as possible to do with him.

Buzzy sat with Peter Galuszka during the press conference. The room was filled with a hundred or more reporters and friends. Paul O'Dwyer began the session by releasing the results and nature of the polygraph test and Dr. Spain's report. I made a statement to clarify why I decided to submit myself to a polygraph after first refusing. The emphasis of both statements was that I could now get on with my work.

Mr. O'Dwyer said that the attack was an "insidious one. It beats anything I have come across in civil rights work and that's a lot." He said that the police were making no apparent efforts to apprehend those who beat me and, thus, had put me in a position of having to defend myself.

Most of the questions focused on Presswalla's motivations. Galuszka and Bissinger were virtually the only ones who didn't raise doubts about him.

The New York, national, and international correspondents were more concerned with the broader story—the possibility of South Africa's involvement in the attack, the motives of the police and medical examiner, etc. We were very careful not to condemn them, much as we wanted to. The Davis Cup was the immediate issue.

Feelings were buoyant and hearts were light as the press conference ended. The tension was broken. Nat Holman, the only living member of the Original Celtics, came over and gave me a big hug. Franklin Williams said, "You just paid South Africa back for what it has put you through."

As the crowd dwindled, Peter Galuszka approached me. He was more cordial now. I remarked that it was all over, that I was looking forward to returning to Virginia later that day. He said that he, too, hoped it was over.

But when I bumped into the correspondent for *The New York Times* on 44th Street, our euphoria became depression. "I have bad news for you," he told us. "I just spoke to the medical examiner and he says he won't change his opinion."

We arrived in Virginia at about 5:00 P.M. Andy Fine and a dozen or so students were there at the airport. It was not exactly a hero's welcome, but I was happy to see them.

The *Ledger Star* was already on the newsstands. At first glance, I thought Buzzy had missed his deadline, for there was nothing about the case in the main section. Then my fears about him were realized. The story was in section B and eight of the first ten paragraphs were on Presswalla's refutations of the polygraph test and Dr. Spain's opinions.

"I am not an expert in polygraphs and have no way of ascertaining what was the significance of it," he stated, and suggested that a medical board of forensic pathologists be appointed to determine if Dr. Spain or he was correct. He then requested that the police release the results of their investigation. I knew this could only mean that Presswalla had seen their report and that it affirmed his conclusions.

Andy drove us home. On the way, we heard the taped "All Things Considered" program and it sounded very good. We arrived at the house in time for the evening news. The local affiliates of NBC and CBS did not even mention the press conference. The ABC affiliate discussed the polygraph but half-dismissed it by adding that it was administered in Maryland where there were no licensing requirements for polygraph operators. I called Jay Moore, the news anchorman, later that evening to inform him that Niebuhr was licensed in Virginia. Moore corrected his mistake on the 11:00 P.M. news. But, as usual, the damage had been done. What began as a day to end it all turned out to be just one more day in the continuing drama.

News stories the next day were mixed. Peter Galuszka wrote a very fair one, extensively quoting from Dr. Spain's report. Part of that report mentioned rope burns on the back of my neck and wrist. Rope burns. The police did not find the rope—that alone should have confirmed that someone had removed it from the office and the building.

I caught an early flight to Nashville where I was to speak at a conference on apartheid. This was the conference that Dennis Brutus and I had tried to communicate about on the day and the night of the attack. I picked up the *Tennessean* at the Nashville airport. Saundra Ivey's article was balanced and, like Galuszka's, appeared on page 1. It concluded with Franklin Williams's charge that South Africa was responsible for the attack. The *Washington Post,* which had sent Athelia Knight to cover the story, printed a lengthy and balanced report on the evidence we presented.

I was picked up and taken directly to a friend's apartment where I was to receive a call from Peter Lamb, the colored member of the Davis Cup team.

We soon realized that someone had tried to break into the apartment through the bedroom window. My friend had already received threats after taking a leading role in the local protests. I insisted that she take some clothes and remain with friends until after the anti-Davis Cup demonstration. She had become one of the primary spokespersons for the protest.

She told me that Peter Lamb had told her that he didn't want to return to South Africa and that he was reconsidering accepting the position on the Davis Cup team.

Even in the atmosphere of fear that pervaded the apartment, I could taste victory. Ray Moore, a white South African tennis star, had already withdrawn from the team after being counseled by Arthur Ashe and, subsequently, Franklin Williams. It would be a great boost to our cause if Peter Lamb pulled out as well.

Lamb's call was a great disappointment. Our conversation was pleasant enough, but he gave no indication of withdrawing.

I was driven along the demonstration route to the site of the proposed rally. I was shocked to see that the rally was to be at the Parthenon, the site of the assassination in the film *Nashville*. Assassinations were no longer only movie themes.

It was good to be at the conference among anti-apartheid activists. It was held at Meharry Medical College, one of the nation's leading black medical schools. The media wanted to ask me about the polygraph test and Dr. Spain, but Dennis Brutus and I had agreed to concentrate on the conference. There was excellent information generated about the reality of apartheid in sport and the false messages emanating from South Africa.

I became faint during the press conference and had to be taken to the office of Dr. Elan, the president of Meharry. I felt too weak to meet the press and John Dommisse, ACCESS's secretary-general, who also attended, brought me to our hotel room.

Sandy called to say how hostile people in the Virginia area seemed to be. She told me of Buzzy Bissinger's follow-up story titled "Lapchick Defense a Media Show." Sandy said she wanted to move away immediately.

I knew things had to be terrible for Sandy to react that way. There were no more flights that evening. Therefore I booked a 9:00 A.M. flight Sunday morning. I didn't want Sandy to feel alone. Several students had arranged a rotating guard schedule so I knew the house was secure, but I worried about her state of mind.

The flight arrived at the Norfolk airport at 12:30 P.M. and I walked to my car. Before leaving Nashville, I had placed a piece of paper in the car door to be able to tell if someone had broken in. There was no need to have done so; the window had obviously been forced open, breaking the window track and leaving it at a sharp angle.

I searched through the engine and under the car for forty-five minutes. I had become so distrustful of the police that I did not want to report it for fear of their saying I had broken into the car myself. Convinced that there were no bombs, I drove home.

Sandy produced an editorial in the Sunday *Virginian Pilot*. It called for a special grand-jury investigation of the case now that "the dramatics of a private investigation had been completed," and claimed that I had denounced Dr. Presswalla at the New York press conference, which was absolutely untrue.

"Of three private doctors who attended him [in the hospital], one conceded that the cuts could have been self-inflicted while another disagreed," the story said. "The deputy state medical examiner for Tidewater, Dr. Faruk B. Presswalla, was emphatic. He said one carving was 'definitely self-inflicted.' Dr. Presswalla, a pathologist with ten years' experience in forensic medicine, went public reluctantly; he too deplores apartheid and sympathizes with the professor's cause."

I began to realize what we were up against in Virginia. I called Charles Hartig, at WTAR-TV, the CBS affiliate. I had been on several of his TV shows and trusted him. Charles advised me to "cool it," that is, to keep quiet for a while so that some perspective on the situation could be gained. He acknowledged that there had been rumors that I would be arrested. The rumors were based on the police report, which no one had seen but many had heard about. Charles added that my taking the polygraph and seeing Dr. Spain had undoubtedly cut short any plans the police might have had for that arrest.

We visited Andrew Fine. He had been upset by the *Pilot* editorial and said he would personally go to the paper to defend me. Andy insisted that I call Hayden about the car break-in, which I did. But before I could complain, Hayden told us that Dr. Presswalla had been very badly hurt by the national attention given to this case, and urged me to hold a press conference, publicly stating my faith in Dr. Presswalla!

When Hayden's "investigators" came Monday, they told

Sandy the break-in was merely one of many car robberies at the airport. They didn't respond when Sandy pointed out that cash and a tape deck were still in the car when I reached it.

I went to see Lambuth Clarke and Dean Wilson on Monday morning. As I entered, two other administrative officers were in Lambuth's office. They left icily, without saying a word to me.

Lambuth said that I was using the college as a platform for my views. He insisted that I was hurting the college in its conservative Virginia community. Lambuth was a nonconfrontational man who did not like to offend people, but he hurt me badly, and it took me some time to understand how disturbed he must have been and how much pressure he had to be under.

Bill Wilson, who was never as warm and easy with people as Lambuth, questioned my priorities. He asked why I hadn't called him to explain that I would be gone for two weeks from my classes.

I tried to explain, starting from the fact that my colleague, Del Carlson, had been fully informed, and that I had left several unanswered messages with Mrs. Baker, Lambuth's secretary, to say I wanted to speak to him.

I could see that nothing was penetrating. Over the years I had always had the feeling that Bill Wilson tolerated me but never that he supported me so I could easily accept his reactions as normal. But Lambuth, who may not always have understood me, had been consistently supportive. I gravely absorbed his attitude.

"The college is my home and its students my family. I would never do anything to hurt it," I said, and agreed to "resign immediately" if he thought it would help. I had a quick vision of a losing coach going to management with such an offer but expecting a vote of confidence. The vision was shattered when Lambuth replied, "You have until May to decide. Don't make your decision today." I knew it was tantamount to an acceptance of my offer.

I had a few minutes before class so I went to my office. Drawers were open and papers were strewn all over the place. I didn't want to touch anything but instead tried to reach Karen Gilbert, who worked with me on our community programs, and Randy Smith, a student who worked with Karen. Both were in my office frequently and I wanted to be sure they hadn't simply left it a mess, although I assumed it had been ransacked. I was unable to reach them before class.

Being back in the classroom was therapeutic. There were not many friendly faces in Virginia, but my students made me feel relaxed. Teaching was a large part of my life and my blood was, once again, running. Pete Axthelm's favorable *Newsweek* column had just come out and several students commented on how good it was.

I finally reached Karen and Randy after the class. They came directly to the office and confirmed that they had not left it like this. We checked the files. The ACCESS and ARENA files were gone, including our mailing lists. I called campus security and Sergeant Hayden. Both said they would investigate, but I have no reason to believe that either ever did.

I stopped by Andrew Fine's house on the way home. He had met with the editors of the *Pilot,* showed them the police photos of the beating, and gone over all the details. Andrew believed they were much more open after the discussion.

He had also called Captain Buzzy of the police department. Andrew had defended the police in several cases and had a good working relationship with them. He asked Captain Buzzy why Presswalla had not retracted his conclusions since I had done what he had asked. Buzzy responded that he was concerned that I would file a libel suit, and admitted that Presswalla had hired an attorney. Andrew explained to Buzzy that I was worried about my family and wanted police help, especially when I was away in Nashville for the demonstrations. Buzzy replied that if I were really so concerned about my family, I wouldn't be going to Nashville.

Andrew asked me if I would agree in writing that we would not sue Presswalla if he retracted his statement. Of course! I assured him.

Bernard Barrow, our neighbor and member of the state legislature, was going to take over the case while Andrew, suffering from exhaustion and the flu, went on a holiday. I went to his house to tell him the plan. As so often before when things looked bright, a phone message from Steve Goldberg of the *Pilot* was waiting to shatter me.

If timing is everything, then Presswalla was a genius. With each shift of momentum, Presswalla came forward to speak to the press. Did Buzzy tell Presswalla about his conversation with Andrew? Or about Andrew's meeting with the editors? Did Presswalla see the *Newsweek* column or Bill Nack's column in *Newsday,* both supportive of me, and, of course, by implication critical of Presswalla? Was it just a coincidence that Faruk Presswalla's written report on the case was given to Steve Goldberg on March 13 when it was given to the police on March 2?

The *Pilot* story, coauthored by Goldberg and Peter, began, "Richard E. Lapchick's shirt was unwrinkled and untorn and every button was in place when police arrived at Virginia Wesleyan College the night he claims he was attacked, a medical examiner's report says. In a written report on the incident, Dr. Faruk B. Presswalla says information about the shirt was provided him by police investigators. He says it helped him reach the conclusion that a racial epithet carved on Lapchick's stomach was self-inflicted."

Goldberg had called me for a reaction on Monday night, March 13, before the story was to appear on Tuesday. I told him Presswalla had never seen the shirt and the police couldn't have thought it important since they told Sandy to take it home, which the official hospital records confirmed that she did.

I told Goldberg that the shirt was still in the bag that Sandy used to bring it home and offered to bring it to him so he could see for himself. He said he didn't need to see it since the police had confirmed Presswalla's report! The shirt had, in fact, been ripped directly down the middle and the reason the buttons looked intact was that they were still in the button holes—fully buttoned.

Presswalla's report said that a Bayside Hospital physician had said there was no blood. Obviously there wasn't; the shirt had been ripped open and didn't touch my body where the cuts were inflicted.

It was a long day; the atmosphere on campus was heavy. Several students whom I was close to shared with me that there was a rumor I had been fired. Did they know something I didn't? I realized after Monday's meeting with Lambuth and Dean Wilson that it was unlikely that I would return next year. Ironically, I had also begun to think that it would be better to be fired than to resign. In that way I would at least be paid a year's salary under American Association of University Professors (AAUP) rules.

I met Dennis Govoni, who had been in the hospital room when Presswalla examined me, in the afternoon. He was upset by the Presswalla report. He clearly remembered the hospital visit, and distinctly remembered my answer of no when Presswalla asked if I thought the attackers were trying to kill me. Dennis also remembered that I said I passed out after the beating on my stomach. He confirmed that Presswalla was not taking notes.

I called Andrew and Bernard. They agreed that Dennis would be an important witness. Andrew said he had spoken to Andy Evans, the commonwealth attorney. Evans insisted that the police had not asked for me to be prosecuted, despite what I might have heard.

Andrew reported he had unsuccessfully tried to reach Presswalla all day to tell him that the police had misled and misinformed him about the shirt. By that time, I had found Mike Mizell, the student who had first noted the carving of N-I-G-E-R in the library. I asked him if he remembered what my shirt was like. Mike confirmed that it was ripped down the middle and hung at my sides, allowing him to see the carving.

Leonard Sharzer, the third doctor who examined me in the hospital, did meet Presswalla that day. Leonard reported that Presswalla was far less decisive than he had been in print, saying that the wounds could have been self-inflicted or the result of an attack. He said he still believed that I self-inflicted the wounds, largely because of the shirt. Leonard said Presswalla was astonished when told the truth about the shirt.

I spoke with Lew Hurst, the highly respected head of the Virginia State Crime Commission. Lew was due to appear in my Urban Studies class. We had been together several times at Wesleyan over the years. I brought him up to date and sought his opinion. It wasn't comforting. Lew indicated that Presswalla's statements, even if retracted, would make it a near-impossibility to bring the attackers to trial.

The Davis Cup matches were only four days away and press interest was growing. Doug Smith of the *New York Post* called to do a story on the reported activities of the Ku Klux Klan in Nashville.

Bill Wilson, a producer on the Cronkite show, called to say that CBS wanted to fly a crew to Norfolk on Wednesday. Several church and civil rights groups had protested that Cronkite had not followed up on the polygraph story.

Tass, the Soviet news agency, called. They wanted to use my case to exemplify United States attitudes toward human rights. I told the reporter I would call him back, not knowing what to do. I remembered that Tass had taken up Harry Edwards' battle for tenure at Berkeley and it had brought results. But Harry was in liberal Berkeley, where Tass endorsement would not be as calamitous as it might be in Virginia. I never followed this up.

Zeke Orlinski called to tell me to get out of Virginia because the police had too big a stake in discrediting me. He hung up and immediately the phone rang again. "If you step foot in Nashville you will never see Virginia Beach again!" a muffled voice warned.

The circus atmosphere—press, police, medical examiners, lawyers, friends and enemies—was alleviated with the late-night arrival of Maggie Kuhn, the founder of the Gray Panthers.

I met Maggie on my 1976 trip to China. I think she was seventy-two at the time. One by one, all the members of the group fell sick under the strain of the constant movement. Maggie, probably fifteen to twenty years older than any of us, kept forging ahead. It was with that spirit that she had built the Gray Panthers into a powerful coalition working for the rights of old people. It was with that spirit that she brightened our home that night.

Maggie gave a speech at Wesleyan the next day. She was sensational. Now Peter Galuszka was with us trying to get a lead on any lawsuit, but I didn't talk to him about anything but Maggie.

That night Bob Lipsyte called to discuss a proposal for a book called *The Last Olympics* that I was contemplating writing. He had talked to several agents and publishers and said there was real interest in it. Bob joked that if I were killed in Nashville this weekend "you would blow the deal and all my efforts would be wasted."

We were ready to go to sleep when Kathy Kent of WTAR called. She had heard rumors that Wesleyan had asked me to resign. The school denied them. So did I. Kathy asked if I was planning to relocate. I answered that such speculation was premature and that I needed to test the climate in Virginia. However, inside I was increasingly certain we would be leaving.

I drove Maggie to her 7:00 A.M. flight and then went to my office. It was the first time I had been in my office in a deserted library since the attack and I went there more to test myself than to do any real work.

After my first class, I went to see Dean Wilson. We had a good open discussion. He remembered seeing a lump over my right eye when he visited me in the hospital emergency room—and suddenly he was a witness. More and more, I saw people not for themselves, but as potential witnesses. Mike Mizell, Dennis Govoni, Niebuhr, Spain, and now the dean: all would testify on my behalf. I wasn't so sure I would have to leave. The mood of relief, as usual, was to be short-lived.

I was walking to my next class when a call came for me in the business office. "If you step foot in Nashville, you won't see Virginia Beach again," a voice said. I couldn't tell if it was the same person who had called the previous night.

I taught my third and final class of the day. My thoughts were more in Nashville than in Virginia Beach, as I tossed over and over whether I should go. I knew I was wasting my students' time that afternoon and didn't like myself for it. I promised myself this wouldn't happen again when classes resumed after spring break.

After class, I reluctantly returned a call to Buzzy Bissinger. He said his "balanced profile" on me was ready and they needed some fresh photos. I told him he had enough photos already, and asked him what he meant by "balanced." He said it was not all good. Buzzy read me a section attributed to an unidentified Wesleyan faculty member discussing my use of my personal "charisma" to sway students. He quoted an unidentified Old Dominion University faculty member, who had supposedly socialized with me a dozen times, as questioning my motives—among other things—saying I controlled the Norfolk press. I congratulated him on his balanced reporting, noting that I did not know any ODU professors well, and had never been with one on twelve or even six social occasions. I was furious. This was the third week he had been writing the story. We were later told that his original draft had been rejected as being too bland. It had certainly been spiced up.

I just sat there in my office for a few moments. The phone rang. I didn't answer it. A minute later it rang again, and I picked it up. The voice said, "Are you going to continue what you have been doing now, nigger–lover?"

I was stopped by Karen Domabyl, the Wesleyan reference librarian, as I left the library. She told me that a man they had never seen before had entered the library and was obviously watching my office. He had told her he was doing research, but he had never opened a book, and had left abruptly after walking around the mezzanine where my office was located. Karen stopped short: she could see how upset I was.

I was trembling as I drove to Bernard Barrow's office to seek his advice. He wrote down the details of the threats and of the presence of the man in the library and told me to call Hayden from his office so he could attest to their being reported. He had his secretary place the call so Hayden know it came from his office. We discussed the pros and cons of going to Nashville, but I knew I had to go. I was much calmer by the time I got home. I had accepted this was the way things had to be.

Chapter 7

Big Rally

It was a rule in our house that we never wake up the children early unless it is essential. But at 6:00 A.M. this morning I went to say goodbye, completely forgetting that they were in Florida! I knew that many friends and some family members felt I had gone too far. Ann Lapchick, my sister-in-law, told Sandy that if she were married to me she would issue an ultimatum: either get out of the movement or lose your family. Others expressed the same feelings.

There I was in Joey's room trying to say goodbye to a child who was a thousand miles away. I had decided to wake him up because I knew it was remotely possible that I would never see him or his sister again.

I had always believed that I hadn't chosen my work in spite of my family but because of them. It tormented me to read about a white cop killing innocent black men in Houston or Cape Town; it tormented me to know that my chances of achieving success in America were directly related to my skin color; to know that the opportunities for blacks on an international level were deteriorating. I wanted to make some contribution, however small, to changing these things so that Joey and Chamy wouldn't be tormented by them; so that Joey and Chamy could really be free.

However, at 6:00 A.M. on the morning of March 17, 1978, standing in my child's empty room, I had to wonder if my being in Nashville was worth the risk. The children were already gone because I feared for their lives. I had even sent Penda, our dog, to my brother's to ensure her safety.

Sandy called to me, "You'll be late. You have to go now." Yes, I *had* to go.

Tom Doyle, one of our rotating student bodyguards, and I were met at the Virginia airport by Sarah Oliver, another Wesleyan student. We were all tense as the plane took off. We had lived in "the South" for eight years, but somehow I felt I was really going to the South now. The Klan would be there in the open, and a tennis team from South Africa would be there as welcome guests. I tried to think of what it must have been like for my father to be driving to Louisville as a member of the Celtics for the first game in the South with the all-black Rens. The Rens weren't welcome in the 1930s, the South Africans were in the 1970s. The world seemed upside down.

Tom broke into my thoughts by describing the man in the library on the previous day and what he had done there. Tom had almost bumped into him in the parking lot. As they stepped back from one another, he had asked Tom where the library was.

Ten minutes later, Tom entered the library and saw the stranger sitting at a table in front of the magazine display, his chair angled toward my office. At first Tom sat down at the next table and then moved over to the table where the man was sitting. He held a folded magazine that he occasionally perused, but primarily he focused his attention on my office.

Mike Mizell came up to Tom in the library after the man had been there for twenty to twenty-five minutes. Tom took Mike aside and described the man's suspicious actions. Apparently in response, the man walked behind the periodical guides desk. Each time Tom looked at him, the man was staring at them.

Mike, never the subtle one, moved toward the periodical guide desk and asked if he was waiting to see me. He answered, "No, I'm here doing research," and abruptly moved to the card catalogue as if to prove that was his interest. But by then he had been in the library for forty-five minutes.

Tom and Mike informed Karen Domabyl about what was

happening and went to get help. The man left in the five minutes they were gone.

Before leaving, he asked Karen about a certain book, went upstairs, and walked past my office. He doubled back past me again, and left the library without a book. Karen watched him walk toward the science building and told Tom about his departure when he returned. Tom dashed outside and saw the man drive away in a brown Cadillac Seville with a tan vinyl roof.

I hadn't said a word for five minutes. When the story was finished, I asked what he looked like. He wore a brown leather jacket, white shirt, brown tie, and black pants. He was white, in his early thirties, about six feet tall with a medium to large build, had brown hair and an acne-scarred face.

I sat quietly for a moment. I didn't know about the acne because of the stocking mask, but the rest of the description could have fit either of the men who attacked me. I tried to be rational, recognizing that it was a description that might fit many men.

I called Bernard Barrow with these details as soon as the plane landed in Nashville. He agreed that the description could be important and assured me he would contact Sergeant Hayden with the information.

We were met at the airport by Mike Mizell, Bob Friedland, and Mary Wells. Mary and Bob were also Wesleyan students who had come down early with Mike to help me.

I taped the "MacNeil-Lehrer Report" that afternoon. Charlayne Hunter-Gault was in the studio and Jim Lehrer was in Washington. The other guests were Bud Collins, the tennis commentator, and Slew Hester, president of the U.S. Tennis Association. I had never met Hester before, although we had exchanged considerable correspondence.

I had assumed that Bud Collins would take a position in support of the USTA, which wanted the matches to take place; however, I was wrong. Hester proved to be very amicable although his thinking on South Africa was, at best, confused. I was impressed by the penetrating questions asked by Charlayne Hunter-Gault. We all felt that the show went very well and served to substantiate our arguments for isolating South Africa.

We drove to the Holiday Inn, where I checked in under the name John Dommisse, ACCESS's secretary-general. I didn't want my name to show up in the register. We had two rooms so several of our student/bodyguards could stay with John and me. A TV bulletin said there were 3,000 demonstrators at Vanderbilt marching in a freak snow storm. Our local efforts were paying off. The demonstrations, which were to be held simultaneously with the matches, were scheduled for Friday, Saturday, and Sunday. The major demonstration was to be held Saturday.

We got to the gym as soon as we could, but the snow and bitter winds had reduced the number of demonstrators to about 500 or 600 by the time we arrived. We were told there were less than 1,000 spectators inside.

We marched for an hour. I was surrounded by Mary, Sarah, Bob, Mike, Tom Doyle, and Tom Hollett, a former student and close friend who had flown down from Washington. The rhythmic chants of the demonstrators let my mind focus on these friends. Whether the threats to me were real or not, they thought they were real and were risking a lot to help me.

As chants of "Sports, yes! apartheid, no! Tennis with South Africa's got to go!" rang through the freezing air, I realized how courageous they were. Their bodies were pressed close to mine to stop a bullet they thought might be meant for me. It was a feeling of dedication and commitment that I had never experienced before and that nothing can ever make me forget. At that moment they made all the Buzzy Bissingers and Captain Buzzys seem irrelevant. If our society was ever to be healed, these would be the physicians. If it would be reconstructed, they would be the architects.

There appeared to be a disturbance ahead of us. Two local demonstration marshalls informed us that our group had been surrounded by Klansmen or what the marshalls believed to be Klansmen. They asked that I leave for my own safety. My thoughts turned to the empty bedroom where I had been preoccupied by such visions twelve hours earlier. What was I doing to my family? "Dr. Lapchick, Dr. Lapchick!" The marshall pulled on my arm, bringing me back to the present. We left immediately and returned to the hotel.

We were joined there by John Dommisse, Lila Miller, and Cary Goodman. Lila and Cary were the first two organizers for AC-CESS. The circle of friends and associates was closing. It would be completed within twenty-four hours. We had a quiet evening, sharing a light supper and a bottle of wine. Tom Doyle, Mike Mizell, and Bob Friedland slept in the two rooms with John and me. Unexpectedly, I slept straight through the night, awakened only by a call at 8:30 A.M.

By 10:00 A.M. our rooms were filled with twenty or so people. Another Wesleyan contingent had arrived at 3:30 A.M. after driving through the night to get there. The group made a collective decision that we should not join the march until it reached Centennial Park. The radio informed us that some 6,000 had begun the march to the park.

The plan was for the demonstration to start at the state capitol and march toward Vanderbilt. The NAACP contingent went to Centennial Park opposite Vanderbilt while about 1,000 students went directly to the gymnasium from Centennial Park.

We met the march just as it was splitting up. It was a strange scene that encompassed both generational and ideological differences. The NAACP contingent consisted of mostly black people in their late thirties or early forties—veterans of civil rights marches of the 1960s, marches to protest racism in places like Nashville. But this was a mass demonstration against racism on the international level, and I felt it was a breakthrough.

The student group was racially mixed although predominantly white. They were in their late teens or early twenties and were notably more strident in tone. For them, the action was at the Vanderbilt gymnasium. They wanted to be exactly where the South Africans were. The slogan "The people united will never be defeated" had replaced "We shall overcome."

Raised and nurtured on the civil rights and antiwar marches of the 1960s, I had increasingly been drawn to more direct action in the 1970s. Therefore, I decided I would participate briefly at the NAACP rally and then go directly to Vanderbilt.

Franklin Williams greeted me at the park and accompanied me up onto the stage. I was the only white person up there with Franklin, Ben Hooks and his wife Frances, Dick Gregory, Joseph

Lowery of the Southern Christian Leadership Conference (SCLC), Judge William Booth of the American Committee on Africa, Carl Stokes, Ossie Davis, and Bayard Rustin. To say that I was honored to be in such company would be a great understatement. Dennis Brutus came a few minutes later. I told Franklin that Dennis, of all people, should be on the stage. Franklin agreed and said he would try to include him.

I quickly perceived the importance of the demonstration for the NAACP, speaker after speaker emphasized the need for strengthening the organization. This was Ben Hooks's first big protest as its new executive director. To have agreed to make such a commitment to an African issue was a brave decision for him. A great deal was riding on the day. I began to understand that he wouldn't want to take a chance of spoiling it with a confrontation with the Klan at Vanderbilt.

The spirit of the moment and the tone of the speeches, even if only for a day, recaptured the high pitch of the 1960s. While it was the feeling of the past, it was the substance of its meaning for the future that prevailed. Everyone seemed to pick up on that—students, old people, even the press.

The speeches were forceful, dramatic, and to the point—racism should be attacked wherever it was found. Particularly good were Ossie Davis, Bill Booth, Franklin Williams, and Ben Hooks. Hooks was especially charismatic that day. Dick Gregory, in his own unique way, was not far behind.

About one hour before the rally was scheduled to break up, Walter Searcy reported that the police had just told him that "all hell had broken loose over at the gym." Walter didn't know what this meant or whether it was inside or outside. I was disturbed, especially considering how well the rally was going. We didn't want news of trouble now, only of protest.

As Franklin was starting to speak, he surprised me by stopping and turning to me. "I want to introduce you to the man who first raised the issue of sports contacts between the United States and South Africa," he said. "We might not be here today if it were not for Richard Lapchick. And what was his reward? Thugs sent by South Africa beat him up and carved *nigger* on his stomach. And Richard Lapchick is a white man. How many white heroes do we have? To me, Richard Lapchick is one of them—to me he is a hero. Please stand up, Richard.'' When I did, the 6,000 or so in the amphitheater also stood up and cheered. I was grateful to Franklin and to the crowd. I was most grateful that our victory seemed assured, and that all the work and suffering had been worth it. It was the proudest moment of my life.

By then Dennis Brutus had finally come on stage. Reports from the gym had made us tense but the speakers were among the few who seemed to have heard that "hell" had broken loose there. I wondered how Hooks would handle it, when it was his turn to address the crowd.

Ben Hooks introduced me again, this time to speak. So much had been said already that I shortened my speech to simply remind the audience that after the representatives of apartheid left our land there would still be much work to do in other areas of the anti-apartheid movement. I told them that this showing in Nashville would reverberate inside South Africa and would deliver the message that the American people would be tough on apartheid in the future.

Ben Hooks was speaking now, and I decided to hear him from a more protected pocket of the stage. He was worth waiting for. He urged the crowd to disband in an orderly fashion and not to go to the gym. This upset some people who were unaware of what we thought were threatening circumstances. In spite of my original inclination, I decided that in light of threats being relayed to me during the rally I would not go there myself. Hours later we discovered that there had been no problems at the gym. I wondered if the threat against me had also been planted to keep me away from Vanderbilt.

The rally broke up. Everyone felt positive, even amid the clouded circumstances of the police reports. I spent several minutes exchanging stories with Dick Gregory, who has always been one of my heroes.

By then I was surrounded by the Wesleyan contingent. They whisked me into a car to go back to the hotel and then straight to the airport. Everyone sat anxiously in the Braniff waiting area until I actually boarded a plane for Washington with Tom Hollett, my former student and now friend. It was extremely painful to say good-bye as we climbed the elevated ramp. My Wesleyan friends had just given so much. The ordeal seemed over, yet deep down I sensed that my career as a teacher was nearing an end. Even though a final decision had not been made, I knew I could no longer be effective in Virginia and the risks to my family were too great. Still, that would be a tremendous price for me to pay. I was going to Washington so I could look for a new job and find a house.

Even as we flew to Washington we knew that the protests had been extremely successful. We outnumbered the spectators over the three days by more than three to one, and the matches were a financial bust. All the manipulating, all the attempts to discredit me and divert attention from the issue were ultimately wasted.

Chapter 8

Final Buzzer

I spent the next week in Washington looking for a job for the following year. It was a time full of soul searching—what type of job did I want, what could I get?

I went to New York to talk to Gene Stockwell of the National Council of Churches about a job. I phoned home Thursday morning to see how Sandy was. Someone had called her to tell her that there was a show on television about our new home. She turned it on to find a program about a jail.

As I flew back from New York to Norfolk it crossed my mind that people might be waiting to arrest me. Everything was so distorted.

The next day was Good Friday. I got up very early and spent the day writing the proposal for *The Last Olympics*. My concentration was interrupted by a woman on the phone.

"Is this Mr. Lapchick?"

"Yes."

"We are doing a survey. Are you a veteran?"

"No."

"Are you and your wife permanent residents of Tidewater?"

"Yes."

"Are you sure?"

"Yes."

"Do you both have a cemetery plot?"

"No."

"You will need one soon."

Joey and Chamy came home on Saturday; I had already come home. Suddenly our lives seemed much more normal. Joey and Chamy were tanned and beautiful. There was no way to see then the deep scars Joey was bearing beneath his external beauty. That pain would gradually emerge later, but for now all was well. (When we eventually got to New York Joey spent a good part of our first year seeing a child psychiatrist. It took the psychiatrist only one hour to conclude that Joey's aggressive behavior was a defense mechanism. As a then five-year-old, he closely identified with his father. To grow up to be like his father meant that he, too, would be attacked. That is a lot for a five-year-old to handle.)

We tried to pretend that all was well now that the children were home and I was teaching again. However, we were still receiving threatening calls, and we still had people living with us as bodyguards. Andrew Fine was still gone and Bernard Barrow had not been able to see Presswalla.

Then, our ultimate vulnerability was exposed. That Friday, at 5:00 P.M., the phone rang in my office. I answered it routinely by saying "Rich Lapchick, hello." The caller said, "Hi, Rich," and I assumed it was a friend.

He continued, "It must be good to have the kids home." By then I knew it had to be a friend since only a few friends and the police knew we had sent them away and fewer still knew they were back.

Then he said, "It may not be for long!" I panicked. "Who is this? Who is this?" I frantically demanded. The only sound was the dial tone.

I immediately called home and asked to speak to Joey. Sandy said she thought he had gone somewhere with a neighbor. I drove straight home without telling her of the call, since I didn't want to alarm her. I was there at 5:30. No Joey. I combed the neighborhood but no one had seen him. I called Sergeant Hayden. He was not there so I told the person who answered to get him because it was an emergency, a possible kidnapping. Sergeant Hayden returned my call two weeks later.

I ran through the neighborhood again. By then it was 6:00 P.M.

and I had to tell Sandy. She was not at all certain now about the neighbors whom she thought had Joey. It had been two hours since she had seen him. We really didn't know these people well. They had lived across the street for only a few months and now they were moving away. Our state of fear even drove us to conjure up thoughts that these people were part of our nightmare.

I went to Bernard Barrow's house, while Sandy remained home to wait for Hayden or his call. There was nothing else to do but wait. As the minutes dragged on, my insides were being torn apart. 6:15, 6:30. Bernard and I walked through the neighborhood again. It was starting to get dark. Joey had never been out of the neighborhood this late. I was becoming convinced that we were about to pay the ultimate price. As we sat there in silence in Bernard's living room I could think of little else but the refrains of unsolicited advice from friends and family that I get out of this work.

My father had prayed when I had polio that if God would deliver me back alive he would do whatever it took to make me whole again. At 7:00 P.M. I found myself offering up the same prayer about Joey. I didn't know what I meant by it. Would I actually stop working in the area of race relations? Would we leave Virginia immediately? Something drastic had to be done. And soon. Every fifteen minutes I called home to hear what Hayden had said or to see if Joey had called. All blanks.

We went outside again at 7:30. It was almost dark now. We stood on the street between the Barrows' house and that of the neighbor whom we hoped had Joey. Cars drove by, their head-lights making it impossible to clearly see who was inside. As none of them stopped, the terror grew. Sandy had joined us, having abandoned any hope of Hayden's help.

I was so distraught as I turned back to Sandy that I was very confused when I saw her starting to run. I turned again and saw the neighbor's car pulling up. Joey seemed to be out of the car before it stopped.

He was in my arms and I buried my face in between his head and shoulder so he wouldn't see the tears. I hoped he hadn't seen the terror and panic on my face. The worst moment of my life was over, but the memories of it may never fade. That was the one price I knew I could never ever pay.

I had arrived at a new low point, having been wrong time and time again for six weeks. Wrong about not going on the offensive versus Presswalla and the police; about the effects of the polygraph and Dr. Spain's report on clearing the deck in Virginia; and especially in thinking that the harassment would end after Nashville.

It was a weekend spent questioning everything; no assumptions went untested. The nightmare with Joey had underlined our vulnerability. With a hostile police force, I knew there would be no safety. With a hostile press, I recognized I could not be politically effective in Virginia. I felt as though the entire community had us in a slowly closing vise. What I needed to know was whether life and work would be better elsewhere. Was all this happening because I was in the South?

This reflective period abruptly ended on April 6 at 9:30 A.M. Ibrahim Noor called from the United Nations Center Against Apartheid. Ibrahim has become one of my very closest friends. As much as anyone else, he helped nurse me back to being a whole person again. But in April 1978, he was Mr. Noor, from the United Nations.

He asked me if I would be willing to come to New York to work for the United Nations for three months. I tried to be cool on the phone but there was no way. As a student of international affairs, as an activist against apartheid, it was almost too good to believe that I would work for the United Nations Center Against Apartheid.

An hour later, I received a call from Nashville. I had been chosen for the Coalition's humanitarian-of-the-year award. That same morning, Pam McAllister called to say that the Federation for Social Action of the United Methodist Church had decided that I should receive their humanitarian-of-the-year award. The contrast in our emotions at 9:15 A.M. and 12:30 P.M. further underscored the mercurial nature of our lives in the recent past. We had run the gamut from despair to hope, from uncertainty to certainty, from painful rejection to warm acceptance. The constant shifting had taken its toll on all of us—our nerves were raw.

Four days later I flew to New York for my three months at the United Nations. I knew I could not return to Virginia for pleasure, that I could not remember that seven and a half of the eight years were very happy. No, this was the South and I was going home to the North. Racism was there, of course, but at least not the racism that deals blows to the body and the mind.

I couldn't know then that those three months would become five years at the U.N.; that the emotional scars were so deep that I wasn't back to full strength until late 1980; that Joey's pain would affect so many aspects of his development. No, all I knew on May 15 when the jet lifted off the ground in Norfolk, Virginia, was that I was on my way home. The relative safety of working for the United Nations was a great security blanket, a warm womb that could protect us physically, emotionally, and financially.

* * *

The womb seemed to explode again in the fall of 1981. The South African Springbok rugby team was set to tour the United States. I became deeply involved in the efforts to stop the tour.

Those 1981 events forced us to see what we had begun to suspect. What had happened in 1978 was not necessarily because we lived in Virginia.

The new trouble began on September 4, 1981, within hours after the city of Rochester became the third city to cancel a game with the Springboks. It looked like the whole tour was about to collapse. Our coalition members were ecstatic when I announced this at our regular weekly Thursday night meeting.

I arrived at our apartment building at 9:30 P.M. feeling very good, only to find Sandy darting frantically about the lobby. Our apartment had been broken into. Valuables, including a camera, watches, jewelry, and cash, were untouched. None of Sandy's, Joey's, or Chamy's things had been disturbed. My things had been thoroughly searched, and, for the most part, ransacked. Nothing had been taken. The nature and timing of the break-in convinced me that it was politically motivated.

The police sent three separate squads that night and they were very deferential. I am sure the facts that I worked at the U.N. set their tone.

Before I went to work the next morning I went to see our new car. We had bought a 1968 Mercedes for $1,000. Sandy had picked it up the night of the robbery. It looked beautiful to me that morning and soothed some of the pain of the previous night.

People at the U.N. were upset about the break-in and the day was spent dealing with both that and the Rochester victory. It was all shattered when Sandy called from Kingston, New York, to say that, as she was driving to Woodstock, the engine of the Mercedes had been destroyed. The oil gasket had apparently been loosened and all the oil had drained out after ninety miles. The mechanic who worked on it said it almost surely had been tampered with by someone. I was frightened.

However, I was not as scared as I was on the following Tuesday when Sandy called to say that our old Volvo had had the grill pried open and the hood was ajar. We had the bomb squad test it, and all was okay. But all was not okay with the Lapchicks. Five days, three major incidents. The last thing I wanted was publicity since I didn't want either the children or my mother to know of the danger.

When the South African team actually got here, Jack Scott, the sports activist who helped launch the athletic revolution in the late 1960s, acted as a bodyguard, shielding my children from any potential danger in New York City. The only game played in public that year was held in Albany, New York. On that day, there were more protesters outside the stadium than there were people in the stands.

Jack was joined by Phil Shinnick, another sports activist and pioneer in the movement that tried to make sports live up to its ideals. Jack, Phil and I were awakened early on the morning of that public match with the news that a bomb had exploded in Albany, near the stadium.

I am grateful to many people in my life. Jack and Phil's help will always remain in my memory and make me grateful to them for risking their lives for me. My entire family was saddened when Jack died in 2000.

The worst of it was that we were now in New York. We could no longer blame it on living in the South. At least the authorities were more responsive to us in New York.

The events of 1978 and later, of 1981, led me to reflect more on my life, especially my childhood and the various influences in it: the events that took place, both within my family and in the outside world, the influence of my education, of my friends, and of the individual members of my family. The chance to write this book enabled me to go deeply into that period.

Part Three
Growing Up in Sportsworld

Chapter 9

Child of Sportsworld

My father always teased me that I was born under the wrong star. My mother was forty-one and he was forty-five when I arrived, surely not a birth according to the prescriptions of Planned Parenthood. Furthermore, almost at the same moment, the United States detonated its first atomic bomb in New Mexico. It was July 16, 1945. Perhaps the upheaval of the earth during my birth planted the antiwar seeds that grew in me twenty years later.

Sports marriages are never easy and my parents' was no exception. Basketball was my father's life for at least six months of every year. As a player with the Original Celtics and as coach of St. John's, he was as frequently on the road as he was at home. Paradoxically, he was an intensely private man thrust into the public limelight because of his exceptional status as a player and a coach. He hated the attention although he accommodated himself to it well.

At six-five he was the first great "big man" in pro basketball. The teams he played for always won. The Celtics were so good that the American Basketball League broke up the team in 1928 to send players to other clubs. For the previous eight years they averaged 120 victories and only 10 losses each season. He was sent to the Cleveland Rosenblums along with other Original Celtics Dutch Dehnert and Pete Barry. Cleveland proceeded to win the World Championship in the 1928–29 and 1929–30 seasons before it folded the next year due to the Depression.

The Celtics reorganized as a barnstorming team and my father played for them with continued success until 1936, when he became coach of St. John's University. In his first tenure at St. John's, his teams won two national championships and he became one of the winningest coaches in the country.

Used to winning, Joe Lapchick became intolerant of losing. His fame on the court increased his time away from home. My mother, Elizabeth, felt abandoned. She began to withdraw emotionally and became a "basketball widow." Wary of the enormous attention given to her husband by the press as well as the local adulation accorded to all famous athletes, she focused her attention on her thirteen-year-old son, Joe, and twelve-year-old daughter, Barbara. Ironically, my father hated the adulation and looked to his home as a refuge from it. Sensing his wife's withdrawal but not realizing why, he felt he was losing in life.

Both parents viewed my birth in 1945 as a way of renewing that life. They lavished love and affection on me. As I grew older and began to sense the importance of the role I was playing, I felt an enormous burden. By the time I was five, my brother and sister were both in college and rarely at home. My parents' love was so great that I could not let them down. When I did, the guilt was tremendous, though it was always self-imposed. Somehow I thought that if I could be a great basketball player I would fulfill their needs. It was a major misreading of those needs.

But such a misreading was understandable. Joe Lapchick had become the coach of the New York Knickerbockers in the early years of the National Basketball Association. The Knicks had been formed in 1946 as part of the Basketball Association of America, which merged with the National Basketball League in 1949 to become the NBA. There were no blacks in the NBA.

Away from home more than ever with the Knicks, his infrequent moments at home were treasured by me. At age five, I began to be brought to Knick games. In the same year, 1950, he signed Nat "Sweetwater" Clifton, the first black player for the Knicks. Occasionally after the Knick games I would descend into the inner sanctum of the old Madison Square Garden on 50th

Street and Eighth Avenue. I actually *knew* Nat, Carl Braun, Harry Gallatin, Vince Boryla, and all the stars. It was a high-altitude world for a five-year-old. I would do anything to be around it and constantly fantasized about being part of it some-day.

But still something was wrong. For all the glamour and fame, I saw the turmoil and agony my father went through in thinking about each game before he drove to the Garden. Sometimes I would wake up in the night to see him sitting in the chair in my room or hear him walking through the house. He would later tell the press that he lived a thousand deaths in defeat. Late at night, I saw many of them. I always knew when the Knicks lost.

Something else was causing him anxiety: the "nigger–lover" calls. I didn't know what a "nigger–lover" was but I was sure it couldn't be good if so many people disliked him because of it; I did not connect Nat Clifton to the calls. When I was in the locker room, Nat Clifton was "one of the boys." I didn't know that once outside the locker room, he became one of a different set of "boys." What I did see was how each call would eat my father up. My brother and sister were both in college and never knew of this. The only reason I did was because I would unsuspectingly pick up the phone upstairs. In the beginning I would go down-stairs to see my father after the calls. He had invariably retreated to the living room and was doubled over in a chair. He never saw me look in and I never said anything to anyone. It was a secret that I shared with him, although he didn't know that I shared it until I was grown up. The confusion was tremendous. As a five-year-old I wondered what awful sin this man had committed to make so many people hate him. He was soft and gentle to me. What must this other side of him be if so many people thought he was so horrible? I didn't really want to know for fear I might hate him too.

Later, when I realized what the calls were about, my feelings of alienation from the racist segment of American society began to grow. My father was hated because he loved. At last this dark burden was lifted from my mind and placed where it had belonged all along—on the fears and hatred that are bred so profusely in America.

But as I was growing up, I left unexamined the traumas my father experienced. I buried the pain of the hate calls. Neighbors and friends told me how I would follow in my father's footsteps.

Christmas and birthdays brought gifts of basketballs, baseballs, baseball mitts, golf balls and clubs. Neighborhood fathers wanted to teach me to shoot, wanted me to play with their kids. As I look back, the draw and power of the sports experience seems even stronger if more bizarre. They were doing this when I was five, six, and seven years old. I felt such pressure from them. I had to be good. The only thing I couldn't understand was why my own father, who would spend endless hours talking to me, going for walks with me, playing word and board games with me, *never* played basketball with me. Never even *talked* about my playing basketball.

My meetings with the Knicks made each time I picked up a basketball a vicarious trip down the Madison Square Garden court. It didn't matter that when I threw the ball up it barely reached the basket, let alone went in. It didn't matter because I was Joe Lapchick's son and I was going to be a star. Everyone knew it, everyone told me. And I believed it.

I was seven and enrolled at the YMCA day camp in Yonkers. We were playing all kinds of sports each day behind Roosevelt High School where the sessions were held. I was in heaven. However, soon after the camp began I got a high fever and had to stay home. Our family physician, Dr. Ahouse, was out of town so they called a different doctor to see me. Everyone was relieved to be told I had tonsillitis. But when the antibiotics and other medication failed to make me better, Dr. Ahouse came.

A warm, wonderful man, he spent an unusually long time with me and then went into the corner of the room to talk to my parents. I remember hearing my mother say, "Oh, my god!" Dr. Ahouse made some phone calls and an ambulance soon pulled up to our house. With tears in his eyes, my father told me that Dr. Ahouse wanted me to go to Grasslands Hospital where they had special facilities to treat polio. I remember he could hardly say the word as he held me. As sick and half delirious as I was, this moment sealed a bond between us. Captured for the first time was that elusive love that comes from total communication between father and son.

The tests confirmed it was polio. When my brother was allowed to come home from West Point to visit me, I knew the sickness was serious. One day a neighbor visited the hospital with the family. "Do the doctors think he will ever be able to play basketball?" he asked my father. Not if he'll be able to walk, not if he'll be able to lead a normal life, but will he ever be able to play basketball. My father was too polite a man to express the revulsion he felt. I was seven years old. I was not a basketball player, I was a little kid.

I don't think he knew that I heard and saw this happen. The next day he sat by my side and asked me if I wanted to play basketball. I enthusiastically, if naively, said "yes." He told me that all he wanted for me was to have a normal and happy life. He said he had prayed that if God delivered me to him in one piece, that he would nurture me back to health, that he would stop everything else to accomplish it. Subsequently, he gave me years of massages and exercise programs.

I realized for the first time that it was unimportant to him for me to be an athlete. Yet, I knew that now more than ever I wanted to be one. Within a year I had recovered from polio. My father's prayers had been answered. Now I had to make my own prayers come true.

As part of my "rehabilitation," my parents bought me a membership at the Jewish Community Center in Yonkers. At the JCC, I was the tall kid with all the potential. I was always high scorer and leading rebounder on the Comets, a club team. My competition was the likes of John Bonito, Fred Fine, and Alan Carmassin, with whom I remained friends for many years. But none of them played in the NBA, or even in college or high school.

My father was doing more and more things with me now. After Knick games he would take me to Mama Leone's restaurant where he would talk about the game with the press. I recall many evenings there, but one stands out in particular. Still unaware of the significance of Nat Clifton in our lives, I couldn't help but be aware of Jackie Robinson. The national sports press was heavily selling his admission into baseball as an indication that sports was the way out of the ghetto for black athletes; it was to become a widely believed assumption about sport and society. By now I was old enough to take an interest in political discussions at home. I had read about Jackie Robinson. I believed sports was the way out for blacks. The press spoke the truth. I continued to believe this for nearly another decade.

While he never discussed racism in sport, my father freely discussed racism in society. I knew it was something he cared deeply about. The Brown *vs.* the Board of Education Supreme Court decision had sparked a major controversy the previous year (1954) when it called for the integration of public schools. It was a decision warmly greeted by my family.

I was relating to sports and not to politics. Anyway, I had read that they didn't mix. Jackie Robinson was much more real and important to me than the Supreme Court. Therefore, when I had an opportunity to meet him at the Garden one day I jumped at the chance. Some sports writers called him "abrasive" and "aggressive." It was only much later that I realized these were code words for blacks that meant they were "uppity niggers." Jackie Robinson shook my hand and spoke to me for two or three minutes. He was neither abrasive nor aggressive, but kind and thoughtful. At Leone's later that night, a member of the press whose name I've long since forgotten asked his colleague, "Did you see that nigger showboating for the crowd?" The friend nodded his agreement. I was nine years old at the time, and my own sports ambitions soon made me try to put this incident out of my mind. But it stuck with me.

My sports progress was measurable. I was euphoric when in the fifth grade I won the school foul-shooting championship; and the Comets and I were tearing apart the JCC League. I was so happy I barely noticed that my father spent day after day in a malaise called losing. Intensely proud, he was about to resign in mid-season, having heard the rumor he would be fired at the end of the year.

My sports development was so good when measured against my competitors at the Jewish Community Center that I barely noticed that the person I wanted to emulate was bleeding to death under my insensitive eyes. My passion to play sports was so distorting my values that my career as the high scorer among eleven-year-olds at the Jewish Community Center was more important to me than the lifetime my father had given to the sport.

The next year I went to Hawthorne Junior High School. The only way a lowly seventh-grader could survive was by being a good athlete. The competition was better than at the JCC but still I managed to make the seventh-grade all-star team. We were to play the eighth-grade champions. For the first time my father was coming to see me play. He had been rehired at St. John's, and he was more relaxed and not traveling as much as he did with the Knicks. The day of the game I couldn't eat. The way I played I might as well not have eaten the week before. I was awful. My father was incapable of lying so he didn't say anything. I didn't dare ask.

The 1958–59 season, his third back at St. John's, was expected to be my father's comeback year. He had a good team returning plus a sophomore named Tony Jackson, the first black basketball player at St. John's in a number of years. Tony was a poet with a jump shot, and he was to lead St. John's to the Holiday Festival and National Invitation Tournament championships in that year.

Even so, I would hear in private the innuendos from the press and from some other students at St. John's—Tony was lazy, not very smart, shouldn't really be in college. They didn't mention that more than 150 colleges had tried to obtain his services. It was funny that you didn't hear these remarks about white athletes, although my father learned that some of them rarely if ever attended classes—an abuse he and his assistant, Lou Carnesecca, quickly corrected. The misuse of athletes was prevalent almost everywhere in the 1950s and is still the norm at many athletic powerhouses. All of this might have been more important in my mind if St. John's was losing. But winning two championships made it seem less significant at the time.

So I vicariously participated in St. John's success. More important, I grew six inches and became one of the biggest eighth-graders in the New York area. Everyone was predicting I would be six-seven or more. I was good for a slow big man and New

York high school coaches were looking at me. I leaned toward Power Memorial High School. I liked the coach, Jack Donohue, and they always had an excellent team.

Everyone in the family pushed me toward Manhattan Prep, which was on the campus of Manhattan College. It had the reputation of a fine academic school and attracted many of New York City's brightest students. I didn't care that much about being a good student. In my own mind I was convinced I would be a very good player. With hindsight, I now realize that *all* ballplayers believe this; even ones who aren't particularly good overestimate their talent.

In trying to prove my ability I was forced to confront racism for the first time. I had made friends with a few of the black ballplayers who tried out for scholarships at Power Memorial. I was drawn to them because they were ignored by the white players when they were lucky; despised and decried when they were not. I think it was at age thirteen that I was, for the first time, embarrassed to be white.

My new friends invited me to their neighborhoods to play that summer. Those neighborhoods, of course, were mostly in Harlem. My white friends from Yonkers told me smart whites didn't go to Harlem. I didn't claim to be smart but I knew I could play good basketball there and that my days with the Comets and Hawthorne Junior High were past.

It *was* good basketball. However, when I visited my friends' apartments I had to contemplate why I lived so comfortably, as did all of my white friends, while they did not. All of my developing friendships in Harlem were with people who had few of the physical comforts I had come to expect.

What was it about this society that prescribed such antithetical conditions for blacks and whites? I was deeply troubled by what I was experiencing during that summer. And then I remembered Jackie Robinson. Sports would surely elevate these talented players out of the ghetto. The only difference now was that I was not sure I still believed in the sports panacea. I wanted to; I needed to; but I was not sure I did.

Having acquiesced to my parents' wishes, I entered Manhattan Prep in the fall of 1959. I was ready to make my mark on New

York City basketball. I soon learned that freshmen had to pay their dues and I mainly sat on the bench for a good Manhattan junior varsity team. It was one of the better JVs in the city. I became reconciled to my role as full-time cheerleader, part-time player. It was enough for me to send a game against my would-be school, Power Memorial, into overtime with a jump shot. Small things had to carry me then. But I was full enough of myself to ignore the reality of not playing. To be on the team was "manly." I wasn't a boy anymore. To be on the team meant having dates with girls. The two went together. Sport was making my transition to manhood easier.

Manhattan was not the place for a pure jock; at Manhattan, the real "brains" looked down their noses at me. Not only was I an athlete but the curse was already a generation old in my family. For these preppies, sport was the height of anti-intellectualism and was to be avoided. They did, however, have a good biting sense of humor. As we took the floor at our first home game, they unfurled a banner the length of the court that read, "Nobody can lick our Dick."

I was so carried away with sports that I rebelled when my father decided to send me to Europe in the summer of 1960. I wanted to stay in New York and go back to the city's playgrounds. Culture had no appeal. Finally, my mother reminded me that the Olympic Games would be held in Rome that summer. That convinced me to go.

I began to read books about the Olympic Games. What greater honor than to represent your country? What an important role to be an ambassador of peace and understanding. It all sounded so wonderful, so meaningful. Africans, Asians, and Latin Americans could forget the colonial and imperial roles of Western nations. The U.S.S.R. and the U.S. could meet harmoniously. In 1959 it momentarily looked like both "Chinas" might be in Rome. The Olympic Movement was a force for peace.

Seeing Europe helped to challenge my mind—perhaps for the first time. There were no sports to divert me. I wouldn't have imagined that I would ever want to go to an art museum. By the end of the summer I couldn't stay away. Raised as a Catholic, I avoided churches on days other than Sundays. Traveling throughout Europe, I loved to visit the famous and historic cathedrals. Concerts, operas, historical museums. I rarely thought about sports.

Most important was the time I spent with my sister Barbara and Roy, her first husband. They were living in West Germany and we traveled a great deal together. They treated me, the fourteen-year-old dumb jock, like one of their own intellectual friends. We discussed politics. They told me about a senator from Massachusetts in whom they had a lot of faith. I had barely heard of John Kennedy. We talked about Martin Luther King. My friends in Harlem had told me he was their savior, not Jackie Robinson. We talked about Albert Luthuli, the chief of the Zulus in South Africa—and head of the African National Congress.

It was at a friend's apartment that I first listened to the singing of a man with a magnificent voice. I heard about Paul Robeson— all that he had accomplished as an artist, all that he stood for as an activist, and all that he had suffered. I wondered if it could be true. How could I not have heard of Robeson? Why did every European white I met speak of him while no white American I knew did? Blacks in Paris and London seemed to be treated differently from those in the United States. Not understanding then the nature of French and British colonialism, I could not penetrate beneath the surface. I knew that all of the blacks I was seeing could not have been former athletes and entertainers who had made it out of the ghetto. Was Europe a model for America?

I returned to New York on the day school reopened with these thoughts buzzing in my head. I would continue in sports, but now life would have more meaning. I began to tell my teammates about Europe. They were bored. I talked to the girls who hung around the team. They found other things to do. When I talked to the intellectual element, they listened, thinking that perhaps I could be "saved" from the morass of sports. But when they listened, a few teammates and some of the girls began to think I was "weird." "Are you becoming a fag, Rich?" I neither wanted to be saved nor a fag, so I reluctantly focused all my attention on the court again. The reluctance soon disappeared. I was starting on the JV. It was now easy to put aside all that I had absorbed that summer. At the end of the year I was brought up to the varsity along with the other JV starters. I was working hard and I was being rewarded for it. My close friend, Billy Jones, had grown several inches while I had not grown a single inch in two years. Now he was the center and I was the forward—the slow forward. But I could shoot. Also, I was studying more and more and had won the academic scholarship awarded to the three students with the highest scholastic average. My family was very proud. My teammates never even knew.

I was also caught up with my father's team at St. John's. Tony Jackson was a senior now and was paying with LeRoy Ellis at center and Willie Hall at forward. Ellis and Hall were both black. It was probably the most talented college team my father ever coached. They were in the Top Ten all year and at one time were ranked second. They played number-one Ohio State in the finals of the Holiday Festival and lost in the closing minutes. We thought they could win the national championship. They didn't. I actually heard St. John's students asking how could they expect to win with three blacks on the front line?

The second major college basketball point-shaving scandal was breaking. As a pro coach during the first scandal, my father had put together a scrapbook showing how the lives of athletes involved had been devastated. He made each player at St. John's read this and sign to acknowledge that he read it before the season began.

It was the time for the St. John's Athletic Awards Banquet. Tony Jackson, as a three-time All-American, was obviously going to get the MVP award. I was going to attend and sit with LeRoy Ellis. LeRoy and I had become good friends. He was six-eleven from Bedford-Stuyvesant, one of the poorest and roughest areas in New York. Sports did bring LeRoy and me together and thirty years later we are still in touch.

But on this day two men from the athletic department came to our house and asked my father to go with them. He walked back into the house alone and went upstairs. I went up after a few minutes to find him staring at a wall, his eyes full of tears.

The New York district attorney advised St. John's not to give Tony Jackson the award as he was "more implicated in the scandal than you can know about." St. John's had agreed and sent their delegation to inform my father. He asked for evidence but was given none. He said he didn't believe it, that it was unfair to Tony since there was no evidence, no proof. Whom was he willing to believe, he was asked, the DA or Tony Jackson, a young man from the streets of New York?

Later I heard St. John's students ask how could Tony Jackson do this to St. John's after it had done so much for him. I heard others say that Jackson had been given the chance to get out of the ghetto but that he had blown it. They had already forgotten that Jackson had led St. John's to three great basketball years and had brought in many new fans. His presence had been partially responsible for LeRoy Ellis enrolling, and he had helped revive interest in college basketball in New York City for the first time since the scandal in 1950. All that seemed to be remembered now was the battle to get Jackson into the school in spite of his low high-school grades; the battle to keep him eligible during his four years at St. John's. All too easily accepted then, it was never proven that Tony Jackson did anything wrong. Tony, a likely NBA star, was blacklisted by the league.

Six years later he was allowed to play for New Jersey in the American Basketball Association where he averaged 19.5 points per game and was one of the league's best shooters. But the fulfillment of Tony Jackson's potential ended that day in 1961. The sports world had made a scapegoat of him, along with Connie Hawkins and Roger Brown, two other black New York players merely "implicated by the DA."

As has become frighteningly obvious over the past three decades, but especially in the 1980s with the scandalous revelations about academic abuses in intercollegiate athletics, the world of college sport was out of control on many campuses.

But when the scandals started to leak out, the question of protecting the athletes was rarely raised. Undeniably, the athletes who actually took money to fix scores cheated. They were wrong and should have been punished. Yet the primary motive for the behavior of many of the athletic departments was simply to protect themselves. The athletes were back on the streets in almost every case. No surprises. Caught in a sports web of cheating, these athletes took the easy way by joining in the cheating. Just more human tragedy. The reality of the sports world was beginning to sink into me ever so slowly, ever so painfully.

I spent that summer at the Friendship Farm basketball camp just being established by Jack Donohue, the Power Memorial coach. There was a big black kid there who was to begin sophomore year at Power in September. It was the first time I had *lived* with someone who was black. He was shy, sensitive, and very bright. He had difficulty handling the racism of some of the others. As he grew taller throughout the summer, racial barbs became more regular. As he began to dominate, there were no more jokes. But one player "niggered" him to death. I got fed up and intervened. Out of sight of anyone else this player decked me. Ashamed of my fate, I never told Donohue. That particular "nigger" is now known as Kareem Abdul-Jabbar, known then as Lew Alcindor. His baiter is now a head coach at a major university. He probably tells recruits of his "friendship" with Kareem to prove how "with it" he is.

I was getting better and better that summer. Playing not only with Lew, but with four others who eventually started at major colleges, I was averaging 10 points a game for the camp team. My only concern was that I was still five-eleven and was now playing guard. I knew I was slow, but hoped my ability to shoot would compensate. Billy Jones was also there and he was growing and improving.

We both came back to Manhattan that fall with high expectations. His were probably real and mine illusory. We both contracted whooping cough before the season began. Billy recovered in time to make honorable mention All-City. I hardly practiced in the first half of the season and became slower and slower on the court. I started to face the fact that I wouldn't be six-seven, and that being Joe Lapchick's son might not be enough to make me great.

I was spending more and more time with LeRoy Ellis. It was his senior year at St. John's and he was about to embark on a fourteen-year NBA career. Usually we discussed basketball, but sometimes we talked about his life growing up in Bedford-Stuyvesant. Without really knowing it, LeRoy had become my professor of race relations. It meant a great deal to me—and I think to him—when we discussed the poverty he grew up in, the loneliness of being black at an almost all-white school, how hard it was for him to deal with his courses after a poor grounding in fundamentals, and how unfair it had been that Tony Jackson was blacklisted by the NBA. My eyes were being forced open as the 1961–62 basketball season was ending. My personal dream had not quite ended, but my belief in the self-proclaimed verities of sportsworld were being shattered.

My own career seemed to be withering away. Suddenly Manhattan's starting backcourt duo became sick before a game with Cathedral. I had brought Janice, my girlfriend and first true love, to the game so that we could go to a party later. It was her first game. I didn't have time to get nervous when told I would start. I scored 18 points and we won easily. Janice was impressed. So was I.

The next day I went to the Manhattan College trainer because I had injured my foot late in the game. He said, "Coach Connington said you played well last night and he wished you weren't so slow so he could use you more." I knew at that very moment that if my coach said this *after* I scored 18 points, I had no future as a basketball player at Manhattan. Maybe I never really had a future. But now I knew. The funny thing was that it didn't hurt at all. From then on I could play for fun. I came out of the closet as a student and stopped hiding my grades from my teammates.

By 1963 my dreams about sports were dying if not dead. In August, as hundreds of thousands of people marched on Washington, Martin Luther King poetically outlined his own dream. Suddenly my experiences in sport—the important experiences—the nigger-lover calls, the games in Harlem, the experiences with Lew Alcindor, Tony Jackson, and LeRoy Ellis—made King's dream the only dream that mattered to me. LeRoy Ellis, by then a pro with the Lakers, had been the only black man in an all-white sea of humanity at Manhattan's graduation exercises two months earlier.

I was speaking directly to LeRoy and my father when I took the platform as the school's salutatorian. I was supposed to greet the people and say some pleasant things about what our experiences at Manhattan meant to us. I did this, but I also talked about all the work we had to do to make our society well again. I talked about racism and poverty to this relatively affluent white audience. I talked about the responsibility of our generation. Then I took my seat to the polite applause of an otherwise perplexed audience. I looked at LeRoy and my father. They understood. I could go on from there. The basketball dream was dead. Dr. King was about to shape a new dream.

Chapter 10

Stolen Ball

I chose to go to St. John's strictly because I was the last of my father's children. My sister had gone to Barnard and my brother to West Point. I knew that I could go to a school with a better academic reputation than St. John's. But I felt that one of us should go even if it was not among the East's academic elite.

When I arrived at St. John's in September I wondered if I would ever want to pick up a basketball again. I had spent the summer as if I wouldn't, working as a lifeguard at the Tibbetts Brook Park Pool, where my father and brother had also worked many years before. I lifted weights all summer, and I was in the best shape of my life. However, it was not basketball shape. I was a very muscular 190 pounds—almost 20 pounds more than I weighed in my junior year at Manhattan. If I was slow at 170 pounds, I was not anxious to know what I would be like at 190.

I met with Lou Carnesecca. He talked to me as if it was a foregone conclusion that I would play freshman basketball. I think he was being kind, for he definitely knew that I was not going to be able to help *this* freshman team. It had been a great recruiting year. There was Albie Schwartz, a Catholic later to be named to the "Jewish All-American" team, Brian Hill, a smooth ballhandler, Billy Jones, and John Zarzicki, a rough aggressive player in the mold of Jim Luscutoff of the Celtics. They were all very good. But the prizes were twin black towers—Lloyd

111

"Sonny" Dove from St. Francis Prep, and Ed Hill from New Jersey. Both were about six-seven. Lloyd, whose life was to end in a tragic car accident in 1983, was already fluid and proficient at age eighteen. He became an All-American and was named MVP in the College All-Star game as a senior. Ed was raw but as time went on showed perhaps more potential than did Lloyd. With such talent on hand, I realized that Lou was trying to be nice to me. I didn't want to expend all the energy practice would take so I could watch the team from the bench instead of the stands. It did not make any sense.

However, four factors made me decide to play freshman basketball. First, I felt a loyalty to Lou, who was treating me so well. Second, I wanted to be around the team to try to better understand what my father went through every day. He would have little to do with the freshman team, but there would be enough interaction. Third, my withdrawal from playing was not going as well as I had thought it would. I wasn't hooked anymore, but I still liked the taste. Maybe I could have fun playing, since I knew I could not compete with the Doves, Hills, and Joneses. Finally, being a basketball player—even a bad basketball player— at St. John's was an ego trip. It was the first time I would be a player at a coed school and players were definitely having more fun—more parties and especially more women. I was insecure around women, and the protective shield of "athlete" became my sliding board into the social world of St. John's.

St. John's was hardly a cauldron of progressive ideas. Thomas Aquinas was its intellectual mentor, while at other universities the shapers were Marx, Engels, Marcuse, and Sartre. Yet even Aquinas was in the shadows. Sports, especially basketball, was the major topic on campus. Being a jock meant being macho. Being white often meant being antiblack. Overtly, there were few signs of racism. "The [black] boys" and their "foxes" had their table in the lounge. At the time I guess this was viewed as full integration. Blacks and whites were marching in the South, fighting for integration. Little Rock, Birmingham, Selma, Montgomery—the capitals of oppression were being transformed into capitals of resistance.

We didn't have to resist at St. John's. Lloyd Dove and Ed Hill were freshmen there. Everyone assumed the other blacks were also athletes. (No one seemed to know that most were pharmacy and science majors.) Athletes were the right kind of blacks—they knew their place—the court, the table, then home. All was neatly laid out for us.

Some of my "friends" were taking me aside to say that others were "pissed off" because I was hanging around with blacks too much. It was one thing to pal around the locker room together, another to go out socially. If sports was helping blacks out of the ghetto, it was not getting them much beyond the locker room.

I decided that my interest had to go beyond empathy. I read John Hope Franklin's *From Slavery to Freedom* about the history of blacks in America, Martin Luther King's *Stride Toward Freedom,* James Baldwin's *The Fire Next Time,* as well as other books on race. I tried to discuss the things I was learning with my friends, but the basketball season was about to begin.

The team was required to spend one and a half to two hours each afternoon in a study hall prior to practice. George Lee was to have been the star of the team. With his academic dismissal the previous year, everyone knew they could not slide by only because they were athletes. However, "gut courses" were still available and many players took them. There were professors who were enthusiastic fans—we quickly got to know who they were. They wouldn't have much to root for if the star flunked out.

Getting by was a process of self-education, of the athletes informing themselves how to "beat the system." I cannot remember hearing about a coach turning athletes in this direction. The coaches, in fact, seemed more serious about academics than the athletes. With all the revelations about academic cheating in the 1980s I now realize that, by comparison, St. John's was far ahead of the field in educating its athletes, even in the 1960s.

Then, it seemed the whole institution was involved in athletics. After all, the administration chose to build the gym before it built the library. St. John's, like many other schools, used its national sports reputation to attract students and broaden its scholastic capabilities. The system was working—while I was there, St. John's became the largest Catholic school in America.

So now the athletes had to produce both in sports and in the classroom. Without the books there would be no sports. Without sports, there would be no more books. Without athletes, there would be no major sports program. It was in everyone's interest, including the athletes, to keep the athletes eligible to play. So athletes found the courses, they found the professors; they reduced their academic load to the minimum; they found friendly students to "help" them in their work; and they did study, at least during the study hall period. All of this was necessary because the pressures were tremendous. I am told that 90 percent of St. John's basketball players who played for four years have graduated since George Lee's expulsion. According to most estimates, that is almost triple the national average for major sports programs.

At St. John's I was never aware of the additional factor of alumni pressure to win. Since my father was the coach, I am quite sure I would have seen it. However, I had friends in other colleges, as did teammates and members of the varsity, and we frequently heard stories of handsome payoffs from alumni. At the time, most of the money was apparently being given in the Southern and Midwestern schools. One St. John's player had been offered $10,000 a year to transfer to a relatively small school-on-the-make in the Midwest. There were many such stories. Direct payments, clothes, cars, women, jobs for family members. Anything one could imagine. The press seemed to be ignoring it.

Reading my father's scandal scrapbook, as all of us had to do just at the start of the season, I was frightened. I was angry. I knew whom my teammates had to avoid. As I began to learn more about alumni payoffs, about their "support" for intercollegiate athletics, I wondered about the bookmakers on the streets. They were teaching the same values—get what you can. But the bookmakers were more open about it. They were not acceptable. The alumni were "friends." Spending time at St. John's in the 1980s, I see that the alumni gave no "big money," and thus, have a negligible role in the sports program.

We freshmen were ready to play against the varsity in Alumni Hall. We knew we had a good team and could win. The freshmen, however, never beat the varsity. This night was no exception. Our freshman coach was Jack Kaiser, a fine, intelligent man who is now St. John's athletic director. He was also one of the most successful baseball coaches in the country. His philosophy was that the freshmen team would prepare those who would later play on the varsity. That meant Ed and Brian Hill, Jones, Schwartz, Dove, and possibly Zarzicki. Not Lapchick. But all would play that night.

Playing for just the last ten minutes, I didn't do anything exceptional, but I didn't make any mistakes either. Against the St. John's varsity!

The next morning my father said two short sentences to me. "You did well last night. You made me proud." It was only the second time he had seen me play in a game.

Now I was free. I had made *him* proud. I finally realized that although he had never once put pressure on me to play, and in fact had tried to direct me *away* from basketball, the pressure had always been there simply because he was Joe Lapchick. Unknowingly, I had been waiting for this moment.

The varsity started the year poorly but finished strong with wins over Loyola of Chicago, the number-one ranked team, and New York University, our biggest rival. NYU had an excellent team and were solid favorites. St. John's built a big lead at halftime and my father literally ran off the court at full speed. The team was shedding its washed-up label. He knew it—the packed crowd knew it. They were on their feet when this sixty-four-year-old lean tower bolted for the exit. The cheering went on long after he and the team had disappeared into the concrete corridors. The second half was an anticlimax. It never was a game and St. John's won by 20 points.

The future was bright. Most members of the varsity were returning. Despite Ed Hill having to leave school for personal reasons, the freshmen lost only once. And there was the prospect that Lew Alcindor, who as a junior was dominating high school basketball, would come to St. John's. With Lew and Lloyd, the national championship would be within St. John's grasp. My father was a happy man.

The summer of 1964 was another turning point for me. The civil rights movement was in high gear and students from the North were heading south to help in the Voter Registration Drive. Spirits were high. The March on Washington had electrified the nation the year before. Martin Luther King was rumored to be the recipient of the Nobel Peace Prize. Students and activists were organizing sit-ins throughout the South. But the Voter Registration Drive had the most potential. The ballot was power.

On June 21, 1964, three civil rights workers—James Chaney, a black man from Mississippi, and Michael Schwerner and Andrew Goodman, both white men from New York, were arrested for speeding in Mississippi. Local police claimed they had released them six hours later. Their burned-out station wagon was soon found without them. It was six weeks before their bodies were discovered, but the nation knew their fate on June 21.

For me, this event dictated that I could no longer simply read about black history. I had to become actively involved. Over and over I read Martin Luther King's "I have a dream" speech. One sentence kept jumping out at me. "With this faith we will be able to work together, to pray together, to struggle together, to go to jail together, to stand up for freedom together, knowing we will be free one day."

I was ashamed. Ashamed to have seen what racism could do and not act to stop it. Ashamed that I had thought of myself as being "free" because my father had told me he was proud of how I played basketball; that he was free because St. John's had beaten NYU. Ashamed that it took the deaths of three contemporaries to sufficiently shake me to see how much I had to learn, how much I had to do.

That summer the police tried to obscure what had happened to Schwerner, Chaney, and Goodman. It took Dr. David Spain, a medical examiner from New York, to ascertain the brutality of their deaths.

In 1964 the work I could do was at best token. I couldn't go to the South—and frankly did not know if I had the courage to do so at the time. I was working seventy-two hours a week as both a lifeguard in Yonkers and as an attendant at the New York World's Fair. With little time to myself, I went to Long Island or Westchester three nights a week to collect newspapers that could be recycled to raise money. The money was then sent to help with transportation costs in voter registration projects.

My job as a lifeguard was helping to crystallize my vision of racism in the North. All we read about was what was going on in the South. However, the Yonkersites who were condemning the civil rights murders were also complaining that too many people from the Bronx were coming to swim at Tibbetts Brook Park where I worked. The "too many people from the Bronx" was code for "too many blacks." Disdainful of the blacks earlier in the summer, the white bathers were more respectful after a serious riot in Harlem. Fear bred respect. It was a lesson not lost on any of us. March, sing, parade, and demonstrate—do that all you want and get few changes. But destroy property—and suddenly whites began moving out of your way. Suddenly whites were being taunted and were taking it just like blacks had to for centuries. You could see it at the pool. You could see it in the streets. You could feel it in the movement. The movement was nationwide.

My sister was talking about leaving for Africa, which she did in November 1964. I knew very little about Africa then. The few references to it in textbooks and in high school were to the slave trade and the colonization of Africa, then equated to Europe's efforts to "civilize" and "Christianize" the dark and demonic continent. South Africa—Christian, civilized, industrialized, and rich—was portrayed as the hope of the continent. That summer I didn't quite understand why this great hope was being suspended from the 1964 Tokyo Olympics. If they were Christian, civilized, industrialized, and rich, then why shouldn't they play? The press condemned the decision, arguing that it was wrong to "mix politics and sport." Most stories explained why. Generally one paragraph near the end referred to the fact that South Africa was expelled because some nations, led by the Communists, felt that it was a racist country. My curiosity was aroused and I began to read about South Africa. The fact that my sister moved to Africa increased my desire to learn more and more. It was in the realm of sports that my education about apartheid had its origin. Many years later I would remember that and try to use it to educate others.

Our family was turned inside out in a matter of hours after my father's annual trip to St. John's to sign his contract. He had always signed one-year contracts. St. John's had been good to him. It had hired him in the 1930s when his playing career was ending. He always said he didn't even know *how* to coach then. And it had rehired him when he resigned from the Knicks. St. John's was about to pay him $12,500 for the 1964–65 season! Yes, St. John's was family. He loved the game and St. John's for letting him play it. But they stole the ball that day.

What he wanted to do most was to help lead it to a National Collegiate Athletic Association (NCAA) title—the national championship. He wanted to give this to his school before retiring. He knew it could be done if he could recruit Lew Alcindor that year. He liked Lew personally very much. Joe Lapchick, the first great big man in basketball, knew what Lew was going through. I counted Lew among my friends. It would be great to see Lloyd and Lew on the same team. There would be no stopping them.

As he was signing the contract, Father Graham, the athletic moderator, said something like, "Joe, we've been proud of our association with you. You've made a great contribution to the school. We hope that your final year will be a great one." He assumed this meant his final year with Alcindor. Of course, it would be a great one. Then they explained to him—for the very first time—that St. John's had set mandatory retirement at sixty-five. Joe Lapchick was devastated.

When I left him in the morning he was buoyant. When I saw him that night he was a defeated and lonely man. I told him we could fight this through the student body. He said no, a rule was a rule. If it had validity, then exceptions should not be made. He called my brother, Joe, who was superintendent of schools in Aspen, Colorado. He told my father that, in general, it was a good rule; in Graham's position, my brother would have done the same thing. For every great teacher over sixty-five there were ten bad ones. Sacrifices had to be made. He only wished it wasn't my father. It was the midnight of my father's life. The man who had spent a significant part of his life fighting for others would not now fight for himself.

He convinced me at the time he was right. The word spread quickly on campus. I remember Lynn Burke, the Olympic champion turned St. John's cheerleader, coming up to me. She was very upset and wanted to do something. Everyone wanted to do something. Protest at St. John's had not been a major activity. I was pleased to see it might be a possibility. On that day, however, I told Lynn that it would upset my father.

Jack Donohue, the coach of Power Memorial High School, and more importantly, the coach of Lew Alcindor, came over to our house that night. He was an outgoing man with a good sense of humor. But that night he was very serious. I had never before seen him like that. He wanted to talk to my father alone. I had never before been excluded. Something had to be very wrong.

Jack Donohue had been asked if he would be interested in being the assistant basketball coach at St. John's. When Lou Carnesecca joined the staff in the 1958–59 season, my father and the athletic department promised him the head coaching job when my father retired. That job had been taken. Jack as assistant coach? St. John's was a powerhouse again. He could move from there into a good head coaching position. Why was he so serious? This effusive man was so timid. Why? At first, my father couldn't understand it. Suddenly, he couldn't miss it.

He asked Jack if St. John's mentioned Lew Alcindor when they brought up the subject of the job. Yes, they had. What a scenario. One of the most renowned figures in the history of sport, the last of the "pioneers" still coaching, was to be mandatorily retired to make room for this high school coach to become an assistant coach. Lew Alcindor would come with Jack. Joe Lapchick would go home with a $100-a-month pension.

It didn't even make sense. First of all, Jack idolized my father. That is why he was so timid that night. I don't think he would have seriously considered the job because of the pain the circumstances would cause my father. Second, even if he would have considered it, St. John's had offered him several thousand dollars less than he was making at Power Memorial. You didn't have to be a wizard with business figures to know that this did not make sense.

Most importantly, St. John's knew my father had a good relationship with Lew Alcindor and with Jack. Maybe they could have considered hiring Jack as an assistant in addition to Lou. Perhaps that would reinforce any decision by Alcindor to come to St. John's.

What they didn't know and what no one knew except Lew himself, was that Lew Alcindor didn't trust Jack Donohue. As Lew related it in a story in *Sports Illustrated,* Jack had told him he was "acting just like a nigger" at the halftime of one game. For Lew, that was the end of Jack. Jack explained that he was only trying to stir him up to get him to play more aggressively; that he had no racial intention. But for Lew, that was the end of Jack.

When I read this, I wondered how many good players had been destroyed by unthinking statements made in the heat of combat by unthinking coaches. Alcindor was strong and could overcome it. How many didn't?

Many years later, Lew Alcindor, now Kareem Abdul-Jabbar, talked about the possibility of being traded from the Milwaukee Bucks to the New York Knicks. Peter Vescey, a reporter for the New York *Sunday News,* asked Kareem why he wanted to return to New York after he had chosen to leave it for UCLA in 1965. He replied:

I will say that the only reason I left New York was because Joe Lapchick was forced into retirement at age sixty-five. I wanted to play for St. John's and Mr. Lapchick but for whatever reason he was squeezed out.

I really liked the man and I found I could relate to him as a human being. I used to see him during the summers at camps and he'd never pressure me in any way.

I remember he'd tell me stories about when he was young and the people in his neighborhood used to gawk as this tall, skinny kid passed by. They'd call him the gypsy. He went through the same things I went through a generation before.

My father had been dead for several years. He didn't know this. Nor did he know that exceptions to the mandatory retirement rule were made after he left. Maybe St. John's finally recognized the cruel effects of the rule. Maybe it was merely the fact that there was nothing to be gained by invoking it.

I could not sleep that night. It was still a month before practice began, but that night my vision was of a packed Madison Square Garden. St. John's had just won their fourth NIT championship and my father was being lifted on the shoulders of a sea of humanity. What a glorious sight. But it was only a vision.

Without any encouragement from my father, mild protests took place on campus over his retirement. There was a petition, a couple of rallies. Lloyd Dove took the podium at a rally on academic problems at St. John's. He talked about the injustice of my father's situation. He talked about how much more Joe Lapchick had to give to St. John's. He asked "if the administration could do this to the best-known person on campus, what could it do to others?" I will never forget Lloyd for that. Not only was he a ballplayer—and athletes never dared to challenge the system in those days—but he was a black ballplayer. It took great courage. Yet, I will also never forget the reaction of some in the audience. No comments had been made after any of the white speakers sat down. But when Lloyd finished, I heard a group of students saying how disloyal he was to St. John's; several claimed that he was inarticulate. This "boy" belonged on the court, not at a protest rally.

Without my father's encouragement, the protests had no force. The opening of his last season ended the students' rebellion but initiated my father's own form of silent protest. He was coaching his heart out, and it almost gave way. Unknown to anyone but his physician and myself, he had two mild heart attacks during games that season. But he couldn't be stopped.

St. John's got off to a great start, including a 75–74 comeback victory over number-one ranked Michigan in the Holiday Festival final. After the tournament each game on the road meant a farewell ceremony for my father. They were all very touching. They were also very frequently followed by a loss. My father attributed the losses, at least in part, to the ceremonies. How could the team fight hard against a school that was being so nice to the coach?

Fortunately, there were no ceremonies in Madison Square Garden during the NIT. St. John's was seeded next to last, yet won the first three games.

St. John's played top-seeded Villanova for the championship, and beat them. For the team, for the crowd, for all New York, it seemed like Joe Lapchick's final game was a crusade. My vision had become reality. Joe Lapchick was riding that sea of humanity. The Garden was in pandemonium. It was the proudest moment of my life. Half of the people must have been in tears. The headline in the next day's *New York Post* was "Joe Lapchick Walks with Kings." He always had. Within a few months he had turned his dismissal from sports into a moment of pure joy, and his tears into his triumph.

Before the end of the season he had been discussing other coaching jobs. He had one offer from the pros and another from the college ranks. I think he probably would have accepted one if he hadn't won that day. But the win simply made him say, "What a way to go!" His intense pride had almost killed him that season, but the victory had made the pain worthwhile.

Chapter 11

Inside Out

My last two years at St. John's were ones of increasing political and intellectual awareness. It was a time when the Vietnam War and the racial situation in America were crying out for change. At Berkeley I would have been a moderate. At St. John's I was a radical. In the real world, I was probably a liberal.

The irony of my father's mandatory retirement was that I was able to have much more time with him. We would sit and talk late into the night. He wanted to know what I thought about the Vietnam War. For him, the war might have meant losing me and that was enough for him to be against it. The geopolitical situation was not the issue. He didn't want me to fight. We watched Muhammad Ali "debate" William Buckley. At the time they were saying Ali was mentally incompetent but that program showed how bright Ali really was. When he was reclassified by his draft board, Ali said, "I ain't got no quarrel with them Viet Cong." In my senior year of college I was the sports columnist for the *Torch,* the school newspaper. I wrote of Ali's courage to stand up for what he believed. My father thought it was the best thing I had written. White students told me it was scandalous, unpatriotic; I was mixing politics and sports. Black students said thanks.

We both read and discussed the *Autobiography of Malcolm X* that spring. My father had always disliked Malcolm X while he was alive, believing the press portrayals of him as a violent, white-hating man. The book was a revelation for both of us. Martin Luther King was still the sun, but Malcolm had become respectable. We were learning together.

In my last year at St. John's I was physically there but felt emotionally removed from it. I shared an apartment with Vincent Ferrandino, probably the most serious and, perhaps, the brightest student I knew at St. John's.

During this time I spent many evenings with Lloyd Dove. We had seen a good deal of each other that year. He was having a great season, leading St. John's to a 23–5 record and an NCAA bid. Lloyd was intelligent and sensitive. He was considered quiet and shy by most students, but this may have been because they were whites viewing a black man in an all-white environment. I had quite a few opportunities to be with him and his black friends, and among them he was a different man.

One evening Lloyd and I went to hear some jazz in Greenwich Village. It was 2:00 A.M. before we headed back to Long Island, and we were both a bit high. I asked him to stay over at my apartment. For twenty minutes he thought of every possible excuse not to. I asked what was really wrong. It was difficult for him to answer, but he finally blurted out that he had never slept at a white person's house before.

Lloyd Dove, sophisticated, intelligent, handsome, All-American Lloyd Dove had never spent the night at a white person's house and, when finally faced with the choice, was apprehensive. I cringed. During my four years at St. John's, I had spent some of my best moments with Dove—double-dating, drinking, listening to music, and sharing feelings. Looking back I think I would rather have been with him than anyone else on campus. Yet here was the bottom line—he was black and I was white. Because of that difference, Lloyd was apprehensive about staying with me.

As on previous occasions, my consciousness of being white swept over me. No matter how close we had become, Lloyd couldn't forget that I was white and, therefore, a possible racist. I am convinced that he didn't believe I was, but there was that hesitation—a self-protective internal mechanism telling black people not to trust white people, not to let the defenses down. I was stunned, and hurt, but in the silence that dominated the end of the ride, the world became more clear to me. That world saw this black man as a jock. As long as he remained a jock, it was color blind. Off court, whether at a white social gathering or at a protest supporting Joe Lapchick, he was invisible. Ralph Ellison, the author of *Invisible Man,* was right.

In the quiet of the car I decided that knowing, studying, and raising money for good causes was not enough. There was too much at stake. I didn't know *what* I would do or *how* I would do it, but I knew then that a major part of my life would be devoted to actively searching for ways to change society. My brother insisted that I was a naive dreamer. Although we were miles apart politically, I had to wonder if he was right.

Lloyd stayed at my apartment that night. We consumed a few more drinks and fell asleep in our clothes at about 8:00 A.M. Poor Vincent. I am sure he must have thought we had had a wild night when he found our bodies strewn about the living room in the morning.

I went home so I could discuss the previous evening with my father. He was sympathetic but not surprised. He mentioned a friend named Bob Douglas whom he knew from his days with the Celtics. They had shared a similar conversation in the late 1940s. Appraising my needs that night, he told me to study—to prepare myself for whatever path I would choose.

Joe and Elizabeth Lapchick had just faced a severe test. Both were Catholics—my mother was devout. Thus it was difficult for them in 1966 when my sister, Barbara, announced that she was divorcing Roy, her Jewish husband.

But the true test came when Barbara introduced her new husband-to-be, Rajat Neogy, a prominent Ugandan literary figure whose parents were Indian. I have known innumerable "liberals" who have balked at sexual relations between the races. For them, any form of integration was positive as long as that sexual boundary was not crossed.

As well as I knew my parents, I did not know how they would react. My father and I watched the sunrise as we talked about Barbara and Rajat. In 1966, such a relationship was virtually unheard of in polite middle-class white society. Then we reached the bottom line. He asked me if Barbara loved Rajat and if they were happy together. I said it seemed so. "Then that's all that should matter," he said. My mother had already given her blessing.

Bill Russell's book *Go Up for Glory* was published in 1966 as Russell's fabulous career with the Boston Celtics was in its final quarter. He would still help the Celtics win more championships, and he had already been a member of the Olympic team and participated in two NCAA championships as a collegian at the University of San Francisco. His Celtics teams won the NBA championships in nine of his first ten years and he was chosen the most valuable player four times by fellow players. He had done everything right in basketball. He should have been lionized.

He should have been—but Bill Russell was black, outspoken, and intimidating. *Go Up for Glory* was, perhaps, one of the first honest sports stories, and these were difficult times to be honest. Protest against the war was threatening all the "yes, sir" people in society, yet Russell criticized America's "yes, sir" mentality. Blacks were rioting in city after city. Respectable black leaders were supposed to calm the waters. Russell wrote about having to confront the conditions that had caused the riots. He wrote:

> The relationship between the white and the Negro is most often represented by the police—the symbol of authority . . . most Negroes look on the police as the white man with a badge, the symbol of the white man's authority. The policeman becomes a natural enemy. . . .
> But it is the people—the whites and the Negroes—who inhabit the battleground day after day and night after night who are the true warriors. Their voices must be heard.

Russell also tackled the sports empire. He told story after story of racism, of quotas in the NBA, of racist fans, players, and coaches. He even discussed the humiliating segregation of the U.S. team's domestic tour prior to the 1956 Games:

> It was a hurting thing. Not desperate. We were men. We had experienced it before. But . . . it was another scar, another slice.

We were representing our nation in the largest sports event in the world. But in our own country we were not equals as citizens.

My father and I both read Russell's book early in 1967, and when I had finished, I told him—for the first time—about listening on the upstairs phone when he was receiving the "nigger–lover" calls. I told him that I had been frightened for him; that I had been afraid to ask him for fear I would also hate him if I knew his terrible secret. I informed him of how many times I had been called a "nigger–lover" for befriending blacks. There was a spontaneous yet enormous emotional release. We both accepted the relief of relinquishing our shared secrets. No words passed between us. We understood each other's pain.

The publication of Russell's book was followed by a public outcry. Critics said that he was only able to write the book because of basketball; he was another ungrateful black man. Russell withstood the attack and grew stronger. But he was, in reality, protected by his dominance as a player. If K. C. Jones, for example, a black teammate of Russell's on the Celtics, had written that book he might never have played again. Russell was just too good; the NBA could not afford to dump him. Sports was supposed to be the great equalizer for blacks. Now it was being described as a racist reflection of a racist society.

My father, for the first time, began to open up about his own racial experiences in sport. The Tony Jackson case bothered him more than any other. He mentioned the early days in the NBA, and the signing of Clifton. But it was when he recalled the all-black "Renaissance Five" (commonly called the Rens) that I became most interested. All my life I had heard that the Original Celtics were the greatest team of all time. Now he told me that the Rens were as good as the Celtics by the early 1930s. What had happened to historical accuracy? This was new information for me.

My father admitted that he knew nothing about black people let alone black athletes prior to his contacts with the Rens. Raised in an immigrant family, he had all the apprehensions about competition from blacks shared by other immigrants early in the twentieth century.

The difference was that he was able to have years of contact with the Rens. They played against each other, traveled to the same cities, competed in front of crowds ready to attack these audacious barnstormers, and finally confronted the stereotypes that each held about the other. At first, the Rens couldn't fully trust the Celtics while the Celtics couldn't fully understand the Rens. Time changed that. However, time moved slowly.

All the Celtics knew was that the Rens could play them even, yet they saw the differences in lifestyle. The Rens traveled in a large bus purchased by Bob Douglas, their founder-owner, so that they could avoid confrontations in hotels, restaurants, trains, and public buses that wouldn't allow blacks. There were some towns where they couldn't be seen by day. They couldn't eat, wash, or even purchase gas in some places. When they could find hotels that would take them, they were usually bug-ridden. On the court they faced hostile white fans, yet they played the game straight and with dignity.

Joe Lapchick found it impossible to even share a drink with Douglas in some places. They integrated arenas in several cities, most notably by playing the first interracial game in the South, but they couldn't socialize together outside of New York and a very few other cities.

For years my father was oblivious to racial slights. He finally asked Bob Douglas about them in New York during the off-season. Douglas replied, "Joe, I can't go where you can go. I'm not going to subject myself to rejection and humiliation." They talked for hours that day and my father realized that previously, in spite of admiring the Rens for years, he had never really learned anything personal about them or about Douglas. It had shocked him that, perhaps subconsciously, he had chosen to ignore the racism around him. My father told me that the talk with Douglas was pivotal in his life—a life he vowed to change.

I had been accepted into a masters program in African Studies at the University of East Africa in Uganda. That is where I wanted to go, but I didn't want to leave the country for long because of my father's health. I chose instead to enroll at the graduate school of international studies at the University of Denver, where

I would major in African Studies. However, Barbara and her new husband invited me to come to Uganda at least for the summer. I hoped that visiting Barbara and studying even briefly at the University of East Africa would show me how to proceed with my life. It only showed me how much I had to learn.

This was Uganda prior to Amin. 1967 was a beautiful time to be there. Barbara ran the Nommo Art Gallery and Rajat was editor of *Transition,* an influential literary magazine. Both the gallery and the magazine were showplaces for talented Africans, so I was exposed to a wealth of African art and literature. Sitting in their house and listening to Rajat, Barbara, and their guests was a living classroom on Africa. Kampala was an intellectual capital and it seemed as though I met every important African writer and scholar that summer. They included Ali Magrui, the African scholar, and Paul Theroux, the well-known writer. It makes me ill to think of what Idi Amin did to this beautiful and rich land.

While I had countless extraordinary experiences, two above all have stayed with me. The first related to sports. I hadn't played basketball in two years yet I was drawn to a tucked-away court on the university campus. I was able to talk to the African students in the classroom but outside I was a social outcast. I was not only white, but a white American. Not only racist, but also colonialist. This wasn't a problem with Rajat's friends, but it was with the students. They had seen too many patronizing Westerners who wanted to "help the natives."

I watched the Africans play basketball, day after day in the melting sun. Bad as I was, I knew I was better than the players I was seeing. After all, I had trained for fifteen years while they were obviously newcomers. I had vowed to stay away from sports a few months before, but I was so frustrated by the alienation I was feeling on campus that I had to play. I hated being stereotyped.

What irony! Here I was almost on the equator in blazing heat. Now I was the white man trying to break into African society by playing basketball. It seemed ridiculous but I was desperate. It worked. We played together. We drank beer together. We talked sports and, here in Uganda, sports really did open a door, at least for me.

The second thing I brought home was the African students' perceptions of black Americans. Black pride was rising in urban American cities. Part of that pride was a cultural identification with Africa and Africans. I quickly learned that in June 1967 it was not a two-way flow. I was abruptly stopped the first time I naively referred to an African as "black." "We are not blacks, we are Africans. Blacks are Americans." I was surprised and taken aback. They did not identify with American blacks at all. In fact, the students criticized black Americans for allowing their oppression to continue. It seemed that they felt African independence movements could be analogous to a black revolution in the United States. I disagreed with their analysis just as I would disagree with Andrew Young ten years later when he tried to compare the civil rights movement in America with the struggle against apartheid in South Africa. I unsuccessfully tried to explain the difference in the situations. What was important was not that I disagreed but that this *was* their analysis.

Perceptions changed one July morning. "Black revolt in Detroit" was the headline in *The People,* a Ugandan newspaper. Racial outbursts, large and small, had spread through urban America in the middle sixties. But Detroit was the bloodiest—41 dead and 347 injured—and costliest in terms of property. There was $500 million worth of damage. Some 5,000 inner-city residents were homeless. But what was most meaningful for the African students was that there were 3,800 arrests.

They believed that this was the start of a black revolt, a black American independence movement. The first American magazines to reach Kampala called it a riot—spontaneous and unplanned. The students didn't believe it for a second. American blacks, they felt, were taking control of their destiny.

We spent much of that summer dissecting Detroit and its aftermath. What was nonviolence? When did a riot become a revolt? What was the future of revolt and what were its consequences? Whatever the nature of the conflict, it was apparent that, once again, violence in America was leading to social change. The men who ruled America could listen to Martin

Luther King, applaud and go to their white suburbs and forget. They could not ignore a Detroit and would rush to take prompt action to quell the riot/revolt. White Americans seemed seized by fear of a reign of terror; black Americans, to their African brothers, seemed equally seized by a vision.

I left Africa and arrived in Denver still searching for ways to participate, ways to contribute. I marched in all the antiwar demonstrations but knew there had to be more. I was away from St. John's, away from sports. The academic demands were enormous. I was reading five to seven books a week on subjects such as international economics, African studies, political ideologies. I met Sandy on my first day there. She was a graduate student in art, an apolitical woman and very different from my deadly serious, highly competitive, very political fellow students.

Professors began to give me direction. George Shepherd taught African studies; Ron Krieger trained us in international economics; Steve Hunter interpreted diplomatic history. All three were political activists in the antiwar and civil rights movements. They demonstrated that one could be an academic activist. That seemed to be what I should do—teach, work with my students to get them involved, and be an activist myself. All seemed to be settled by the third quarter. I was confident as a student and, for the first time in my life, had a concrete concept of what I would do. Additionally, Sandy and I decided to get married in June.

Then one April evening my confidence crumbled. Martin Luther King was assassinated in Memphis. I was all at once filled with sorrow, fear, and rage. I called home for comfort, but there was none. It was a weepy conversation. The apostle of nonviolence, armed only with moral courage, had met—inevitably, perhaps—violent death. As inner city after inner city erupted, I began to see that revolt just might be underway. I feared for the U.S. for I believed that sustained violent revolt by black America could lead to only one thing—massive retaliatory repression against blacks.

Mostly, I hated America—that is, white America. For King, the philosophy of nonviolence could only be effective if it pricked the conscience of a moral society. This society seemed to have no conscience and was not moral to this twenty-two-year-old. In Asia, we were killing Vietnamese by the thousands to save them from Communism. In Memphis, we had killed a black leader trying to make things better for his people. I wanted to get out. By midnight I decided I would leave the country and join Barbara and Rajat in Uganda. Then I realized that I could afford to go to Africa, get my degree there and work *because* I was white and had the money. Most blacks in Denver or New York cannot pack up and leave.

By 4:00 A.M., I decided to stay and fight. By eight in the morning I had written to Wilt Chamberlain, then playing for Philadelphia, LeRoy Ellis, who was playing for Baltimore, and a host of other professional basketball players whom I knew. I wrote to Jim Brown, the great football player and social activist. I wrote to Coretta King. The idea that I was proposing was to form an organization called PRIDE that would help to introduce black and African history and culture courses into the curricula of high schools around the country. While the time for the idea was ripe, I did not expect a serious response. Then Wilt and LeRoy endorsed the idea. Brown, through John Wooten, his associate, wanted to meet me in Cleveland. I began to see the potential linkup between sports and politics at close range. With the athletes' endorsements, I was able to get Walter Mondale, Jacob Javits, and Hugh Scott, then Senate minority leader, to join PRIDE's advisory board.

That year saw several other linkups between sports and politics. It had been announced in November 1967 that a number of black athletes would boycott the 1968 Mexico City Olympics to protest racism in American society. The efforts were being organized by Harry Edwards, a former athlete then teaching at San Jose State. Harry, along with Jack Scott, was to become one of the major shapers of the oncoming athletic revolt.

In February 1968, South Africa was readmitted to the Olympics when the International Olympic Committee (IOC) met in Grenoble, France. The reaction was instantaneous. All African nations except Malawi announced they would boycott. They were joined by most developing countries from Asia and some from Latin

America. The Socialist nations threatened to pull out. With the potential for racial violence already illustrated by the assassination of Martin Luther King and an attack on IOC President Avery Brundage's hotel in Chicago by blacks, the IOC voted South Africa out again in April.

In both cases, the media criticized the attempts to mix sports and politics. It gave extensive coverage to black athletes like Jesse Owens, who opposed the boycott, and to Brundage, who continued to insist that politics had no influence on the IOC's decision to bar South Africa.

I returned to New York at the end of May before the wedding. Most of the daily discussions were of what I would do in the future and about PRIDE. After my New York friends had a bachelor party for me I arrived at our house in Yonkers weary from too much to drink. Sandy called and said, "Did you hear? Robert Kennedy was shot last night in California." Suddenly sober, my body became rigid, my mind became numb. I couldn't believe it.

At the time I was an RFK supporter and thought he was our best hope for real change in America. We had recently met on his campaign stop in Cheyenne, Wyoming. We briefly discussed PRIDE, the concept of which had been endorsed by all the presidential candidates except Nixon. He told me how much he admired my father and wished me luck. I could still feel his firm, reassuring handshake.

My father had been keeping a vigil all night. For him RFK was the hope to end the war, to heal the cities, to bring peace to the world and to the country. It was too much to take. When would it all end?

I tried to postpone the wedding date. Not only was it scheduled for the night Kennedy was to be buried, but it was to be held in Rockville, Maryland, just outside Washington. Tent City and the Poor People's March were in Washington. Kennedy would be buried in Arlington. But Sandy's parents insisted that the wedding be held as planned, and I acquiesced.

I went to Cleveland to meet Mayor Stokes, Jim Brown, and John Wooten on Monday morning at the offices of the Negro Economic Union, which had been cofounded by Brown and

Wooten. But Stokes remained in Washington after Kennedy's funeral and Jim Brown was in Los Angeles. So Wooten and I met to talk about what the Negro Economic Union was doing and what PRIDE hoped to do. We felt that Cleveland might become a test city for the introduction of black history and culture courses in the schools.

Aside from the business aspects of the meeting, I left with a real understanding of the faith of a large part of the black community in the Kennedys. John Wooten, a serious, astute man, talked about looking forward to the Kennedy children growing up and entering politics. In 1968, it seemed like a long time for the black community to have to wait. The black community is still waiting.

Whether it was inspired by or fearfully reacting to the potential of a black Olympic boycott, *Sports Illustrated* published a five-part series by Jack Olsen called "The Black Athlete: A Shameful Story" in July (discussed in detail in Chapter 13). It was the first investigative report I had read on how pervasive racism was in professional and intercollegiate athletics. It confirmed all that I had come to believe about the nature of sports in America, and seemed to add fuel to the controversy about any black role in the Olympics.

Lew Alcindor, along with UCLA teammates Mike Warren and Lucius Allen, had already boycotted the Olympic basketball trials. Up to that point I had not known what to think about the idea of a boycott. However, I respected Lew's judgment enough that I began to support the idea. My father strongly disagreed with me on this, although paradoxically he respected Lew Alcindor more than ever for his decision. He knew it was a decision based on principle and my father thought Lew had made a courageous personal sacrifice.

I watched part of the Olympic Games with my father in New York. Any illusions I had had about the Olympics had been destroyed a long time ago. The pre-Olympic "ceremonies" in Mexico City included a three-day student riot in which thirteen were killed and hundreds more injured. Striking students claimed that the incredibly high cost of staging the games was a national disgrace.

While the boycott itself had been called off, everyone knew something would happen. The goals of a total boycott were expressed in the simple gesture of two young black men. When Tommie Smith and John Carlos raised their clenched, black-gloved fists on the victory stand, they eloquently expressed what white America had tried to ignore: sport, like society, was racist.

The importance of that gesture became evident in the ensuing reaction. White society was quick to punish Smith and Carlos immediately in Mexico and for many years after as both became unemployable. The sports establishment, from Avery Brundage on down, did everything it could to pretend nothing had changed. In response to a question about how the Olympics could survive as long as politics continued to become more and more a part of the games, Brundage replied, "Who said that politics are becoming more and more involved in the Olympics? In my opinion this is not so. You know very well that politics are not allowed in the Olympic Games."

However, that memory of Smith and Carlos on the victory stand would not go away. It became *the* Olympic picture. Everything had changed. Black athletes were vigorously speaking out. And my father, initially spurred on by Bill Russell's writings, resumed telling me of the forms of hate he had encountered in sports because of his racial views.

Suddenly horror visited our own family. We got the news that my sister's husband, Rajat Neogy, had been sent to Luzira Prison in Uganda. The date was October 18, two days after the Smith-Carlos raised fist salute. We could no longer think about the Olympics, the Rens-Celtics saga, or about the integration of the NBA.

Rajat had been charged with sedition. The charge stemmed from his printing a letter to the editor in *Transition,* the magazine he edited, that said that Uganda should Africanize the courts, that is, the judges should be Africans. The trauma lasted for five months.

The case was clearly racial and political. Rajat was an Asian Ugandan. By 1968, Asians had become scapegoats for all the ills of Ugandan society. The trial became an anti-Asian showpiece and, in the process, Rajat had his Ugandan citizenship revoked.

When the jury handed down its verdict, Rajat was ruled innocent. But the mental anguish for my sister continued when he was rearrested at the conclusion of the trial. Knowing that all mail would be opened, she sent a letter back to us with friends. Her baby's nursemaid had turned out to be a police informer. Now Barbara was unable to sleep because each night she listened for the nursemaid's steps that signaled the arrival of the police car to collect the day's information. Joe Lapchick, who said he died a thousand deaths in defeat, was dying once more through the suffering of his daughter. My mother and father drew very close together during this period. The weight of the horror was finally lifted when Rajat was released in the spring of 1969. He and Barbara rushed to leave Kampala and all they had there before President Obote could change his mind and rearrest him. It was over for all but Barbara and Rajat, who had yet to work out their private nightmares and inner fears. More than twenty years later, Rajat still has deep scars.

*   *   *

The events of the previous four years had a tremendous impact on my father. Joe Lapchick had been known as a man who shaped the destinies of others. He had tried to instill pride in being self-disciplined and honest, and pride in being able to accept victory and defeat in the same way.

The press described him as a humble and self-effacing man. An event in the last full summer of his life underscored this. The Maurice Stokes NBA All-Star benefit game was being held at Kutscher's Country Club.

There were mobs outside the arena when my father arrived. At six-five his head was way above the crowd. No one else in line was connected to the game. He could have signaled Kutscher's employees at the gate, said "excuse me," and gone right through. In spite of wanting to see Lew play against Wilt, he refused to use his influence to go ahead of those who had arrived before him. If you didn't know him, this almost seemed absurd. The first great big man of basketball refused to use his fifty-year-old reputation to obtain a seat to see two of the greatest big men square off. As my father told a reporter that night, "It wouldn't have been right. These people have come a long way to see the game and if I had forced my way in, one of them would have been turned away." He never saw the game.

I spent two weeks at home during the 1969 Christmas holidays. The events of the 1960s were forcing my father to look at the dark side of his life; to acknowledge to himself the cumulative effect of the series of racial incidents he had encountered in sports. In the course of our conversations, it became even clearer that his lifelong friendship with Bob Douglas had been pivotal for what my father did in race and sport. I hated for that Christmas vacation to end. As much as I thought I knew my father, I was learning more and more. I was about to move to Washington where I was to do research for my Ph.D. thesis on the racial factor in American foreign policy. Being so close to New York, I felt I would continue to learn more about him.

Back in Denver to prepare for the move, I met Dennis Brutus at a reception in his honor. Dennis, as I've already said, had suffered for years because of his efforts to end racism in sport and apartheid in South Africa. This meeting took place less than a week after I left my father. Dennis and I talked nonstop for four hours, finally finishing at 3:00 A.M. Race and sport—I couldn't get it out of my mind. I decided to submit a new dissertation proposal, this one on the politics of race and international sport. I never went to sleep that weekend and finished the new proposal early Monday morning.

The proposal was approved and we canceled our plans to go to Washington. Three weeks later I was in London where I did the bulk of my research. By the time I returned to begin teaching at Virginia Wesleyan College, my research had shown to me that racism and politics in sport were not products of American society but were global in scope.

My mother came to visit in Virginia on August 4, 1970. She was unpacking when we received a phone call from Monticello, where my father worked at Kutscher's. He had had a heart attack while playing golf. The doctor said we should come right away. We drove straight through the night, arriving at 6:30 A.M.

My father was in the intensive-care unit. My mother went in first. Because of the rules, I had to wait one hour before I saw him. His spirits were good but you could see that his body had taken a terrible beating. We joked with a nurse about allowing our dog, Blivit, my father's constant companion, into the room to sleep under the bed. He complained that we had driven there "for nothing." He repeated this when my brother Joe arrived. But he lit up with a broad grin when told that my sister was flying in from Greece, where she and Rajat had been living since fleeing Uganda.

My father seemed to be doing better and there was hope. I was at the hospital most of the day. He was talking about going home. He couldn't wait to see Barbara. She was due in Monticello at about 8:30 that night and he asked that she wait until the next morning to see him.

Suddenly I heard a commotion in the corridor. The door swung open, and the intensive-care unit took on a cocktail party atmosphere. Five or six people entered. One man talked to a nurse on duty. I was incredulous. She looked at me and shrugged her shoulders as if to say "What can I do?" The people, one of whom was carrying a small dog, stood around my father. The man introduced himself as one of the principal owners of the hospital. He said how proud they were that Joe Lapchick was with them and that they wanted a photograph with him. They got it.

Joe Lapchick, a man who sought privacy but was denied it throughout his life because of his fame in sports, was even to be denied it now. Late that night, he took a turn for the worse. By 7:45 A.M. on Monday he was dead.

We were called at 7:15 about his condition. My sister and I rushed to the hospital at 7:30 in the hope of snatching one final moment, one last touch that would have to last a lifetime. We rushed into the intensive-care unit to see his body wrenched across the table with his legs dangling off one end and each arm floating over a different side of the table. His face was frozen in pain. Barbara, who had traveled thousands of miles, kissed him tenderly.

I met with his attending physician in the corridor. He told me they did everything they could, that he was sorry, and then tried to explain the mass visit on Sunday.

They were bracing for a lawsuit. But this was Joe Lapchick,

the man who had fought battles for others. Our family would never have allowed the last moment of his life to precipitate a legal battle. He would have been very unhappy.

His death was widely covered by the media. We would go home late at night to see clips of him speaking on the news. We couldn't let go. He was still with us. Hundreds of friends came to the wake in Yonkers. St. Denis's Church was jammed for the funeral. Television crews were there. The stories kept coming. All emphasized my father's qualities as a human being and the contribution he had made to basketball and to his community.

On the last night of the wake I noticed several black men staring at the drawing of my father above the closed casket. The same men were seated together at the funeral and stood together at the burial. I walked over to introduce myself and to find out who they were. The first man I went up to said, "I'm an old friend of Joe's. My name is Bob Douglas." They were the remaining members of the Renaissance team. I was deeply touched. Mr. Douglas took me in his arms.

Part Four
Teamwork: The Rens and the Original Celtics

Chapter 12

Caged Superstars

When men commence to make money out of sport, it degenerates with more tremendous speed and inevitably results in men of lower character going into the game.

Dr. Luther Gulick, 1898

As the new century dawned, America discovered a new diversion. It was conceived by James Naismith, who had been hired by Dr. Gulick to invent an indoor winter sport for the Young Men's Christian Association (YMCA). It was not meant to be a sport for the masses but a genteel sport by which the Y-types could keep physically and morally fit during the frigid winter months. It would keep the young men busy with a civilized outlet for their excess energy, teach discipline, and above all, strengthen the YMCA's ability to mold them into the upright Christian image that was to be imbued and projected among the elite.

But basketball was also being played on the streets, especially in immigrant communities. There it became a contact sport, which it has remained until today, despite denials that this is the case. In 1894, the YMCA published a series in its *New Era* magazine entitled "Is Basketball a Danger?" It pointed out problem areas such as increased jealousies and rivalries, the loss of interest in class work, rowdyism among spectators, and, finally, rivalries caused by unfair officiating. Four years later, before it could reach its international network, basketball was thrown out of the YMCA. Men of conscience like Gulick gave up, as boys of "lower character" took up the game.

Compared to today's sport, basketball as played in its infant days in the Y was very crude, with peach baskets serving as the nets, irregular floors, and balls that sometimes bounced and sometimes didn't. But compared to street basketball, playing in the Y was pure luxury.

Never dreaming that it would become a fifty-year professional career, Joe Lapchick played street basketball in the Hollow in Yonkers, New York. "Teams" consisted of as many of the children from the Czech community as would be on the streets and want to play. A street team could have three to ten boys on it without anyone caring. Naismith's "Rules for Basketball," published in 1892, said, "The only limit to the number of men that can play is the space. If a great number of men wish to play at once, two balls may be used at the same time, and thus the fun is augmented though some of the science may be lost. . . . As many as fifty on a side have been accommodated." Rules about numbers were confusing anyway, as basketball was officially being played with seven, then nine, then eight to a team.

Discarded soccer balls were always prize finds, as they were stuffed into a cap and used as a basketball. Baskets were another matter. Usually, throwing the ball onto the roof of a shed was a goal. At a young age, strength to reach the roof and not accuracy was the key.

When they were ready, young boys joined the bigger boys in weaving around moving ice wagons. Passes had to go under the bellies of the horses. Tossing the ball between the legs of the walking horses was a score. Wagon operators were very angry at the games, as the children frequently startled and upset the horses. It gave operators great pleasure to see the children slip on the "gifts" left behind by the horses. Frances Lapchick could never understand why her son smelled so bad until she happened by a "game" one afternoon. There was no supper that night for young Joe, who didn't want his father to know that he spent his time playing instead of working to supplement the family's meager income. There were four sisters—Anne, Emily, Frances, and Florence—in addition to brothers Ed and Bill. As the eldest child, Joe was expected to help with the family's finances. Although life had gotten better for the family when the elder Joe Lapchick became a trolley motorman (after careers as a coal miner and hat finisher), they were still poor by any objective standards.

Young Joe opted for bed that night, but was back on the streets the next afternoon. He made a deal with a friend who agreed to keep a separate set of playing clothes at his apartment. Joe never had the tell-tale odor and Frances thought he had reformed. This arrangement worked well until the day when Joe went to his friend's house and discovered that his mother had found Joe's clothes and burned them. Playing on the streets was over, but it didn't matter. At twelve, Joe was 6 feet 3 inches tall and weighed 140 pounds and was playing indoors for the Trinity Midgets and Public School Twenty.

The philosophy of the so-called sports reformers underwent a dramatic change. Men like Dr. Gulick, who tried to freeze out immigrant children at the YMCA, now became advocates of bringing them in. As the American industrial machine grew and capitalism adjusted to the changes, it became obvious that immigrants and their children would be valuable as crucial labor cogs in the industrial wheel. Team play would yield a cooperative spirit, loyalty, self-discipline, self-sacrifice and group control. Gulick himself became a leader of the Playground Association of America and helped found the Public Schools Athletic League in 1903. Cary Goodman, in his book *Choosing Sides,* argues convincingly that the organized play movement which began during this time was designed to acculturate immigrant children to American capitalist ideas. The playgrounds, settlement houses and forms of supervised recreation were to be training grounds for the inculcation of the American dream and the American spirit.

For young Joe Lapchick that dream was close enough to touch. He had been a caddy on a golf course every weekend since he was nine. One advantage of being so tall was that he could pass for the requisite twelve years of age for caddies when he was only nine. He carried bags for many top golfers, for Christy Mathewson, Fred Merkle of the New York Giants, sportswriter Grantland Rice, and entertainment personalities such as Al Jolson and Douglas Fairbanks, Sr. At dusk each Saturday and Sunday he himself would play. He was also learning to play baseball and was the water boy for the top local baseball team. He was convinced that his dream would be realized by playing either baseball or golf. Meeting these celebrities and seeing their wealth fired that dream. He could taste it. He would do anything to realize it. All he wanted was success.

In 1914 Joe had to leave school after the eighth grade. He went to work for the Ward Leonard Electric Company in Bronxville, New York, making 15 cents an hour for a 10-hour day. He played sports each night and on weekends.

Beginning in 1915, Joe used to hang out at Lou Gordon's sports shop in Yonkers. He listened intently to all the stories of the athletes so he could pick up pointers. Gordon, noting his size and interest, sent Joe to see Jimmy Lee, who managed the Hollywood Inn basketball team. The Inn was a private athletic club for affluent businessmen. It sponsored a team which was made up of former high school stars. Lapchick recalled the times:

> I shall never forget the afternoon that I entered the sporting goods shop. I had never thought of it before but the suggestion stuck and I went down and tried out. Even then I was 6 feet 3 inches tall. I was skinny as a rail and quickly proved I was the greatest floor man ever to be in the game. I did this by remaining most of the time flat on my backside.
>
> I got broken up a good deal. Arms and ankles were cracked and dislocated, and for a season or two I was quite miserable. But finally I began to catch on to the tricks and was able to take care of myself. In those days, brute strength and the ability to take it and dish it out were the chief requisites.
>
> Players then were admitted roughnecks. If a man began to show too prominently in a game, his opponents ganged up on him and tried literally to break him in two, frequently with considerable success.
>
> I have had as many as a half dozen jerseys torn off me in one game, and I remember one night when three opposing players picked me up and threw me into the fifth row of chairs.

There were no coaches or training as we know them today, so Joe began his own training program to improve his coordination. He would go behind the Alexander Smith carpet mills at night. He ran and ran, forwards and backwards, practicing starts and stops, directional changes, and pivots. It began to pay off when he joined the professional Bantams, who played in the Hudson Valley. He was paid $5 per game minus expenses. "I netted the grand total of $15 the first year and $18 the second year."

However, this wasn't so bad during the war years, as money and everything else was scarce while Americans went to war to make the world safe for democracy. But it was only a white world which had secured that safety. Blacks fought in the war in large numbers with distinction. But when they returned home there was great disappointment and the realization that life had gotten worse for them instead of better.

The Klan, playing on the knowledge that there wouldn't be enough jobs for all returning soldiers, stood up for jobs for the white soldiers. Within a year after the war ended, membership in the Klan had increased from several thousand to one hundred thousand. It operated in the North and Midwest and spread its particular brand of terror as never before. There were seventy lynchings in that year. Ten returning soldiers were murdered. Eleven blacks were publicly burned alive before the eyes of men, women and children. In the summer of 1919, there were twenty-five race riots. But the mood had changed; the riots were characterized by blacks rebelling against whites, not whites attacking blacks. Blacks resisted and showed new self-respect and determination. They had a sense of togetherness and unity in the urban communities which was little known in the rural South.

Whites were also disillusioned. Wilsonian idealism had lost much of its appeal after the war. The public was in the mood for withdrawal. In foreign policy this meant isolationism. At home, it meant perhaps the first term of "benign neglect." Warren Harding was elected president on the basis of his call for a "Return to Normalcy." This meant refueling the industrial engine, consequently pitting blacks against immigrants in the competition for industrial jobs, increasing racism. There were two things that weren't so normal. First, many blacks were now proud and resistant. Second, the economy became so hot that even the poorest people seemed to be doing better. The masses became absorbed in the pursuit of prosperity and wealth. Immigrants and blacks alike felt they were doing better. Left alone, life was just fine.

It was in this context that professional basketball took off. It was a place where the public could seek escape. Pro players became relatively rich men. Between 1918 and 1922, Joe Lapchick, the man who had earned a total of $33 in the previous two years, was making $75 to $100 per game. He was playing on four teams in four leagues at the same time: the Visitations in the Metropolitan League, Holyoke in the Western Massachusetts League, Schenectedy in the New York State League and Mt. Vernon in the Interborough League. Needless to say, he couldn't play in all the games of each team, so he, like other rising stars, put himself up on the bidding block. Whoever came up with the highest bid won the services of young Joe Lapchick for the night. By playing owners off against each other, he successfully increased his market value from $5 a game in 1916 to twenty times that in 1918. With no income tax, Joe Lapchick was rich for an immigrant boy. Not only could he touch that American dream, he almost owned it now.

Players of the same class would gather in New York's Grand Central Station. Honey Russell, Elmer Ripley, Dave Wassmer and others met there to discuss which team they should play for that night. The owner's agents would likely be there to bid. Then they would board the train for Schenectedy, Holyoke or wherever.

The men also discussed the game, but never in terms of who won or lost. The question was "How did you do last night?" It was a triumph if you personally scored more points than your opponent; otherwise, it was a defeat. Obviously there was no room for team loyalty in such a system. Winning was a personal victory not to be shared.

Bill Hoffman, a sports columnist for the *Yonkers Herald Statesman,* described Joe at the time: "What a basketball player—and what a 'brute.' The feminine trade will just adore him." Sports groupies did not just appear with Joe Namath; there were always women around for the sports celebrities. This became especially true for Joe Lapchick after he bought a big car. It was a time for heads to swell. He would cockily drive to an arena with his date, get out and throw his equipment bag in the air. Whichever kid caught it entered the arena with Joe and carried his bag. It was a great break for the kid who would both meet a star and save the fifty cents admission price.

While Joe was playing for some good teams, Schenectedy was not the Original Celtics. And Joe Lapchick was not Horse Haggerty. Horse was the burly, aggressive center for the Celtics, who began to remind Joe of his more humble origins. Lapchick said Haggerty would beat opposing centers down with his bruising play: "It would take me two weeks to recover after playing against Horse."

The Celtics were founded in 1912 by Frank "Tip" McCormack to play for the Hudson Guild Settlement House on New York's West Side. The Settlement House, like others around the city, was doing its part in the organized play movement in getting kids off the streets. McCormack organized the Celtics to play on what was known as the "dance hall circuit." Promoters knew they couldn't draw enough fans just to see a ball game, so dances were held before and after the games to attract more people. In 1916 they transcended the neighborhood and became the New York Celtics. McCormack went off to fight in the war and returned to find that Jim Furey had taken over the team, along with its name and several of the original players. When the team became professional in 1918, only Pete Barry and John Witte were left from the first Celtic team. Hart, Goggin, Mally, Calhoun and the McCormack brothers were gone. When Frank McCormack sued Furey over the use of the team's name, Furey agreed to call his team the "Original Celtics."

The team played at the Central Opera House and later at the 71st Regiment Armory on Park Avenue and 34th Street. In 1920, Furey signed Johnny Beckman and Dutch Denhert. With Beckman, Denhert, Barry, Haggerty and Witte, they were a formidable team. Beckman was a real fighter on the court. He was a leader and was considered by many to be one of the best scorers in Manhattan. Denhert was solidly built and would become one of the game's first innovators; he invented and then perfected the pivot play. Pete Barry, a member of the first Celtics team, was its master strategist. He was credited with being the smartest player on the court and was one of the finest rebounders in the game, although he was only 5 feet 11 inches tall. Haggerty was the enforcer. He was so strong and tough that no one wanted to mess with him. Witte was the "coach," a term used loosely at the time. The coach's main job was to get the players out of the bars in time for the game.

By 1921, the only real rival was Tex Rickard's Whirlwinds, who played in Madison Square Garden. A three-game series with the Celtics was set up. The Whirlwinds, whose stars were Nat Holman and Chris Leonard, easily won the opener 40–27. The Celtics won the second game 26–24. The rubber match was canceled because the promoters claimed they feared violence from the fans. It was more likely that they were hyping the fans for a bigger payoff in 1922. It was not to remain a rivalry, however, because Furey signed Holman and Leonard to play for the Celtics. Holman, from an East Side tenement, was later to be considered perhaps the greatest player in the 1920s. He could shoot the eyes out of the basket, especially from the outside. He averaged nearly ten points a game for the Celtics—a figure almost unheard of in that period. While playing, he earned a physical education degree from Savage Institute and then coached at City College of New York.

In 1922, Furey revolutionized the game by signing players to exclusive one-team contracts for guaranteed salaries. This allowed a stability that never existed in pro basketball. It created the first real "basketball team" in that sense.

In 1922 the Celtics lost two of three games to the South Philadelphia Hebrew Association team, also called the "Wandering Jews." Their star was Davey Banks, who Furey then signed to play for the Celtics. Banks, only 5 feet 7 inches tall, became the fastest member of the team, and was also a great shooter.

Joe Lapchick began to outplay Haggerty, although Horse still won the physical battles. He punished Lapchick more with each game as he saw what was the inevitable end. Furey signed Lapchick in 1923 and he replaced Haggerty.

He didn't fit in right away: "I was only a beginner in the type of game the Celtics played. I was frustrated because of my ineptness, and the resulting anger which shot through me every time I made a mistake was no help. I had been bred to the theory of individualism, whereas the Celtics were devoted to a team effort."

But it was only a matter of time. In those days there was a center jump after each basket. At 6 feet 5 inches tall, Joe Lapchick nearly always got the Celtics the ball.

By the time he learned what he had to, no one could beat the Celtics. Joe Lapchick had realized his dream and reached the top of his world. He earned $10,000 the first year and $12,000 soon thereafter, making him, along with Nat Holman, the highest paid player in the land.

It sounds unbelievable today, but in his first year (1922–23) the Celtics record was 193–11. In the next year, it was 204–11. In 1924–25, they traveled 150,000 miles and were 134–6. In 1925–26 they won 122 and lost only 7 times. They were playing everywhere east of the Rocky Mountains, drawing huge crowds. Ten thousand people jammed Madison Square Garden and an incredible twenty-four thousand came to a day/night double header in Cleveland on February 22, 1924.

The greatest money was to be made as a touring team like the Celtics. But by 1925–26, the owners in the new American Basketball League refused to play against the Celtics, forcing them to join the league in the 1926–27 season and to cut back their touring. They won the "world championship" in the next two years while compiling a 236–15 record. Bringing the team into the league backfired on the owners, as fans lost interest because the Celtics dominated the league. The Celtics were about to be dissolved.

The Celtics did not know the world north of Central Park. Harlem was swelling with blacks who had been migrating from the South for several decades. Racial tensions increased after the war as city after city experienced riots. Those white residents of Harlem who were still there left soon after the war as Harlem became America's black capital city. The black press discussed racial injustices, called for change and served to unify blacks in

Harlem. It was like a magnet for black writers, musicians and actors. The spirit of black defiance that was growing in the post-war era was being reflected in the emergence of new literature. A fresh, clear vision of social, economic and political freedom was being expressed through culture.

The Harlem Renaissance was under way. Black theater thrived. There were musical reviews and serious music as well. But it was the writers who had the greatest impact. Claude McKay, one of the many Jamaicans who had come from the West Indies to New York, was the Harlem Renaissance's first great writer. Countee Cullen and Langston Hughes followed. The Twenties were a period of high black culture.

To be sure there were blacks who were not so defiant and willing to give the white man what he wanted. One of Harlem's most famous night spots was the Cotton Club which catered to an exclusively white clientele. There, black art was tailored for white taste and therefore seriously compromised. It was near the Cotton Club that the Renaissance Casino Ballroom opened in 1922.

Bob Douglas was born in Jamaica in 1882. He arrived in the United States four years later. Douglas labored as a courier and porter for almost a quarter of a century in New York, but his love was always basketball. He was thrilled by the rise in popularity of the sport and dreamed of having his own team. Just as Joe Lapchick didn't know where his dream would lead him as a young boy, Bob Douglas couldn't have known that the opening of the Renaissance Casino Ballroom would start him on his way and that once begun, his team would join the Celtics as one of the only teams to be inducted into the Basketball Hall of Fame.

Douglas was in contact with some of the better black players in the New York area. However, while everyone bid for the Celtics and the better white teams, Douglas knew the extent to which racism in America would limit his chances of success. He needed a place to call home court. The opening of the Ballroom cracked the door. He became manager of the Renaissance Casino Ballroom and started a team in 1922. Douglas named them the "Rens" after the Renaissance Casino. Like the white teams of the era, they played on the dance floor. The team did well against weak competition in the early years. The money was coming in and Douglas signed James "Pappy" Ricks in the 1925–26 season. Ricks was a great shooter and the Ballroom filled up more and more after his arrival. Clarence "Fat" Jenkins and Eyre "Bruiser" Saitch joined Ricks. Jenkins stood only 5 feet 6½ inches tall. Like Davey Banks of the Celtics, Jenkins looked like a midget when standing next to his teammates. However, Jenkins was the team leader and captain. Douglas gave him control of the offense. Saitch added size at 6 feet 1 inch and was very agile on the court. Saitch was also one of the first black tennis stars and twice won the National Negro Tennis Championship.

With these three stars, the 1925–26 season marked a turning point. Unofficial records show that the team won 81 games while losing only 17. Word of the Rens began to spread. Promoters suspected that confrontations of white and black teams would draw crowds. They were right, and the Rens began to play the white teams and win consistently. They continued to prove their artistic value as well as their financial value over the next two seasons when they went 84–19 and 111–20. They were playing regularly against the Celtics and caught the attention of the sports world by splitting a six-game series with the world champions in 1926–27. They would not match them this well again for several years, but they had made a point. The press called them the "Colored World Champions."

The Celtics found themselves without a financial backer. In a column he wrote for the *Yonkers Herald Statesman,* Joe Lapchick said,

> There was no backer or money man. On the first page they (fans) may have noted the demise of one James Bugs Donovan, who was shot full of lead on the west side of New York due to his operation in the beer business. He had quarreled with his erstwhile partner and was an obituary figure within two weeks.
>
> Bugs Donovan was the owner of the Celtics though the Celtics supposed their owner was a man interested in real estate. We attended the wake and our boss's body was a mess—they must have used old fashion cannon-balls on him.

It should be noted that prior to Donovan, the Celtics "owner" was a department store cashier. The Celtics sometimes had to go to the store to collect late payments. They were having too good a time to wonder where the money was coming from until they read that the cashier was indicted for embezzling $190,000. The Celtics then suspected that some of this was their money, but it was too late.

In 1927, league owners, who originally boycotted the Celtics to force them to join the league, now plotted to get rid of them. Fans were losing interest as other teams simply couldn't compete with the Celtics. The owners tried everything to subvert the Celtics. Pete Barry was told that a family member had a serious illness, so he went home and missed a game. Johnny Beckman disappeared before one game; he had been a temporary kidnap victim. Davey Banks was not admitted to the arena one night. Nothing worked, and the team continued to win. The owners decided to break up the team.

The owners understood the importance of ethnicity to the fans. Thus, Nat Holman and Davey Banks, the two Jewish stars, were given to the New York Hakoahs. It seems ironic that the game which today has become a black-dominated sport at the highest levels was so successfully played and sometimes dominated by Jewish players in the Twenties, Thirties and Forties. Stereotypes prevailed. Ed Sullivan, later to be a great TV star, wrote in his column, "Sports Whirl": "Holman, Jewish star of the Celtics, is a marvelous player . . . Jewish players seem to take naturally to the game. Perhaps this is because the Jew is a natural gambler and will take chances. Perhaps it is because he devotes himself more closely to a problem than others will." Davey Banks was known as "the Rabbi" according to writer Lank Leonard in his column entitled "Tall Pole and Little Jew Shine Brilliantly for New York Celtics." The "tall Pole" was Lapchick, who was Czech.

Lapchick, Denhert and Barry went to the Cleveland Rosenblums. In effect, they became the "Rosenblum-Celtics" after they won the league championship in 1928–29 and 1929–30. The Celtics would regroup and barnstorm the country after the season ended. The high-living style continued unabated since the team made the same salaries as when they played in New York. The Celtics traveled first class in Pullman cars on the train, stayed in the best hotels, and ate at the best restaurants. The camaraderie and fellowship was remarkable. They really were a family that nurtured and protected each other.

Bob Douglas continued to expand his family and the Rens became more and more successful. The pieces continued to fit together. In 1929 Douglas got his big man for the center jump. Charles "Tarzan" Cooper, 6 feet 3 inches tall and 220 pounds, was brought to New York via the Philadelphia Colored Giants. Cooper was born in Newark, Delaware in 1907. He went from a Philadelphia high school to the Panther Pros in 1925, and then played for three years with the Giants. Joe Lapchick, whom the white press acknowledged as the greatest center of his time, said that there was no doubt that Cooper was the best by the early 1930s. John "Casey" Holt and Bill Yancey, a star in the Negro Baseball league, also joined the Rens. Against stiffer competition, they went 120–20 in the first year that the six played together.

While the Rens were making almost as much money as the Celtic players, their lifestyle was a reflection of the racial realities. Their tremendous financial success inspired promoter Abe Saperstein to found the Harlem Globetrotters, the "clown princes of basketball." In an interview in *Sports Illustrated* just before his death in 1979 at age ninety-six, Douglas said, "Abe Saperstein died a millionaire because he gave the white people what they wanted. When I go, it will be without a dime in my pocket, but with a clear conscience. I would never have burlesqued basketball. I loved it too much for that."

For Joe Lapchick, the early games against the Rens were life and death struggles on the court. Much more importantly, he experienced the consequences of racism for the first time. In spite of the radically different lifestyles off the court, the Celtics and Rens built a shared brotherhood on the courts. As the two best teams in the country, everyone was out to get them. The players today would barely recognize the game.

Games were usually played in dance halls so crowds could be increased by the lure of dancing before and after the games. To accommodate this, the floors were highly waxed. It was very difficult to run without slipping on such courts, so both the Celtics and Rens developed a passing game that became their trademark.

Bounce passes were discouraged because the balls used were so inconsistent; they were just bladders covered by leather. You never knew which way the balls would bounce or if they would bounce at all.

The name "cage" or "net" game originated when many courts were surrounded by a rope or wire "net" or "cage." The intention was to keep the ball in play as there were no out-of-bounds lines. However, the nets were often used to pin the ball and the opponents.

Sometimes games were played in church basements. There would be pot-bellied stoves at one end. Players had to be careful not to get burned on the stove. There were often posts in the floor of the court in such basements. Running opponents into these concrete "picks" was the origin of the term "post play." Inexperienced players were often victims of the play and incurred serious injuries.

Injuries were especially common early in the season as there was no such thing as a training camp. You had to play your way into shape. Old timers claim that today's players pamper their injuries. While this is surely a disputable point, one has to understand how rough the sport was and how old timers had to keep on playing despite injuries if they were to make a living. Elmer Ripley once knocked out Joe Lapchick. Although he had a deep gash on his left forehead, stitches allowed Joe to play. Two weeks later, an elbow opened up a large gash over his right eye. He played for six straight nights, getting new stitches after each game to replace those that were knocked out. On the seventh night another elbow fractured two ribs. He never stopped playing. Lapchick wrote, "If you complained about anything, you were gutless."

Beckman was the Celtics "doctor." His prescriptions were based primarily on the theory of "survival of the fittest." If you were strong you survived. If you were weak, you could be crushed. If you admitted to a weakness, you became weak.

One night Lapchick's arm became painfully swollen. He could barely raise it and went to see the doctor: "Becky, I don't think I can play tonight." Beckman gave Lapchick his famous guilt-producing stare and said, "What's the matter, no guts, you yellow-livered louse? Who do you think is going to get the tap for us? Since when does a basketball player run on his arms?''

Lapchick played and ruptured a blood vessel. The arm became black and blue from the shoulder to the wrist. Beckman told Lapchick not to play and to see a real doctor. Lapchick replied, ''To hell with you, I'll play.''

On another occasion, Lapchick's arm became badly infected by scratches. Beckman placed a steaming hot towel on his arm, soaked it, pulled off the scabs, and poured a bottle of whiskey over the open wounds. Lapchick played the next night with an arm that was green and with pain such as he had never experienced before. Many years later he described this to a real doctor who, slightly horrified, told him it was a miracle that he didn't get gangrene and lose his arm.

The basketball players' uniforms helped prepare them for the battle. They wore padded pants, knee guards and elbow guards. They wore sweaters not only to warm up but to stay warm; most arenas were not heated. As a testament to the importance of the Celtics and Rens, the Rome, Georgia, *News Tribune* announced that the gym would be heated for them—a rare occasion. Uniforms were worn game after game. The only light they would see was during game time. Ultimately, they were to be discarded and replaced—never washed. This unsanitary practice, combined with the cheap green dye used in the uniforms, was a frequent cause of infections for the players. Basketball shoes were of such poor quality that they frequently wore out during a game.

Officials were not highly thought of by either the Celtics or the Rens. They frequently took the side of the local team. Lapchick said:

> The umpire at that time was a joke. No one, least of all the players, paid the slightest attention to him. If he tried to assert his authority in any way, the players would curse him out; and if he still proved officious, they'd run into him and knock him flat.

Horse Haggerty once got so angry at a local referee that he knocked him out. After the game, Haggerty was attacked and beaten by a local gang. That taught the Celtics never to move alone.

The fans also went after the referees. Between spectators and players, the ref's white shirt would sometimes be covered with blood by the end of a game. Police protection for the ref was often provided. A referee named Chuck Solodare had his neck broken during a game and was hospitalized for nineteen weeks.

The problem of refs and fans was different for the Rens. Eric Illidge, the road secretary of the Rens, told *Sports Illustrated,* "In all those years, the referees gave us nothing. Sometimes we had to fight just to stay alive." In a game with the Goodyear Tire Company in Akron, Ohio, Wee Willie Smith was hit with "a vicious elbow during the game and Smith broke the offending player's jaw right there on the spot." The player's name was Schipp "and evidently he didn't like colored people."

The referee threw Smith out of the game but said nothing about Schipp, who had started the action. Illidge argued with the referees that both should be ejected. The coach of the Goodyear team agreed. The refs refused to continue. Illidge recalled: "That's when all hell broke loose. We had to form a circle in the middle of the floor and fight back to back. I had my pistol out and Fat Jenkins pulled out the knife he kept hidden in his sock. We were ready to fight our way out, but the riot squad came and saved our lives."

The fans were also rough on the players. While the manager watched the promoter to be sure he didn't run away with the money and the "sixth man" watched the time-keeper to help him remain objective, fans near the net would stick hat pins into a player's backside or burn him with a lit cigarette. Fans who were out of reach of the court threw cigarettes and cigars through the net. Bottles were thrown at foul-shooters. In industrialized towns, fans threw small store bolts at out-of-towners or shined mirrors to reflect the lights into the eyes of the shooters. In coal towns, miners would wear their helmets to the games and shine the lights into the eyes of the visiting team.

The abolition of cages and nets gave fans a field day. They could shake the backboards of the visitors to throw off shots. Fans ran out and tripped the players. When the Celtics played in a northern Michigan town, a fan attacked Nat Holman while he was dribbling up the court and landed a solid punch to Holman's head. The spectator became the town hero.

The fans, opponents, referees, injuries, inconveniences—none of these were very important. The Celtics and the Rens were self-contained families. They were the best in their business and had enormous pride in what they were accomplishing. Basketball was their whole way of life. The members of these teams knew each other better than they knew their parents, brothers and sisters, wives or children. When they were together on and off the courts, life was secure emotionally and financially. It was a high life for men of such humble origins.

Chapter 13

On the Road

The high life came crashing down with the onset of the Great Depression, as the American Dream suddenly ended in an American Nightmare. The gyrations of industrial machinery began to slow. Consumer goods were now outside the reach of the growing poor. The ranks of the tramps and unemployed swelled. Suicides skyrocketed. The bellies of more and more Americans cried out for food. With so many rural Americans sucked into the temptations of urban living, slums sprouted everywhere. The greed that fueled the Twenties made the Thirties harder to accept. If the spirit of the country had not died, it was certainly on its deathbed.

While the Depression was undeniably tough for everyone, it was especially hard on blacks. In the urban areas, they were the first to lose their jobs, while in the South they worked for almost nothing. There was nothing for them to fall back on. By 1934, 38 percent of the black population was unemployed and considered to be incapable of self-support; this compared to 17 percent for whites. Their relative economic prosperity had been snatched away by the Depression. The Harlem Renaissance, which had been so inspirational, effectively ended in 1930 as it became harder for artists to sell their work.

Sports historians write today about the Celtics and the Rens in the Thirties as if little had changed. Sportswriters at the time continued to mythologize sport—it would go on and so would American life. While fans weren't losing interest, it was becoming harder and harder to pay the admission price.

The Rens tried to keep playing out of the Casino Ballroom. The "Rosenblum-Celtics" tried to stay alive in the league. Based on the theory that dwindling fan interest was based on a stagnant style of play and seeing the "same old players," the American Basketball League abolished the famed pivot play and instituted a rule that each team must carry two rookies. But owners blamed the fans and the players just as industrialists repeatedly blamed softened workers. The press trumpeted the reflection of society as viewed from the top.

When Max Rosenblum decided to withdraw his championship team from the league, he proclaimed that his dedication was to the game and not to making money. He said, "I have placed my wholehearted efforts for many years into the promotion of professional basketball in Cleveland—a promotion upon which there was never based any intention of profit."

Playing for the dance-hall crowds was no longer possible for the Rens. Almost simultaneously, the Rens and the Celtics decided that their survival was based on barnstorming across the country. The Rens got into their bus and took off. The remaining Celtics bought themselves a Pierce Arrow for $125 and followed. Each team cut itself adrift from the familar in search of emotional and financial solace from the Depression. Emotional relief came; financial comfort never really followed.

The formula was simple. First, all the overhead expenses were to be cut down. That, of course, was easier for the Rens, who didn't have that many to begin with. Second, the teams would play anywhere they could obtain a guarantee—with sharply reduced expectations. Third, they would play local teams and try to hype interest in the match-up as if it would be a real barnburner even if the local team was terrible. Finally, in big cities they would match up against each other and exploit the black-white conflict with the media and the fans.

It was a conflict that the proud Douglas was willing to exploit, but on his own terms. He knew, as did the Celtics, that it was a gamble. The Harlem Globetrotters had become white America's image of what a black basketball team should be. As long as blacks were clowns, tricking rather than outsmarting their opponents while speaking barely recognizable English, they were allowed to succeed. This was especially true if the profiteers of this showmanship were whites like Abe Saperstein, owner of the Globetrotters. The players were merely his field hands.

After all, this was the heyday of *Amos 'n Andy,* a radio show that whites loved and blacks despised. Freeman Gosden and Charles Correll were the Sapersteins of radio. These two white men, whose voices portrayed the black pair, exaggerated every stereotype white Americans had about the blacks. Amos 'n Andy were the Globetrotters of the airwaves—they succeeded by trickery, conniving and breaking all the rules.

Douglas said that what he wanted to offer was simply good basketball. The Depression-era match-ups between the Rens and the Celtics were classics on the court even if there was some artificial hype off the court. Both Douglas and Lapchick believed it was the greatest basketball rivalry ever seen. Neither would claim that his team "was the greatest team of all time," although many called them that. In fact, Lapchick called the Rens the best team of the mid-Thirties, while Douglas said the Celtics were the best prior to that time.

The Celtics wouldn't be rich anymore, but they would still be together. Max Rosenblum decided to back the Celtics, who still used Cleveland as a home base in deference to the Rosenblum patronage. But it was no longer that great 1920s unit. Lapchick, Denhert, and Barry came from the Cleveland franchise. Nat Hickey and Davey Banks rejoined them. Carl Husta, who had played for Cleveland, joined the barnstormers. He was a smooth shooting guard who had his basketball beginnings in Kingston in the New York State League. For $75 a month, he set up the chairs, drew the court lines, played the game, showered, and then returned to join the orchestra for which he played the drums. So the Celtics, even the Depression-era Celtics, were the big time.

Joe Lapchick said, "We looked at the time romantically. We were going to survive, overcome and still be the champions. But, the truth was, we were becoming old men." The aging Celtics played without Holman and Beckman, their two best shooters from the Twenties. The new rigor of their lifestyle made it still harder to meet their old standards. However, they still had that spirit and belief in themselves, and their competition was rarely up to even this somewhat antiquated version of the glory team.

The Rens were another matter. First, they didn't lose any of their players. They were younger than the Celtics and were used to a lifestyle which denied sleep and normal bodily comforts. Most importantly, they completed their roster with the addition of the powerful Wee Willie Smith. Standing 6 feet 5 inches tall and weighing 225 pounds, Smith was an imposing figure on the court. Ironically, he came from Cleveland, which the Celtics called home. In other times, he might have joined the Celtics and allowed them to continue as unchallenged world champions.

Instead he became the capstone for the Rens' "Magnificent Seven." He was the perfect complement for Tarzan Cooper since hostile opponents could never gang up on both big men. The whites accused Smith of being a "dirty player." Lapchick said it was just the opposite: "He was big and strong. Refs frequently ignored it when opponents roughed up Smith. It was when the game got out of hand that fights started. I never saw Smith start a fight." With Smith and Cooper getting the ball; with Ricks and Yancey shooting uncannily; with Jenkins controlling the pace and Holt and Saitch ready to pitch in, the Rens dominated basketball for the next four years. They won 473 games and lost only 49 during those four years. At one point, they had won eighty-eight consecutive games. No white or black team could consistently beat them. Only the Celtics could beat them, but by the 1933–34 season even they could not win the season's series.

The formula for success of both teams became the formula of survival. The Rens always lived an unpretentious style on the road out of necessity. They usually had to sleep in their bus because they were denied hotels. They traveled by bus because many forms of public transportation wouldn't have them. They ate on the bus when restaurants refused to serve them. Segregation may have been the law in the South, but discrimination was the accepted practice in the North. Life worsened for the Rens only in the sense that the road became endless in the Thirties and there was less money to put on the bus. However, their basic lifestyle outside of New York was quite the same.

The sports press wanted America to think that the life of the Celtics was the same high life they had enjoyed before the Depression. The champions had to be an example of reward for hard work and persistence. A column written by Bobby Norris in Macon, Georgia, in January 1935 was typical:

> Naturally, the champions must stop at the finest hotels and travel in style. Not entirely for the sake of appearance but for the comfort that is necessary to sustain their perfect physical trim all season. They are an expensive lot. Joe Lapchick, who serves as coach and boss of the crew, once was recognized as the highest salaried star in basketball. He was pulling in $10,000 per season then.

The Celtic promotional materials exhorted fans to "forget the Depression and have a good time."

Both teams were playing almost every night and twice on Sundays. The managers who booked the games were not masters of geography and were just as likely to arrange for back-to-back games three hundred miles apart as they were to arrange them for nearby towns.

By driving all night, the teams saved the expense of hotels. Even if there was no time to eat, the Celtics would always pack in a case of 3.2 beer. Denhert told a reporter, "The malt tonic, taken in judicious quantities, gives us something to wear off in games." This was a real indicator of the times. The Celtics were always a hard-drinking crew. When they had traveled in style before the Depression they didn't have to be refreshed in their car.

Life without hotels and Pullmans and without much leisure time or money was certainly less fun than it was in the Twenties. Moreover, packing six to seven large men in a car, night after night, was taking its toll on their aging bodies. In 1934, the average age of the Celtics was thirty-four. Most of the players had trick knees, charlie horses, sprains, bad backs, colds or all of the above. Their ankles swelled up after sitting for hours in the car. Usually two men would be assigned the night's drive. It was not uncommon for gas station attendants to mistake the Celtics for gangsters when they pulled up in their big limo late at night. But at least they were sure of getting gas; the Rens, on the other hand, had to learn which towns sold gas to blacks.

The players learned to compensate for each other on the court. Those who had driven the previous night were on the court less and were expected to do less when they played. Columnist William A. Spring of the *Yonkers Herald Statesman* praised Lapchick for pacing himself:

> It is the effortless ease with which Lapchick works that makes him a master of the art. After his 200th game, no doubt, he realized that all this running around got him nowhere. Basketball players who tear around the court like so many deer really are not traveling at all, and accomplish about the same thing as a six day bike rider who pedals around and around and never gets out of the same square block.

He didn't realize that they had no choice. In 1934, for example, the Celtics played on Christmas night in New York City. They piled into the car and drove all night through a blizzard, arriving in Johnstown, Pennsylvania, at 6 P.M. without sleep. They gave a clinic from 7 P.M. until game time at 9 P.M. Exhausted, they coasted and were losing 51–49 with ninety seconds left. Lapchick called time out to say that they should play all out. They won 56–52.

The previous year, they had played eleven games in ten nights. Their bodies aching and their tempers short, the Celtics lost a game to the Yahoo Center Five. They were about to graciously accept defeat when an opposing player told the Celtics that they should retire and not drag down their glorious traditions. Lapchick was furious and called Nig Rose, their booking agent, at midnight. "Get us a game with these punks as soon as you can. We'll play them anywhere and for nothing." The match was set for two weeks later. The Celtics were confident, so Lapchick told the player who had derided the Celtics that this would be the Celtics' last game if they lost. The cocky opponent nodded his appreciation for Lapchick's newly acquired wisdom. The Celtics won 61–8.

The Celtics traveled to Baldwyn, Mississippi, in mid-January 1934. According to Rose, the Celtics' car stalled some eighty-five miles outside of Baldwyn. The players pushed the car for several miles while unsuccessfully trying to jump-start it. They finally hitched a ride in a cattle truck and arrived at 7:30 for a 7 P.M. game. They looked terrible and played even worse. With seven minutes remaining, they were losing 26–7. The fans were screaming—not with joy for the locals' apparent victory but because they believed the Celtics were deliberately losing the game. The Celtics could barely walk, let alone run. Losing, although never welcomed, was more acceptable at that moment even though it had been a great year. They were 50–1, having lost only to the Rens 44–40. A record of 50–2 wouldn't be so bad under the circumstances, but the cries of fix from the fans ignited them, and the Celtics outscored Baldwyn 19–1, only to lose 27–26.

Once again Lapchick called Rose. There were no open dates and a number of upcoming games with the Rens. They were to play the Rens in St. Louis on January 31, in Evansville, Indiana, on February 1, and in Dayton, Ohio, on February 3. On February 2, they were to oppose the Earle (Arkansas) Cardinals in Memphis. Lapchick told Rose to make it a doubleheader. They beat the Cardinals in the opener 33–20. Baldwyn came on the court knowing the Celtics had not had a day off since December; geography told them that the Celtics couldn't have slept between St. Louis, Evansville, and Memphis. Nevertheless, Baldwyn could only watch with awe as the Celtics won 40–27. The pace never let up. The Celtics played thirty-two games in twenty-eight days. This included a tripleheader in Nashville one day, an afternoon game the next day in Indianapolis, and a game that night in Dayton.

The Rens had much the same fate, since duress and exhaustion could lead to inconsistent play and irate fans. But it was always more dangerous for them because they were a black team in a white world. The Rens took off for Chicago after an easy game in Wisconsin. They had the next night off and looked forward to some relaxation in Chicago, one of the few cities where they could stay in decent hotels. They used such cities as bases when they were scheduled to play in towns where they couldn't stay.

The bus broke down and the Rens pushed and shoved it for almost ten miles in the ice-cold Wisconsin winter. They finally got to a town with a railway station. Their night off was spent in the station as they couldn't find food or hotel rooms. The morning train brought them to Chicago in time to play that night. Their minds were present but their bodies were back on that Wisconsin highway; they lost. The spectators were sure they had intentionally dumped the game and stormed the court. They had to escape through a back door and get a police escort to the station. It was neither the first nor the last time the Rens fled from a belligerent white crowd under police escort.

Another episode in Akron, Ohio, has already been mentioned. Akron had also brought bad luck for the Celtics, who approached the town on a foggy night for a game with the Firestone Tire Company team. Nat Hickey was driving when he spotted a freight train through the thick fog. Hickey slammed on the brakes, but they didn't hold. Carl Husta and Davey Banks jumped out of the car as it careened wildly over an embankment. The car landed on a lower road. Hickey was too nervous to move. Lapchick and Denhert went back to discover Banks unhurt in a snow drift and Husta nursing his newly bruised back on the icy pavement. The Celtics won that night all the same.

On another occasion they traveled to Butler, Pennsylvania, from Pittsburgh after six weeks in the South. It was a bitter cold night. One of the tires blew out, the brakes froze and the carburetor developed trouble. It took five hours to travel the thirty-four miles to Butler. They arrived in a frozen state, greeted by an impatient crowd that had waited one and a half hours for them. The arena manager insisted that they start without warming up.

Butler scored the first nineteen points and led by twenty-three at the half. The Celtics sent for a bottle of Scotch and allowed it to warm them up. Relying on Lapchick to get the center jump after each basket, the Celtics scored twenty-nine straight without Butler getting possession of the ball. Nig Rose called it a performance that had never been matched. The Celtics weren't convinced it was worth the price their bodies paid. But complaining wasn't part of their style.

Hearing reports of an impending blizzard, the Celtics arrived early for a game in Webster, Massachusetts. The poster on the arena announced the game for the following night. They checked their route book and, sure enough, they were booked that night in Westfield, Massachusetts—some fifty-four miles away.

By then the blizzard was in full-force. They called the Westfield promoter to cancel the game. His arena was filled with anxious fans and he refused, informing the Celtics to get there however they could. They stopped at each town to call and plead with the promoter. He wouldn't listen. Arriving at midnight, they drank a bottle of brandy and beat the locals before a packed arena.

In spite of all the hardships, the owners loved the Celtics' dedication and willingness to sacrifice. In February 1934, Nig Rose discussed the Celtics' current methods of operation with a reporter from the *St. Louis Post,* contrasting them to teams in the old professional leagues. He said that previously there had been too much luxury overhead. Referring to the possible reestablishment of a pro league, Rose said:

> When it does return it will have to be on the basis established by the Celtics—that of a sensible budget. Extra fare trains and Pullmans, high priced hotels, $2 luncheons and all that sort of stuff will have to be squeezed out. The sport can't stand that sort of overhead. The Celtics have solved the transportation and living problems and that will set the standard for a revival of professional basketball on a reasonable expense basis.

The Rens and the Celtics promoted themselves and made their managers' jobs easier. They both knew that, for different reasons, fans wouldn't want to see them badly defeat a local team. Before the game, reporters would be told to expect a close battle. After the game, they would be told how much the team had improved. All the while, the Celtics and the Rens were carrying their opponents to make them look good.

The Rens tried to avoid fights because they added nothing to the game and might make white spectators antagonistic and threatening. The Celtics had their own code of conduct for a physically aggressive opponent. They would concentrate on him by blocking him out of the play and having his man shoot all the shots until the coach had to remove him.

In the fall of 1935 they played a local all-star team in Ohio. The All-Stars used brute force in every play. The Celtics called time-out and the fans were sure they would reciprocate. Pat Herlihy tipped the ball to Paul Birch, who threw it to Banks. He scored *for Ohio*. Herlihy repeated this on the center jump. The crowd went wild. They did it again after a beautiful display of Celtic ball-handling wizardry. The Celtics were very serious and shook hands. Ohio, suddenly enjoying a two-point lead after the Celtics had scored six for them, was humiliated, and the rough-house tactics stopped.

Lapchick explained the philosophy to a reporter:

> If a team is reasonable with us and does not rough us and try to take advantage of the fact that we are pros, we'll let them down easy and make a good show of it. Occasionally, though, we run into a team that gets too enthusiastic and we have to put the pressure on.
>
> A short time ago, for instance, we were playing in a certain southern city. At the half we were leading by only one point. The team came back in the second half, apparently thinking it had a chance to win, and started out roughing us up unmercifully. Furthermore, the referee was accommodatingly blind to their tactics. I called time-out and we decided to settle it then. We won by 53 points.
>
> Of course, there's no fun in that because when you're playing for blood the crowd doesn't particularly enjoy it. After all, we must entertain them so they'll come to see us next year.

Once they played the Indiana Omars in Indianapolis. One of their players began to take underhand shots from forty to fifty feet out. Chris Leonard, the best man on defense, couldn't contain his laughter when he saw this man's technique. He never went near him until it was too late, and that man scored six baskets to help the Omars win.

Ed Sullivan, then a sports columnist for the *New York Graphic,* later went over to the manager to get the player's name and was told, "Homer Stonebreaker." Sullivan, apparently feeling this was as funny as his technique, laughed and asked his real name. "Homer Stonebreaker" was again the reply. The Celtics had a rematch with the Omars in Cleveland. Leonard was all over Stonebreaker who never scored a point. Leonard scored 12 points and the Celtics won easily.

Professional athletes respected players who could compete in more than one sport. The Rens had several pro baseball players and a tennis champion on their team. Lapchick had played pro baseball and golf. Lou Gehrig toured each winter with an All-Star team under his name. He came into the dressing room before a game with the Celtics and pleaded, "Please don't rub it in tonight." The Celtics assured him that this was not their intention. With five minutes left and the team down by 3 points, Lapchick called time-out and said, "Let's go!" Gehrig's All-Stars won by two. After that, the Celtics decided to put the game away first and then let their opponents score.

The Celtics and the Rens both possessed a balance between enormous pride in themselves and compassion and respect for their adversaries. They wanted to win but not to destroy. Lapchick called the felling one of "quiet fierceness." A column by Wirt Gammon in January 1935 illustrated this. The Celtics had asked how Adolf Rupp's Kentucky team had done. When told that Rupp had sent his first team back in with the score 66 to 19, Gammon wrote, "Lapchick registered genuine disgust" and said,

> Why does coach Rupp do things like that? I just can't understand it. Those coaches are all in the same boat, have the same problems. I can't understand why they can't appreciate each other's position and not jeopardize each other's jobs.

The Celtics never complained about ethnic references to them in the press. It was another way to promote fan interest. The Celtics were also called "the Shamrocks" and more rarely, the "Irish." The *Atlanta Constitution* ran an article by Jimmy Jones in January 1934:

> The Celtics are a colorful crew, too designed for crowd appeal. Denhert is a Dutchman; Lapchick a Pole or something; Davey

Banks is Jewish; Barry and Herlihy are Irish and Hickey is a French Canadian. They are reinforced this year by Carl Husta. Husta must be Hungarian since there are no nationalities left.

The scientific method was not one of Mr. Jones's tools of inquiry. Denhert was German and Lapchick was Czech. Hickey was from Hoboken, New Jersey. Even in 1934, there were several nations left to choose from besides Hungary for Husta. The Birmingham and Chattanooga newspapers referred to Herlihy as "a new Jewish star," "the Jewish luminary," and a "scintillating Jewish product."

Lapchick wrote of a treasured ethnic moment for the *Yonkers Herald Statesman:*

An incident I shall always remember happened after a game in Chattanooga. While dressing there was a great rumpus outside the door. Pushing aside all opposition was a burly Irishman, who opened the door and said: "Glory be praised—Shamrocks." Leonard grasped the situation and introduced everyone thusly: Barry as Barry, of course, Banks as O'Brien, Denhert as O'Flynn, Holman as Shaunessy, and me as Flavin. A big smile beamed across his good–natured pan and he cried, "Oh, me buckies 'tis glad I am to see some faces from the old sod!"

Fans also came because of the team's ability to perfect their own game and to create innovations that would revolutionize the game. The Rens were pat in personnel while the Celtics were changing some. Paul Birch joined them to replace Pete Barry who retired at age forty-one. The powerful Pat Herlihy played more and more for Lapchick. Even with the changes, the Celtics had basically played together even longer than the Rens. They knew each other's moves inside out and could anticipate where their teammates would be without seeing them go there. Reporters, fans, coaches, and players all agreed that no one could handle the ball better than the Celtics and the Rens. Even when the games got rough, they were graceful on the court.

And there can be little doubt that they were the greatest innovators the game has ever seen. The Celtics originated the switching defense, the give-and-go offense and the pivot play under game conditions, usually after building up a big lead.

Before the switching man-to-man defense, players judged their performance solely on the basis of how many points they scored in comparison with the man they guarded. This was all a logical outgrowth of the team concept of the game that Lapchick had so much trouble adjusting to when he joined the Celtics:

> The Celtics never practiced so I couldn't figure out how they were switching. I was always in somebody's way and my teammates were getting picked off right and left. They were angry and told me how dumb I was. But I couldn't understand. Then Johnny Witte told me, "Joe, it isn't how many points you score or how many times you get us the tap. We know you will be great in those areas. But to be a member of the Celtics you have to also contribute without the ball." That helped me to understand. The team was the thing. We were five green shirts playing together and not five individual performers.

Lapchick described Dutch Denhert's discovery of the famed pivot play:

> We were playing one night in a game that was a total walkover. Denhert walked under the basket, turned his back on it, and began to kid the other team by receiving a pass and throwing it back to the player who had thrown it to him.
>
> Suddenly one of our team, receiving a pass from Denhert, found himself completely unguarded. This happened again and again and we thus saw that what Denhert had conceived as a joke was really a powerful offensive threat. We began to study it until we worked out the swiftest possible manipulation of the ball.

The Rens perfected all these plays. In addition, Tarzan Cooper and Wee Willie Smith are credited with the invention of the double-pivot play in a game in St. Louis in 1933. With the game safely in hand, Smith moved in front of Cooper. They passed the ball back and forth from the pivot line. Smith batted the ball back over his head to Cooper who then batted the ball to players around the foul line. The newspaper story said they "knocked the patrons out of their chairs and befuddled the opposition."

The crowds dwindled. However, wherever the Celtics and Rens played each other, every coach within a hundred miles would bring his team to see the masters teach their trade. There were always dozens of yellow school buses outside the arena. When the Rens played the Celtics in St. Louis in January 1934, more than one hundred fifty teams came to witness the master teachers of the era. When they played other teams, they did not always have the energy to teach during the whole game. They would play as the Celtics and as the Rens for enough of the game to both assure victory and show the fans how the game was supposed to be played. However, when they played each other, there was no time to innovate, no time to rest. They respected themselves too much to do anything short of playing the entire game as if it was the last minute of a close encounter.

It was easier for the Rens to do this in the Thirties. The Rens were in a period of heady ascent, while the Celtics were making their last stand. Lapchick and Denhert were playing less and less. Barry was forty years old. Lapchick talked seriously to a reporter in Waco, Texas, in 1936: "No, we don't disguise our ages. We think that's in our favor. Paul Birch, who joined us only this season, is twenty-three. We sorta watch out for Paul—watch his morals and so on—he's so young."

Gradually all the Celtics realized that being legendary was not the same as being immortal. Playing in Buffalo for $100 before one hundred twenty people was not the same as it used to be. Ironically, it was the Celtics and not the Rens who began to try everything to fill the arenas. They held clinics before almost all the games to assure that at least local players and coaches would attend. They added new men like Herlihy and Birch. They even persuaded W. L. Stribling, then boxing's number one heavyweight contender, to join the team on a southern tour only three weeks before he was to fight Max Schmeling for the championship. As a rule, they drew fair crowds in the North and Midwest and good crowds in the South.

Famed singer Kate Smith backed the players' salaries in the mid-Thirties. Her patronage promoted fan interest for a while.

This was especially true whenever she attended the game. She brought the house down when the Celtics played the Young Men's Hebrew Association (YMHA) at Duquesne University's gym. With the Celtics ahead 39 to 18, she was introduced between the third and fourth periods. Kate Smith, even then an impressive figure, announced, "May the best team win." Even the YMHA team couldn't contain their laughter.

The Celtics started new antics on the court. With Denhert only able to perform a few pivot plays and Lapchick a few palms, the burlesque began to entertain the fans. They used the hidden ball trick when Herlihy put the ball under his shirt. They passed the ball to the referee.

But it was Banks, the lightning-like wisp of a player, who became the real clown. He would sit in the stands while the team played defense. He would flirt with women spectators. Sometimes he took popcorn from children and sat courtside to eat it. Then he would call for the ball with popcorn blowing everywhere. Pat Herlihy would lift Banks onto his shoulders for jump balls. When Banks shot the ball, he would sometimes fall to his knees to pray while it was in the air.

The crowds loved all the tricks. Many believed that the Celtics were better at them than the Globetrotters at this time. After all, the Celtics weren't paying refs and the opponents to make them look good as Abe Saperstein was doing. Even so, the Celtics weren't happy that they had to do these things to survive. They loved the game too much to make a joke of it and soon after they were forced to do so, Lapchick and Denhert quit. The fun was gone, and now what that Yahoo Center player had said about quitting before they destroyed the Celtics' honor and glory struck home.

Earlier in 1933, Lapchick had told a reporter:

Some of us are getting older now. We pack and jam ourselves somehow into a big automobile going from city to city, playing somewhere every night. It's a terribly hard life, but I don't believe you could prevail on any one of the boys to quit it. Basketball is in our blood. We love the game, we always have and we always will.

But much of the fun of the old barnstorming days is gone. It has become a hard racket now and the fun of the thing is lacking. There was a time when backers fought each other to underwrite the tours. Crowds have fallen off and the backers are unwilling to take a chance. So we players underwrite it ourselves and make the tour on our own account.

During those last years, games with the Rens were the only thing that brought the Celtics back to their best days. Each match-up was like the Super Bowl in the minds of the players. Nat Holman sometimes rejoined the Celtics for these big games.

The white press, which rarely mentioned the Rens in the North and never mentioned them in the South, now paid attention. These writers had already dubbed the Celtics the greatest team ever. The Rens could only call themselves "Colored World Champions." But this was hard to explain when the Rens won the series with the Celtics in 1933–34, the same year they had won eighty-eight straight games.

For many spectators, the match-up was black versus white. If there were any "incidents," the fans were ready. It was a test of racial pride. For the players, the match-up was the chance to test who was best. Over the many years of the series, the Celtics won most of the games. Losing the series to the Rens in 1933–34 was a first, although the Rens had previously come close when they split the 1926–27 series. The Rens had some scores to settle, but it was never easy and the Celtics began beating them again in 1934. It was a war on the court. Bob Douglas told me, "We always played in a war, but often it was a race war. When we played against most white teams, we were colored. Against the Celtics, we were men. Over those last years a real brotherhood was born out of competition and travel."

However, the Rens had much to be bitter about, as recognition from the press was hard to win. Even when they had it, a subtle racism could be read into most of the stories in the white press. Words seemed carefully chosen to protect the stereotypes. Thus the *Dayton Herald* of February 5, 1934, described "the shifty Renaissance Five" versus the "matchless Celtics." Blinky Horn in his column called the Rens "the Sepia Squadron" and wrote that the "Rens clowned and grinned their way through a combat with a local colored team last night." Of the Celtics he wrote, "They come as near to being the poetry of motion as it is possible in basketball."

Sid Keener of the St. Louis *Star Times* wrote of the "Renaissance tossers" and the "Celtic shooters." The Rens were "lightning fast," the Celtics "steadier and more accurate." Others wrote that the Rens "outmuscled the Celtics" or that the "Celtics outsmarted the Rens." Most of the stories granted some throwaway line like "the Rens represent among their own race the greatest in the court game." They were still the "Colored World Champions" playing the real World Champions. The press was very free in questioning Dutch Denhert, who, aroused by his Celtic pride, made statements like "They have a great bunch of players but we generally succeed in outsmarting them one way or another and they are inclined to let down when you get ahead of them." The white Celtics were smart, steady, accurate and graceful poets. The black Rens were shifty, strong, and fast grinners. The media, after all, was serving the nation. The nation it served was white.

The press made their competitiveness seem like a bitter personal rivalry rather than heat generated by the battle of the giants of the game. Stories before the games repeatedly predicted fights. When fights occurred, it was generally the Rens who were blamed. A typical account appeared in the Brooklyn *Times Union* on April 6, 1933:

> Pat Herlihy was the innocent victim of an attempt at peacemaking. Willie Smith of the Rens . . . and Nat Hickey locked up arms on a play near the sidelines and just as it looked as if blows were to be struck, Herlihy stepped in and locked Smith's arms in the hope of averting trouble. The other players rushed in and separated them and just as they stepped apart Smith let a right fly that dipped Pat on the chin. Pat, being Irish, decided that peacemaking wasn't in his line and tried to return the compliment. . . . A moment later Herlihy and Smith were in a tangle and before they could be stopped the crowd surged out onto the floor.

Note that Herlihy was a peacemaker because he grabbed opponent Smith's arms. It was fine for him, as an Irishman, to fight back against the ungrateful Smith.

Another especially rough game was reported before a home-town crowd of seven thousand five hundred in Cleveland which the Celtics won 44–34. It was noted that "all the grips and holds commonly believed to be only in the wrestler's stock and trade and not a few hefty punches were shown by the fighting-mad cagers." When fights didn't happen they wrote about the number of fouls, as if it were the same thing.

There were many fouls. But it must be remembered that in those days a player was not ejected because he exceeded a certain limit. After a key game in St. Louis in January 1934, Denhert said, "We're bitter rivals and they'd give a right arm to knock our ears off. Naturally, when they turn basketball into football, the Celtics must fight back." Forty-six fouls were called. Banks had committed twelve violations and Smith eight. After the game Banks said, "Those Rens are too tough for experiments and trick plays. We have to play all out."

Perhaps that game typified the series. According to the St. Louis papers, whoever won would break the series tie and be the champion. The two teams were labeled "bitter enemies" and fights were predicted. The Celtics were 60–2, having lost to the Rens 44–40 and to the Baldwyn, Mississippi Athletes. The Rens were 45–1. Their loss was delivered by the Celtics 44–36.

A huge crowd of 8,513 came to see them play. Some one hundred fifty high school teams attended. The Rens got off to a fast start and led 33–29 with less than five minutes left. However, the Celtics rallied to win 38–35.

The next day the papers reported that the series would continue. Each pre-game story said that the series was tied and that game was for the "championship," but the series seemed to go on forever. The next night in Evansville the posters announced:

CELTICS (World's Professional Champions)
versus
NEW YORK RENAISSANCE (World's Colored Champions)

Under the "Seats for Colored" heading, the promoter promised that "as usual there will be a section reserved for colored people." After a Celtic doubleheader in Memphis, they played the Rens again on February 3 in Dayton, Ohio. All the Ren-Celtic games were billed by the local papers as being for the "World Championship." The Celtics won in Dayton 42–39.

The Celtics seemed to be in high gear and good form in February 1934. The northern press asserted that they were on top of the basketball world again after these key victories over the Rens. The Rens were almost never mentioned in stories about the Celtics in southern papers. On February 18, James Saxon Childers of the Birmingham (Alabama) *News-Age Herald* naively asked Joe Lapchick if the Celtics were the greatest team in existence. Even after the recent wins, Lapchick responded, "No, the Renaissance, the Negro team, is the greatest basketball team of the day. Over the years we have beaten them 6 to 1, but recently they have beaten us. I believe they can do it again." Douglas later said that this type of acknowledgment meant a great deal to the Rens. It was especially important that it came in the South, where the Celtics and Rens played the first game between blacks and whites in Louisville, Kentucky.

Dutch Denhert still wouldn't let go. The 1933–34 series ended in a virtual stand-off. It was a new year in 1935 when he was interviewed by Harry Martinez for his column "Sports from the Crow's Nest." Denhert seemed to acknowledge the greatness of the Rens and yet attributed part of their success to ex-Celtics:

> They're a fine team all right, but they haven't beaten us so much, only about 25 percent of the games we've played against them in the past 10 years. They have been in existence about 10 years and in the beginning of their career, we beat them regularly. But they stuck together so long that they began to learn how to play the game well, what with some of our ex-players coaching them. And then it was they who gave us hard fights.

The series that year was also a stand-off. The Celtics were in Chattanooga and Wirt Gammon of the *Chattanooga Times* asked Lapchick if he thought the St. Louis Americans were the next best team after the Celtics:

> The Rens and the Celtics are far ahead of the rest of the pro basketball field and have been for years. They (Rens) are our closest

rivals. Every year we play a long series with them for a sort of unofficial world championship. When the returns are added up at the end of the season we were always ahead—except two years ago when they had a slight edge.

Lots of cities clamour for a game between us and when they want it badly enough we give it to them. But it is nothing like one would think. There is no time for putting on a show for the fans. The going is rough with everyone bearing down every minute. The fact that each team knows the strong and weak points of the others very well results in the contest being a very bitter and rough game.

A month later the Celtics played the Rens in St. Louis. The Rens led the series 5–4 and this was reported to be the last game of the series that year. The arena was so crowded that the game started at 9:20 P.M. instead of the scheduled 8:30 P.M. time. It was very rough going with forty-seven fouls called. Lapchick, who was playing less and less against other teams, played almost the entire game. He and Pat Herlihy had seventeen fouls between them. Tarzan Cooper had seven. The Celtics pulled away at the end to win 50–41. The series was tied again, but it wasn't over; the teams drove to Kansas City for a game the next night "for the world championship." Such championship games proliferated as both teams relied on the rivalry to pay the bills. The season was even extended into April. They played in Saratoga, New York and the Celtics prevailed 49–44 after outscoring the Rens 11–2 in the closing minutes. The *Saratogan* described the game: "Both teams were out for blood and the spills were frequent. Players from both teams suffered minor injuries, cuts and bruises."

While this series kept them going, it was becoming harder and harder for men like Lapchick and Denhert to go on. Lapchick was married to Elizabeth Sarubbi in 1931 and had two small children. He began to feel like he knew none of them. His home was Cleveland and the road. From November to April he might spend two to three days in New York where he could be near his family in Yonkers. He couldn't quit because he didn't know what else he could do besides play basketball.

The Celtics compromised and moved back to New York. Without the Rosenblum patronage, there was no necessity to be in Cleveland. So, with the agreement of the players and Kate Smith, Lapchick and Denhert came home.

Joe's wife was happy; she had felt forced to live with her mother and father during those years. At twenty-seven, she had married late for those times. Living at home, even though she was married, made her feel like the proverbial old maid. She was sure that his return would help relieve the burden of raising two small children by herself.

It didn't work out. No matter where one called home, the only home for a barnstorming team was the road. Now, without the support of her parents, it was even harder for Elizabeth Lapchick to raise the children. The crowds grew smaller still, and what little fun and excitement had remained was gone. Lapchick knew it was over for the Celtics. They could still rise to the moment in head-to-head battles with the Rens, but it would take days and sometimes weeks for Lapchick to recover from the bruising play. This made him unable to play much, if at all, against other opponents. The same was true of Denhert. While players like Birch and Herlihy were exceptional athletes, the fans wanted to see Lapchick and Denhert.

In January 1936 the Celtics played the Rens in St. Louis. It was the same type of game as always—hard fought, bone-crushing, and exciting. Forty-nine fouls were called. The Rens led the series 5–4 before the game and the Celtics tied by winning 51–41. It should have been a great moment. Davey Banks, Herlihy and Birch were ecstatic. But Lapchick and Denhert knew the only statistic that counted. In 1935, 8,500 had come to see them. Now it was 3,400. The series was dying and the death of the Celtics would surely follow.

At this time Lapchick was asked by Father Rebholz, the Athletic Moderator at St. John's University, to succeed the great "Buck" Freeman, coach of "the Wonder Five" at St. John's. Lapchick jumped at the opportunity, although he was afraid he would not know how to coach or how to talk to university men with his eighth-grade education. But it was a way to stay in the game he loved. Nat Holman had successfully made the transition at City College. So life on the road came to an end for Lapchick. New York would really be home.

Birch, Herlihy and others continued to play under the name "Celtics." But writers and fans marked 1936 as the real end of the Celtics' dynasty and domination. The time had come to mythologize them, to embellish the already rich legends.

The timing could not have been worse for the Rens, who were reaching their peak in 1936. They would go on playing and even occasionally be called "world champions" by the white press, but without the Celtics to be measured against, it was an empty accolade. They played on into the mid-1940s, adding such stars as John Isaacs and "Pudgy" Bell. In 1939, they won a tournament for the world title by beating the Harlem Globetrotters and the Oshkosh All-Stars.

Harder still for Bob Douglas was the unending recognition given to the Globetrotters. Then Rens dominated the sport for a decade as pure basketball players. Individually and as a team, they were incomparable. Yet the fans and the press adored the Trotters.

Bob Douglas fought for the dignity of his team and its individual black stars. He never compromised them as black men just as they never compromised themselves. Some said he paid them more than he could afford and bought that well-fitted bus so they wouldn't have to endure the rampant racism on every street corner in America. Yet the press called Abe Saperstein "the Jewish Abe Lincoln." The press made the Trotters into the living proof that America allowed blacks to "make it." The Trotters were purportedly showing America and the world how sports could help overcome racial prejudice. The media portrayed them as a high-living, highly paid team taking their happy message from city to city and country to country. The Globetrotters, unlike the Rens, received enormous press coverage, drew large crowds, and eventually were the subjects of a movie and a television cartoon show. The message they brought, of course, was exactly the one that Bob Douglas desperately avoided, even at his own financial expense. The Trotters were, quite simply, white America's acceptable image of blacks—lazy, lackadaisical, and inept, able to entertain with their bodies without threatening whites.

For many, it was just as disillusioning to find out that the "Jewish Abe Lincoln" was no more a racial emancipator than the original model himself. The Trotters were woefully underpaid, lived the lifestyle of the 1930s Rens and Celtics even into the 1960s, and, worst of all, were the subjects of derisive if humorous thought by the hundreds of thousands of whites who would watch them play. When the time was eventually ripe for blacks to join the NBA, it was none other than the great emancipator himself who tried to stand in the doorway to block them.

As the Thirties faded into the Forties and Fifties, life for the old Rens became more difficult. Everyone remembered the great Celtics. The Trotters were still going strong, shuffling from station to station. The individual Celtics had, for the most part, gone on to better things. Pete Barry coached Kate Smith's Celtics. Dutch Denhert coached the Detroit Eagles to pro titles in 1940 and 1941 and also coached the Sheboygan, Wisconsin, team. He also owned a bar and grill in New York. Johnny Beckman coached Baltimore in the American League. Lapchick and Holman became as famous as coaches as they were as players.

But it was quiet obscurity for most of the Rens. Tarzan Cooper, the greatest center of the Thirties, was typical. He left the Rens to paint houses so he could have a steady income. Legends in the black community, few whites remembered their greatness or, for that matter, that they existed at all. The media buried them while it breathed life into the Globetrotters.

However, the Rens were suddenly rediscovered in the 1960s as cities began to burn. Douglas, embittered because the press seemed to deliberately ignore the Rens, was wary of the new attention. A bright, racially aware man, he wondered if this acknowledgment was a symbol of progress or an easy way to diminish white guilt for having denied blacks in those days. He wondered where these people who enshrined the Rens in the 1960s had been the previous forty years.

The years no doubt make memories softer and the times seem better then they were. Events are embellished and become fact.

Legends and myths become mixed. The Celtics and the Rens were and are legendary. The passion and love they shared for the game may not exist in the world of sports today. In spite of the struggle for survival and the intensity of the rivalry between the Rens and the Celtics, new meaning in life grew out of those times. Certain moments, long forgotten by everyone else, helped sensitize Bob Douglas and Joe Lapchick to black-white relations.

A month before his death in 1979 at age ninety-six, Bob Douglas told me, "I read about what happened to you in Virginia. It was awful, but I was glad to learn about what you were doing. It didn't surprise me. I always said the acorn doesn't fall far from the tree. Joe Lapchick was my best friend, in or out of basketball." Joe Lapchick used to call Bob Douglas his teacher. They had learned together.

The learning was acquired slowly for Lapchick until that conversation in New York which followed so many deferred invitations to Bob Douglas. Until then he had assumd that being around and playing with blacks was enough to break the psychological barriers that existed between blacks and whites. When Douglas kept saying "Not tonight" to Lapchick's eager invitations to join him for a drink, Joe Lapchick never thought anything of it, assuming that Bob must have had other plans. Lapchick had never given much thought to the indignities suffered daily by his black contemporaries. Never having really socialized with blacks, Lapchick didn't know that some places wouldn't allow blacks to have that drink. He couldn't have imagined that for Douglas it would be even worse to go to a bar where he would be served but where white patrons would render him numb with their icy stares. He never knew that if Douglas had stayed to have that drink, he often would have had to get on the bus and leave for one of the cities where the Rens could spend the night. Joe Lapchick didn't realize how much he didn't know about Bob Douglas.

The New York conversation had shaken Joe Lapchick. He was disgusted with what he learned. He wondered why he hadn't learned it before. It was just as instructive to Lapchick some twenty years later when he mentioned this conversation to Douglas to learn that he had forgotten it. Profound, meaningful, perhaps life-changing for Lapchick, the conversation wasn't even recalled by Douglas. Douglas was used to talking occasionally to white men—reporters, players and fans—about the conditions suffered by blacks. He saw surprise and sometimes even concern in their faces. But he also saw them turn and walk away untouched.

But Lapchick was always sensitive to the hurt felt by others. He wanted to protect his family and his friends. It was he to whom his brothers and sisters turned when they were in trouble. Many of his players would later say that this was the reason for his success as a coach. He was not a master strategist or great technician of the game. But people came to know that he genuinely cared about them. Players felt tremendous loyalty to him and that personal loyalty was a major motivating factor for them on the court. His life with the Celtics had taught him how to relate to people, to make the individual believe that he had a part to play in the larger whole whether on the team or in society. Before his last game at St. John's in 1965 for the National Invitation Tournament Championship, his players were in an emotional uproar to win it for "the coach." One of the stars, Ken McIntyre, was asked by a reporter how he felt about Lapchick. He said, "I believe in him. If he asked me to run through a wall, I would only ask, which wall?" When he died five years later, his last team acted as honorary pallbearers. Bob Douglas was there. He saw it. He knew what Lapchick stood for. When he had given him his first lesson on race in New York, Joe Lapchick was just another white man who happened to be a basketball star.

Once the Depression started, the Rens and the Celtics had shared a more similar lifestyle. As crowds dwindled in their traditional game cities in the North and Midwest, the Celtics moved south. The crowds were bigger, the gate receipts fatter and the weather warmer. The warmth was attractive as it allowed the increasingly injured bodies of the Celtics to heal faster—or, at least, to make them think that they did.

There had never been a professional game in the South between blacks and whites. Lapchick began to suggest to Douglas that the Celtics and the Rens play there.

Douglas's initial response was that there were enough hostile white crowds to face in the North. Douglas knew that they didn't stop at shouting "Nigger, nigger" in the South. They lynched blacks. In the year the Rens were founded, the NAACP had initiated a campaign to get congressional legislation passed to punish the crime of lynching. In the years he had lived in the United States, the NAACP estimated that 3,436 people had been lynched by mobs, mostly in the South. A newspaper in Tennessee had invited local townsfolk to come out to witness the burning of a "live Negro." Three thousand responded and watched. Douglas said it might be one thing for two black teams to play against each other. But, as much as he loved beating the Celtics, he didn't want to beat them in the South. For Douglas, the cold of Wisconsin must have appeared much more appealing than the type of warmth that might await his team in Alabama and Mississippi.

Eventually, faith and courage rose up and the game was set for Louisville, Kentucky. Both teams were a little apprehensive and tentative in their play. Used to being rough with each other, they held back that night. No one had suggested it, but it happened nonetheless. There were no incidents and Lapchick later said that the fans seemed to enjoy the quality of play. After all, even an apprehensive and tentative game between the Rens and Celtics was better than an all-out game between any of the local teams. Lapchick realized that something significant had happened that night. The game itself was enough of a breakthrough; after the game, the two teams returned to business as usual, with the Rens sleeping at a local black college while the Celtics stayed in one of Louisville's best hotels, the Depression not withstanding.

Many of Lapchick's most important experiences of this type took place in the South or in places where racial struggles were rarely won. Douglas also sent the Rens on southern trips to give impoverished rural blacks a chance to witness the Rens.

Local promoters were not always terribly honest. The Celtics' usual deal was a guaranteed flat fee or a percentage of the gate. For most of their playing days the latter was more profitable; the Celtics would always try to monitor the counting of tickets sold since payment took place in cash on the spot. There were a few times when the local promoter vanished with the money or could not meet the guarantee. On at least two occasions, the Celtics walked off the court when it appeared that they were being had. Douglas had told Lapchick about having received more than one bad check. There was a simple rule that everyone agreed to—cash in hand or no game. It was easier for the Celtics to enforce than the Rens.

Lapchick frequently handled the Celtics' business affairs on the road. Such was the case in one of the first contests with the Rens in St. Louis, a town where in the 1930s "integration" was a dirty word. The crowd was a big one. Lapchick was pleased when he was given an envelope with the cash but he noticed that the envelope marked "Rens" was very thin. After he counted the money he asked about the other envelope. The Rens were to be paid by check. Lapchick called over several members of the Rens and Celtics. They agreed that the Rens would get the money and the Celtics would accept the check. From the look on the face of the promoter, Lapchick was sure that his expenses for the game had just doubled.

Over the years, Lapchick developed great respect for the Rens' road secretary and business manager, Eric Illidge. After the ice had been broken with the Louisville game, others in the South followed. Illidge and Lapchick were to appear on a radio program together in Alabama to promote a game. Illidge was already in the studio when Lapchick arrived. Lapchick was shocked to find out that Illidge had to use the service elevator when he came to the studio. The studio manager, of course, thought he was being liberal for interviewing a black and white together. He thought nothing of the indignity caused to Illidge but was speechless when Lapchick chose to ride back down in the service elevator with Illidge.

The two businessmen also broke the ice in Evansville, Indiana. The Rens had a last-minute cancellation of a game there against a local team. Eric Illidge finally asked the local promoter, Mr. Grubbs, what the problem was. Grubbs admitted that an Evansville reporter told Grubbs he would have to leave town if he ever brought a black team to Evansville.

Illidge asked Lapchick to assist him in convincing Grubbs to go ahead with the game. Grubbs finally got up his nerve. A good crowd watched the Rens run up a 10–0 lead by repeating the same play five times: Wee Willie Smith tapped the ball to Cooper who sent a screaming pass to Yancey for the easy score. But five times in a row? The Evansville coach called time-out. Illidge listened to the team in their huddle. The Evansville players did not know who to guard because "all the niggers looked alike."

These incidents were important, but there was so much more to learn. After Lapchick went to St. John's, the contacts were fewer but were always meaningful.

Lapchick was saddened to watch the Rens in decline in the early Forties, to hear about players like Tarzan Cooper painting houses instead of coaching. Tarzan lay dead for days before his body was discovered in late 1980. James "Pappy" Ricks, the master shooter, had his career shortened by his taste for liquor; Douglas blamed it on his inability to handle the money he made. Casey Holt had it better for a while after he became a member of the New York City police force. He was off-duty when a friend asked him to investigate a robbery. When uniformed police arrived and mistook him for the thief, Holt was killed before he could establish his identity. One has to wonder if he would be alive today if he was white; would the officers have assumed he was the thief? Wee Willie Smith drove a bus in Cleveland and then did janitorial work for the schools. He never recovered after his son was killed in a car accident. Smith later had his leg amputated and hardly resembled the man he was in the 1930s.

The way the story was told, the Rens had little education and no skills outside of the arena. Therefore, their fate was to take up menial jobs when their playing careers ended. Aside from Nat Holman, the Original Celtics also had little education. Yet Witte, Denhert, Barry, Beckman, Hickey, Holman and Lapchick all had coaching careers and years of glory. Banks owned a lumber company, Denhert a bar and grill, and Herlihy a baking and confectionary business. Their fame, as individuals and as a team, grew. Lapchick saw that the only blacks who became popular heroes other than the Trotters were Jesse Owens and Joe Louis, who humiliated the Nazis for America. The Rens had none of it. He saw what was happening. He just didn't know what he could do that would make any difference other than to his friends and family.

Chapter 14

The Nets Fall

It is ironic that Lapchick's coaching career was launched by two referees who recommended him to St. John's Athletic Moderator, Father Rebholz. Dave Walsh and John Murray told Rebholz that Lapchick would be a natural. As a player Lapchick had a reputation of being a "referee baiter" with little respect for the early breed. An incident in Nashville in 1935 made him rethink his position.

The local opposition was stretching the Celtics to the limit and Lapchick believed the refs were assisting the locals. He blasted them after each call. One ref stopped the game and took Joe Lapchick aside saying, "I heard so much about the great Joe Lapchick and was really looking forward to meeting you tonight. I'm sorry that I met you. All you are is an animal."

Lapchick went into the dressing room after the game, concluded that the ref was right and returned to apologize. He never stopped protesting the calls of referees, but after the Nashville incident he realized that most refs were professionals trying to do a job.

Lapchick built a great reputation as a coach at St. John's. However, it was not an easy transition for him. Although he was nominally the coach of the Celtics for the six previous years, this meant driving the car, getting the players out of saloons in time for the game, and keeping track of the money.

"I was scared stiff at the idea of speaking to college boys, let alone coaching them," he confessed. On the first day of practice the team gathered around their new coach with great expectations. Lapchick realized that he had no idea what to say, so he instructed them to practice shooting. Three days later they were still shooting when Jack Shanley, the captain, asked, "Coach, don't you think we should try something else?"

The coach said they should scrimmage and divided them into teams. He escaped to the top of the bleachers so Shanley couldn't question him further. He thought it also made sense because:

> I had read that a coach should get up high and look down at his team. So I walked back and forth at the top of the bleachers in the old De Gray gym for the whole preseason. It was the beginning of my insomnia. I couldn't sleep because I was being paid for nothing. The only reason we did well was because the captain and a few other players managed to get along without any help from me. A faculty member asked one of the players about me and was told "Lapchick stinks." I was told to throw him off the team. I couldn't because as far as I was concerned the boy was absolutely right. That season was a nightmare.

Lapchick sought help from Clair Bee at Long Island University and Nat Holman at City College of New York (CCNY). But it was Father Rebholz, the man who hired him, who gave Lapchick the confidence he needed in himself. Lapchick tried to resign first as baseball coach and then as basketball coach after the season. Rebholz said he wouldn't accept the resignations and that Lapchick would be a certain success in both sports.

Lapchick began to analyse the Celtics' style of playing the game in order to teach it at St. John's. As success mounted, he said, "I was never afraid again." St. John's was consistently invited to the National Invitation Tournament (NIT), the oldest of the postseason championships.

They won the 1944 tournament with such stars as guards Hy Gotkin and Larry Baxter, center Harry Boycoff, and Fuzzy Levane. Both Levane and Boycoff were pros after the war. Hy Gotkin became a lifelong friend of Lapchick.

The next year Boycoff, Levane and Baxter all were in the army. Although invited to the NIT as defending champions, St. John's was seeded seventh in an eight-team field. It was a great field featuring three of the best big men of the era—Bob Kurland of Oklahoma A & M, Don Otten of Bowling Green, and George Mikan of DePaul. Otten played in the NBA until 1953 while Kurland and Mikan were voted into the Hall of Fame. Mikan, of course, dominated pro basketball for a decade with the Minneapolis Lakers.

St. John's made it to the finals against heavily favored DePaul and Mikan. Lapchick was known as a nervous coach and this game, which turned out to be one of his greatest victories, was also one of his most embarrassing moments as a coach. St. John's was ahead by five points with the second half about five minutes over. It appeared as though the heavy underdogs might win. When George Mikan fouled out, Joe Lapchick passed out. He regained consciousness ten minutes later when St. John's had a 12-point lead and had sewed up the championship. "I dealt a helluva blow to coaching strategy that night," he joked.

While Lapchick was complementing his fame as a player with an illustrious coaching career, the college game flourished. The slower, more methodical and rougher pro game was alienating fans who were increasingly turning to the college games. In addition to those mentioned, Lapchick developed other St. John's stars such as Dutch Garfinkel, Howie Vocke, Bob Tough, Bill Kotsores and Dick McGuire.

In the meantime, a new pro league, the National Basketball League had formed in 1937 with mainly midwestern teams. It adopted many of the college rules and went after college players, landing such stars as John Wooden and Red Holzman who went on to become famed coaches after their careers ended. The league was very unstable and dwindled to four franchises during the latter years of the war.

However, the end of the war and the signing of George Mikan breathed new life into the league. Mikan played for Chicago that year and they won the championship. In 1947–48 he joined the Minneapolis Lakers and they won the championship, easily defeating the Rochester Royals in three out of four games. The

Lakers then played in the last "World Tournament," where they were stretched to the limit, narrowly beating the Rens, 75–71. Thus, as late as 1948, with an older team of less publicized stars, the Rens were still near the top of the basketball world.

It was a year of great hope for Douglas and the Rens. Branch Rickey of the Brooklyn Dodgers baseball club had signed Jackie Robinson to play for the Montreal Royals in 1946. Rickey signed other black stars like Don Newcomb and Roy Campanella. It was sad to see that the great old stars of the Negro leagues weren't being signed. But the big breakthrough came as Robinson started the 1946 season with four hits, including a home run. He never let up and in 1947, after all the years of forced exile, blacks were in the major leagues in baseball. Douglas was sure that the new rise of pro basketball would mean integrated league teams.

An equally important sign to him was the creation of the Basketball Association of America (BAA) in 1946. He saw this as the big league. Ned Irish, who had done so much to popularize college basketball, was behind the New York franchise. Walter Brown was in Boston. Teams were also located in Washington, Philadelphia, Cleveland, Chicago, St. Louis, Detroit and Pittsburgh among others. These were big cities with large black populations.

By 1947–48, the second year of operation, four of the original eleven teams had folded. But Douglas saw this as an opportunity to bring in the Rens. Moreover, Ned Irish had signed Joe Lapchick to coach the New York Knickerbockers.

The league owners met in Philadelphia in the fall of 1947. Bob Douglas could taste victory; he bought a new car and drove to Philadelphia for the meeting. On their agenda: the admission of the Rens to the league. Bob Douglas recalled the day with Bruce Newman of *Sports Illustrated:*

> I'll never forget that day as long as I live. . . . They invited me to sit in on their discussion before they voted. I remember that at one point an Italian fellow from Providence stood up and said the league could get along fine without us. Then Joe Lapchick, who was with the Knickerbockers, got up in front of his boss, Ned Irish, and said, "I may lose my job for saying this but I'd play against the Rens any goddam day. To me they're the best."

Douglas was asked to leave the room before the vote was taken. Leaving with confidence, he was stunned when he was informed that the motion didn't pass.

Joe Lapchick and Douglas shared time together after the meeting. Bob Douglas was despondent. Emotionally scarred, he was convinced that the door might be forever closed to blacks in the game he loved. Lapchick told Douglas that had it not been for their conversation in New York almost two decades earlier, he would probably never have stood up in that meeting. That conversation had helped create a consciousness about race that few others of his time shared. It was then that Bob Douglas told Lapchick that he couldn't recall the conversation. He had had so many similar ones without any expectations or results.

By 1947, however, Douglas knew Lapchick was different. Douglas had heard people tell him that Lapchick was anti-black since his St. John's team was all-white. Douglas pointed out that there were virtually no blacks playing at predominantly white colleges. Critics said Lapchick joined an all-white pro league. Douglas said it was really the only major league and that the National Basketball League, which by then had Dolly King playing for Rochester, was not as significant.

Douglas told Lapchick of these charges and said that he always chewed up anyone who made them. Although he had forgotten the earlier conversation with the man who was then just another white man who happened to be famous, his respect for Lapchick had grown tremendously as he saw Lapchick prove himself time after time.

Lapchick was relieved that Bob had brought this up. He had heard the charges but said there was no way to deal with them other than to persist in the pursuit of his principles. While he could do that, hearing them always made him sick. Here was a man who felt he truly believed in equality in an era when not many did. He felt that Nat Holman was of the same mind, but few others were. He wondered what possessed people to say such terrible things.

Douglas said to him:

Joe, in all our years together, I have always enjoyed our relationship. I must admit that I usually thought the basis of it was the love of the game that we had in common. I never could fully trust you or any white man. My black heart told me that if I was together with two white men and we were told that only two of us could live, it would be the whites who would survive. Whites would always choose whites. I knew you were very different, Joe, but today, for the first time in my life, I know there are whites who would risk everything for blacks.

My father told me about this conversation when I came to him to relate what had happened to me on the night Lloyd Dove stayed in my apartment. Like him, I had thought that I had as full and totally trusting a relationship with Dove as he had thought he had with Douglas. He had thought that years of playing together, eating together and standing up together meant there were no barriers. I too had thought that my years of friendship with Lloyd had left no barriers. Yet there I was in 1967 making that total breakthrough for the very first time like he did in 1947.

Joe Lapchick was no crusader. He didn't plan to stand up in that meeting. But when the situation arose, he knew he could do nothing less. Although he failed, he gained solace from the fact that Bob Douglas, at last, had completely understood his real beliefs.

Lapchick considered resigning from the Knicks, but ultimately believed that it would not serve any purpose. On the contrary, he believed that he could be instrumental in breaking down that wall against color. But the league would have to stabilize first.

Douglas didn't want to go on and turned the Rens over to Eric Illidge. The National Basketball League (NBL) lost four of its best teams to the Basketball Association of America (BAA) before the 1948–49 season. Rochester, Ft. Wayne, Indianapolis and George Mikan's Minneapolis teams all switched leagues, leaving franchises like Waterloo, Oshkosh, Sheboygen, Hammond and Anderson in the NBL. When the Detroit franchise folded a third of the way through the season, Illidge was offered a replacement franchise in Dayton. However, a boycott by the fans destroyed any chances of success and Illidge took a large personal financial loss as the NBL moved close to collapse.

The BAA, strengthened by the addition of the new franchises

in Minneapolis, Ft. Wayne, Rochester and Indianapolis, was becoming a big league operation and 1948–49 proved to be a good year. George Mikan led Minneapolis over Coach Red Auerbach's Washington Capitols for the championship.

The leagues merged before the 1949–50 season and formed the National Basketball Association (NBA). The NBL franchises such as Anderson, Waterloo and Sheboygan couldn't make it. So as the 1950–51 season approached, only major cities with major arenas were left in the NBA. The time for racial integration had come, although there were still obstacles.

Abe Saperstein, sensing the imminent integration of the NBA, began lobbying against it. At first, he told league owners it would be bad for blacks, just as major figures in the Negro baseball leagues had argued that integrating the major leagues would hurt black baseball players a few years before. After all, he was the "Jewish Abe Lincoln" and he was out to protect black players. When the humanitarian approach failed, he tried power. He said that the Trotters would not play in the arena of an owner who signed a black player.

But the time had come. Walter Brown and Red Auerbach were in Boston and Ned Irish and Joe Lapchick in New York for the 1950–51 season. Brown had drafted Chuck Cooper from Duquesne University. When Saperstein threatened to boycott the Boston Garden, Walter Brown told him he didn't have to withdraw because any team of his would never be allowed to play there. Irish and Lapchick went one better and signed Nat "Sweetwater" Clifton right off the Trotters' roster. The door had finally been opened.

The integration of professional baseball made the entry of Cooper and Clifton into the NBA far less dramatic. They didn't face most of the public abuse hurled at Jackie Robinson. Clifton certainly didn't see himself as a racial frontiersman. He played good solid basketball even though the race bar delayed his entry into the league until after his prime years. Joining the Knicks at age twenty-eight, Clifton averaged ten points a game over the next eight years.

However, Clifton was somewhat tentative in his first year and was getting pushed around a lot under the boards. Lapchick called him over on a train ride back from Indianapolis and told Clifton to push back. Nat didn't reply. "Can you fight?" Lapchick asked. "Coach, I'm terrible," Clifton answered. Lapchick could not understand. He had seen Nat play for the Trotters and had told Lou Effrat of the *Times* "Clifton owns the most beautiful hands and arms in basketball. They extend almost to his knees and make him a 6 foot 9 inch athlete. Besides, Sweetwater is an excellent hand-off man and outstanding underneath the boards, on defense as well as offense."

He reminded Clifton of these attributes that day on the train and said, "Terrible or not, I never saw a basketball fight where a guy really got hurt. So you go in swinging if you have to." Clifton opened up and explained that he was trying to make a good impression since the color bar had just fallen. Lapchick was sympathetic after all the years of seeing what white crowds, refs, and writers did to the Rens when they got into fights. But he told Clifton that the times had changed and that he could act freely. Nat improved that year but was still not up to his potential.

In his second year Clifton was hit hard by Boston Celtic Bob Harris after he pulled down a rebound in an exhibition game. They exchanged words and Clifton started back down the court. Harris chased him and they squared off. The Boston bench got up almost as a unit when Nat pulled his arm back. The punch floored Harris. Clifton turned toward the onrushing Celtics. When they saw Harris's fate they stopped dead in their tracks. Lapchick laughed, "You could smell the rubber burning on their shoes as they screeched to a halt."

Lapchick was ecstatic to see the fired-up Clifton who then went on to become one of the better rebounding and most respected forwards in the league. "I thought you told me you were a terrible fighter," he reminded Clifton. Clifton replied, "Coach, what I meant was—I'm terrible when I get mad."

Clifton actually got his professional start with the Rens. During the war he had served in Italy with Sonny Woods, another Ren. He joined the Trotters for two years while he played first base for the Wilkes Barre affiliate of the Cleveland Indians. He hit .321 there in 1950 before deciding it was to be all basketball for him in 1951.

Clifton developed an easy relationship with Lapchick. The coach was never big on enforcing rules with grown men and usually did so only after he was forced into it. One Sunday Clifton missed the curfew in the Knicks' training camp in Bear Mountain, New York. Lapchick happened to meet him at the door where Clifton explained that he had gone to nearby Highland Falls for a haircut. Lapchick laughed at his creativity.

Clifton was often teased by the New York press for his large facial features. Lapchick announced one day, "You know, you've made the all-ugly all-star team." Clifton countered, "Then I reckon we're still together because you must have been named coach."

That fondness between Clifton and Lapchick never bred a close personal relationship; Lapchick believed that there must be some professional distance between coach and player. There would be time for that later and he would become close to Carl Braun, Dick McGuire, Harry Gallatin, Vince Boryla and others who eventually joined the coaching fraternity.

Joe Lapchick didn't discuss the "nigger–lover" calls with the team or anyone else. It would be almost two decades before he knew that I had overheard some of those calls. Likewise, he didn't discuss the charge that he was anti-Semitic, which was apparently leveled by a Jewish ballplayer whom he had cut from the Knicks prior to signing Clifton.

This was even more ridiculous than the anti-black charge. He had Jewish teammates on the Celtics, many of his St. John's players were Jewish, his best man at his wedding was Jewish and two of his children had Jewish spouses. He knew more Yiddish than any other language. He discussed this with me in his last year. There was nothing he could do but continue to live by the moral code he had adopted so many years before. However, that didn't assuage the pain of thinking that someone—anyone—could believe he was something less than what he believed himself to be.

While he buried these things inside himself, Lapchick could not hide the anguish of coaching in professional basketball. In an article he wrote for *Collier's* in December 1954, titled "Each Game I Die," he wrote:

Within the first month of the season my weight drops from 195 to 178 pounds. I can no longer eat a normal meal and, unable to get a normal night's sleep, I have to rely on sedatives. My cigarette consumption goes up from one pack a day to two, and during a game I may have two or more cigarettes burning on the bench at the same time. One night, in fact, Bud Palmer sat on one of those hot butts. I have walked off the court unable to keep from crying.

He collapsed several times during his tenure with the Knicks. His health deteriorated badly in the later years as the pressures increased. At one point, the team had lost four straight before a game at Madison Square Garden with the Boston Celtics. Three of his regulars were out with injuries. After hours of tossing in bed the night before, he finally fell asleep only to wake up in a nightmare. His body was soaking wet and he was shaking. He had dreamt that the Knicks did not score a point! The Knicks won that day, but the nightmare never went away. Along with many other varieties of nightmares, it kept Joe Lapchick tossing and turning each night before and after a game. Each game was a doubleheader—the one on the court and the lonely replay in bed.

It was all part of his style. Leonard Koppett once wrote, "He was always a pro at heart. And to him being a pro meant putting out all the time as hard as you can. Many men in sports know this, feel it, and act upon it. Lapchick has the additional asset of being able to convey it. When things went bad for the Knicks, players weren't ashamed to be identified as Knicks, they felt ashamed to face Lapchick."

Things were not great for Lapchick or the Knicks in his last two and a half years. While always in the playoffs, they had not reached the finals since 1953. Lapchick was increasingly second-guessed by Ned Irish, the Knicks' boss. Irish was perhaps basketball's most successful entrepreneur, but he was not an affectionate man. Lapchick never criticized Irish publicly and was loyal to the man Roger Kahn later described as "the perfect mortgage forecloser."

By the beginning of the 1955–56 season, it seemed as though Ned Irish was ready to foreclose Lapchick as coach of the Knicks. Irish didn't fire him outright, but set up the situation so that Lapchick had no choice but to resign. Leonard Koppett wrote on January 30, 1956, that "Irish undercut Lapchick's authority by knocking Knick players, second-guessing the coach and interfering in decisions that should be strictly a coach's province. He did these things openly—sometimes in print, sometimes in the presence of players. He made it unmistakable that he no longer had confidence in Lapchick's judgment, thereby destroying the club's morale, shaking Joe's confidence in himself and finally tying Joe's hands . . . and his players were the first to realize it."

It was a far cry from the day Lapchick signed with the Knicks in March 1947 to become the highest-paid coach in basketball history. Citing "poor health and too many sleepless nights," Lapchick announced his resignation in January 1956.

It was surely the open rift with the Garden management that caused the final break. A glaring sign of this was the fact that Walter Brown and the Boston Celtics gave Lapchick a public send-off in the Knicks' last game in Boston, while the Garden management refused to even allow a local New York committee to stage a Joe Lapchick Night at Madison Square Garden. Leonard Koppett called the decision "a display of pettiness and blindness."

The New York press immediately took up the Lapchick case. Red Smith of the *New York Herald Tribune* wrote:

> What the Giants have been to professional football in New York, Joe Lapchick has been to basketball, both college and professional . . . nobody in any game has lent greater dignity to the American sports scene.

Leonard Koppett noted in the *New York Post* that "Joe Lapchick has one important failing as a coach—he's a nice guy . . . and soon Irish may find a song from 'Damn Yankees' haunting his thoughts. A man doesn't know what he has until he loses it." Warren Pack of the *New York Journal American* said, "We, the sports writers, will miss him at the Garden for he was always ready to give out with the truth, even when it affected him."

Jimmy Cannon of the *Post* reported:

You're Joe Lapchick who plays every game twice . . . you're haggard and jumpy . . . you've sickened with defeat in other years. You've taken the game to hospitals with you . . . you're part of the mythology of basketball . . . you and Irish have grown slowly apart. Few people like the guy. You do. You defend him. You tell people he's a good guy. This is a professional matter between an owner and his coach. The boss wins them all. Owners don't resign because they don't get along with the coach. The coach and the manager take the fall. The owner stays.

Arthur Daly of *The New York Times* concluded that:

No coach in memory went through the agonizing torments of Lapchick during a game. . . . He talks of going into public relations. He should. Being a man of vast charm, amiability, graciousness and winsomeness, he would do well in that field. If he returns to basketball, it will kill him. Despite his all-encompassing love for sport the big fellow should be too smart to toy with suicide. . . . The world of sports will be poorer without big Joe. But he may be a much happier man elsewhere.

Joe Lapchick didn't take Arthur Daly's advice because he couldn't accept defeat. He had to return to coaching. He had to recapture the rhythm of winning. But he had a perspective on coaching:

There are no geniuses in coaching. The players always make the coach, and we must never forget that. Sure, we make a contribution to direct them to the type of game we want them to play. But the coach isn't more important than the talent and commitment of his players. A coach is never greater than his team.

Whatever the combination of talent and coaching, Lapchick's St. John's teams won again for ten more years upon his return. His intensity didn't change. "The game still tore me up inside, but I only go through it twenty-five times a season instead of the seventy-two I had with the pros, where you either win or get out."

Still worried, Arthur Daly wrote about the game between St.

John's and national champion Ohio State in the 1961 Holiday Festival:

> The tall and lean Lapchick looked like a man striving to achieve a mental breakdown. He was worse than he had ever been during his palmiest and balmiest days with the Knicks. He kept edging ahead in his chair until he pitched forward onto one knee at courtside. He would leap to his feet, screaming, exhorting and pleading. He'd let go withering blasts at the referees. He'd pound hands to temple when things went wrong. He'd untrigger himself by trips to the water cooler at the far end of the bench. Before the first half was over he had taken 24 such trips. Then count was lost.

There was to be a lot more winning and a lot more pain. The triumphant ending at Madison Square Garden in 1965 topped the cruel news of his mandatory retirement, just as his comeback at St. John's restored his pride after he had left the Knicks.

Perhaps what Joe Lapchick said about cutting a player in the *Collier's* story told me more about how he felt about being let go himself than anything else: "When a kid fails you can't dismiss it by saying, 'Well, he just went home.' He didn't just go home. In many cases he's a hero in his hometown. Before he left they had a dinner for him and gave him a watch. There were write-ups in the paper. How is he going to feel when he goes back? How am I going to feel?"

He couldn't allow himself to fail, although Ned Irish in the mid-Fifties and St. John's a decade later made the ultimate cuts. If they understood this deeply sensitive man, they didn't show it. But Lapchick tried to ease their embarrassment at hurting a popular public figure. He never publicly criticized either decision. He decided first to prove them wrong and second to take them off the hook. He later said of Ned Irish, "He was a tough man, but he took basketball out of the dance halls. He gave it the respectability it deserves. No one ever did more for the game." As for St. John's, he never stopped being a fan.

Once he had achieved that last conquest at the NIT in 1965, he said, "I shall settle for the todays because all your tomorrows soon become yesterdays and then who gives a damn." It was an ironic statement for a man who had experienced so many yester-days: the Celtics . . . the Rens . . . St. John's . . . the Knicks. For him they would last for the rest of his life. As he aged his yesterdays did become his tomorrows. The game and life all seemed to stand still. He could only passively watch basketball on television instead of on the sidelines; he could only passively watch the news about deteriorating race relations without the forum he once had to make his own quiet but meaningful changes through his sport. Whatever changes were to come, he knew that he would not take part in creating them. But Joe Lapchick helped build the stage so that those changes could someday begin. Sport's flickering torch would have to be picked up by others.

Part Five
Race and Sport in The
New Millenium

Introduction

In the past, sport and sportsmanship may have been a force to better society and in the future it may be so again, But I am not sure that it functions so positively in the present. For more than a decade, race took center court as the most important issue in sport. Yet sport often fails to maintain ethical standards or provide opportunites irrespective of race. Chances for college and professional sport to lead the way to change are slipping away.

No one can deny that sport, whether at the Division I college or the professional level, is a huge business. Big-time sporting events such as the Olympics, the All-Star games, the NBA and the NHL Finals, the World Series, the Super Bowl, college bowl games, and March Madness for men's and women's college hoops get fans excited while advertisers pay huge sums of money to sponsor broadcasts.

In such an enthusiastic atmosphere it is easy to forget the unsportsmanlike behavior of many athletes such as Latrell Sprewell and P. J. Carlisemo, NHL players who shout racial epithets, or Charles Barkley, who threw a man through a window. Baseball and football players spit at other players. Many athletes engage in gay-bashing as a means to psyche out other players. John Rocker is infamous for his vitriolic speech, while Allen Iverson's rap lyrics degrade women and gays while preaching violence.

Many of us involved with college sport were feeling very good about the level of reform and progress over the course of the 1990s. Scandals in athletic departments were on the decline and graduation rates were climbing for both white and black student-athletes. Then in mid-1990s *Emerge Magazine* began to publish its "Bottom 50" list of schools with the worst graduation rates for black student-athletes and the bubble burst.

To avoid *Emerge*'s list in basketball, a school merely had to graduate one percent of its black student-athletes. Not one of the fifty schools listed in the year 2000 had graduated a single black athlete over a six-year period. Since black college students hold more than 45 percent of all football scholarships and 55 percent of all basketball scholarships in general, American colleges and universities must take notice so that student-athletes will have a real chance to suceed academically.

The sports business, including the sports media, must change if sport is to deliver on its promises. Fully half of black high school student-athletes now think they have a real shot at becoming professional athletes. All involved in sport must let children know that only one in 10,000 athletes will make it as a professional athlete. If the true statistics remain hidden, sport remains a cruel illusion of fairness for too many African-Americans who see that hundreds of African American professional athletes are millionaires. They see only the stars and the money, not the thousands of athletes who did not achieve fame or multimillion-dollar salaries.

Do we need the Reverend Jesse Jackson to publish a "Fairness Index" again or to have the Black Coaches Association threaten to take action? Maybe. But if we did the right thing in the first place, we wouldn't need such actions. Publications such as the *Sports Business Journal*, *Sports Illustrated*, and *The Sporting News* need to provide those in the business and on the field with the necessary information to make the right choices. Then the world of sports will get a new chance to be a great model for America.

I have written this part of the book to portray what I consider the current situation of race in sport in the United States in the new millennium. There is no way to do this without some historical and descriptive overview. Thus, chapter 15 begins with a look at what has transpired since Jackie Robinson broke the color barrier in 1947 through the most recent data on who plays our games and who runs the games they play. It examines the new dimensions of diversity, especially the issues facing Latino, international, and Native American athletes, the opening up of tennis and golf to athletes of color, and the issue of how race is presented in the media.

Chapter 16 examines the opportunities for young people, male and female, to play sport in America. Although participation in sport benefits young people, few opportunities exist for urban youth to participate in sports programs. Chapter 17 deals with the two-fold challenges that women of color have to be successful as both athletes and professional administrators in sport. Chapter 18 analyzes issues that cross racial lines, but that may at the same time most directly impact athletes of color. This section includes material on academics—both the opportunities to get an education and the obstacles to academic achievement—as well as drug use among athletes and the power of addiction over those who fall prey to it. The last part of chapter 18 looks at athletes' potential to act as athletes and model citizens, issues of gun control, and the use of cheap labor in Asia and Latin America to produce American sporting goods. It also discusses league-wide efforts to affect change and athletes providing public-service announcements.

Chapter 19 deals at length with the stereotyping of athletes. One of the most serious issues in sport today is the public's assumption that athletes are more likely to violate social norms than nonathletes. Although statistically this is not true, this impression reinforces the belief that when one or more athletes commit a crime, it implies something about the sport they play and about athletes in general. Since many of the crimes committed by athletes and reported in the press involve football, basketball, and baseball players, this stereotype disproportionately implicates athletes of color and can reinforce prevailing prejudices.

Chapter 20 is a compilation of recent stories about athletes that shed light on the continued presence of racism in sport and in our society. They include stories about Reggie White and the burning of black churches; Michael Watson, a victim of a racial assault; and Ray Seals and police brutality against blacks.

The final chapter presents stories of transformation involving such individuals as Muhammad Ali, O. J.Simpson, and Clifford Moller, a student-athlete who returned to get his degree thirty-three years after his freshman year. It describes LaGrange, Georgia, a community known for Ku Klux Klan activity that opened itself to change after a group of African athletes lived there. It juxtaposes John Rocker and Hurricane Carter and introduces an eighty-year-old man in South Florida whose words made me believe that change is always possible.

The conclusions that follow part five take a penetrating look at the future of race and sport in America.

Chapter 15

Historical Overview: The Changing Face of Diversity in Sports

---

Fifty years have passed since my dad helped integrate the National Basketball Association as coach of the Knicks. That was three years after Jackie Robinson blazed a much harder trail as the first black player in Major League Baseball. Robinson had two dreams—the integration of the players and the integration of management. The first seems complete. The integration of blacks, Latinos, and international players onto American professional and college teams is nothing short of remarkable. The second part of Robinson's dream is far from complete.

Until very recently, discussions on the issue of diversity in sport focused almost exclusively on black and white players, but sport in America is no longer a snapshot of black and white. Diversity is being redefined for the new millennium.

In November, 1999, Northeastern University's Center for the Study of Sport in Society released its tenth annual report regarding the racial composition of players, coaches, and key administrators in the NBA, the WNBA, the NFL, Major League Baseball, the NHL, Major League Soccer, and college sport. The report, long known as the *Racial Report Card*, was renamed the *Racial and Gender Report Card*. The data on African American participation appears immediately above. Despite the widely held per-

Table 15.1   African American Players in Professional and College Sport (from 2001 Racial and Gender Report Card)

League	Year	Percentage of African Americans
National Basketball Association	2000–01	78%
Women's Nat. Basketball Assoc.	2000	63%
National Football League	2000	67%
Major League Baseball	2000	13%
National Hockey League	1999–2000	2%
Major League Soccer	2000	16%
NCAA Basketball	1998–1999	56%
NCAA Football	1998–1999	46%
NCAA Baseball	1998–1999	2%
Other NCAA Division I sports	1998–1999	25%

ception that the number of black athletes continues to soar in the major sports, these tables reinforce the conclusion that racial diversity in sport will no longer be only about black and white.

Since the early 1990s, the percentage of black players decreased in all professional sports as well as at the Division I collegiate level. The percentage of black players in Major League Baseball hit a ten-year low point in 2000. In Division I men's college basketball and baseball, the percentage of black student-athletes was at the lowest level since 1991–92, while the total percentage of black student-athletes playing Division I sports dropped from 25.2 percent in 1991–92 to 25 percent in 1996–97.

For the most part, these declining numbers have remained stable or, in some cases, decreased further. As of November 2000, blacks made up 78 percent of the players in the NBA, 63 percent in the Women's National Basketball Association, 67 percent in the National Football League, 13 percent in Major League Baseball, 56 percent in college basketball, and 46 percent in college football.

On the other hand, the percent of Latino players in MLB in 2000 reached an all-time high of 26 percent, and that number is climbing. Their presence continues to grow in Major League Soccer. In Division I college sport the total number of players of color reached 32.1 percent of all student-athletes, due in large part to the increase in the number of Latino, Asian, and Native American student-athletes.

In the 2000 WNBA season, 34 percent of the players were white, 63 percent were black, and 3 percent were Latino. In the 2000 NHL season, 2 percent of the players were black. There were also three Asian players, and six players from other minorities. In the 2000 Major League Soccer season, 63 percent of the players were white, 16 percent were black, 21 percent were Latino, and 1 percent were Asian American.

International players control 11 percent of the slots for players in the NBA, 18 percent in the WNBA, 3 percent in the NFL, 12 percent in MLB (excluding American-born players of Latino descent), 25 percent in MLS, and 6 percent in college sports.

The NBA consistently holds the best record for opportunities for people of color and women in management positions. Among the new men's leagues covered for the first time in the 1999 *Racial and Gender Report Card*, Major League Soccer had the best record for racial diversity and the NHL had the best record for opportunities for women. In light of the small number of NHL players who are racial minorities, the NHL had a better than expected record on racial diversity especially in the league office. By comparison, the colleges and universities had the poorest record of all once again.

Who Runs the Games? Management Positions in Professional Sport

Off the playing fields and courts, Jackie Robinson's second dream remains unfulfilled. The 1999 *Racial and Gender Report Card*

Table 15.2 International Players in Professional Sports (from 2001 Racial and Gender Report Card)

League	Year	*Percentage of International Players*
National Basketball Association	1999–2000	11%
Women's Nat. Basketball Assoc.	2000	18%
National Football League	2000	3%
Major League Baseball	2000	12%
National Hockey League	1999–2000	26%
Major League Soccer	2000	25%

shows that while hiring practices in sport have improved for people of color and women, there is clearly room for progress in all sports. Yet, according to the Federal Glass Ceiling Commission Report (FGCR), pro sport was far ahead of society in these matters. Whereas affirmative action programs have been under siege in many states, both college and pro sports assert that their goal is to embrace affirmative action.

One of the most important findings of the RGRC was that the growth of opportunities for women continued to exceed those for people of color by significant numbers for professional off-the-field positions in both college and professional sports. However, many of the jobs held by women indicated that there is still a gendered division of labor in sport. Despite important gains, women are overrepresented in support staff positions and are underrepresented, aside from in the NBA, in senior management.

When compared with the league offices in the NFL and MLB, the NBA had the highest percentage of employees of color (22 percent) and female employees (45 percent). The total percentage of minorities in the NBA league office was down only slightly from 30 percent in 1997 to 29 percent, while in the NFL league office the total percentage of minorities was 23 percent, up slightly from 1997. At the NFL league office, people of color held 21 percent of professional posts and women held 26 percent.

Since 1997 there has been a one percent increase in the number of black employees and a 4 percent increase in the total number of minorities at the executive and department head level in Major League Baseball in central offices. Overall, minorities make up 26 percent of all MLB personnel. However, the percentage of women represented at the executive and department head level dropped 9 percent from 1997.

In the NHL in 1999, 19 percent of the professional staff was made up of people of color and 41 percent were women. At the MLS league office, the professional staff was 81 percent white, 17 percent Latino, 2 percent Asian, and 47 percent female.

Val Ackerman, president of the WNBA, is the only woman to head a major professional sports league. In 1999, 31 percent of WNBA league office employees were minorities. Women made up 69 percent of the total staff at the office. In addition, 31 percent of the WNBA head coaches were black, of which 13 percent were black women. Though many staff members of the WNBA's central offices are shared with the NBA, all data referred to here are for all personnel employed only by the WNBA.

There were no black or Latino majority owners in the NBA, the NFL, the NHL, the WNBA, Major League Soccer, or Major League Baseball. There was one Asian majority owner in MLS and one in the NHL. Three majority owners were women: two in the NFL and one in MLB.

The NBA, the NHL, and MLS all had people of color as team presidents or chief executive officers (CEOs). However, the NFL and MLB did not report any people of color holding the positions of board chairs, presidents, or CEOs. Marge Schott was once the only female president/CEO in MLB, then heading-up the Cincinnati Reds. In August 1998, Wendy Selig-Prieb assumed that role with the Milwaukee Brewers.

As of May 2001, the three major professional sports leagues combined reported 19 head coaches and managers who were persons of color an increase of 6 from 1999 and a new all-time high. Major League Soccer had two Latino head coaches. At the start of the 2000–01 NHL season, persons of color held none of the head coaching positions.

The number of people of color in the role of the ''principal in charge of day to day operations,'' positions such as general manager or director of player personnel, also increased by June 2001. There were six African American general managers in the NBA, 4 in one NFL and one in MLB where the Chicago White Sox had baseball's only black general manager. In the 2000–2001 NHL season, as well as Major League Soccer's 2000 season, no persons of color held a similar position. Lynne Meterparel, general manager of the San Jose Clash, was the only female general manager in men's professional sports. Of the five general managers in the WNBA, three were women and one was African American.

Latinos in the Front Office

With the exception of Major League Soccer, gains for Latinos on the field have not been matched in the front offices, or in college athletic departments. Tony Bernazard, a long-time Major League Baseball player who is now an executive with the MLB Players Association, is convinced that more Latinos need to be in decision-making positions in baseball's hierarchy. "Until we routinely get those positions, we will not make progress in the lower level professional posts in baseball."

Given the increasing number of Latino players, it is hard to believe that:

- Linda Alvadrado (Colorado Rockies, baseball team) was the only Latino to be part owner of a professional sports team. As of 2001, no professional sports team has ever had a Latino or African American majority owner.

- As of 2001, no Latino has ever been general manager of a Major League Baseball team.

- Omar Minaya became baseball's first ever Latino assistant general manager when the Mets hired him in 1997. There were only two in 2000.

- In 2001 Felipe Alou of the Montreal Expos was Major League Baseball's only Latino manager.

- In 2001 only 4 percent of the executives and department heads in Major League Baseball's central offices were Latino.

- The 2000 Los Angeles Dodgers, San Francisco Giants, Florida Marlins, Houston Astros, San Diego Padres, Arizona Diamondbacks, and Detroit Tigers were the only teams that had Latino team vice presidents in MLB.

- As of the 2000 MLB season, there was no Latino chief financial officer, director of public relations, or director of community relations in MLB.

- In 2000, Dan Guerero and Rudy Davalos were the only Latino Division I athletic directors.

People close to the game argue forcefully to raise a related issue: that there is a need for a cultural transition program for Latino players. José Massó, the Senior Associate Director of Northeastern University's Center for the Study of Sport in Society from 1997 to 2000 and previously an agent who specialized in Latino players, saw first hand how difficult it is for players to break through linguistic and cultural barriers. "The players need help as soon as they are signed. They need to learn English as a second language as well as [receive] instruction to know how to handle their new life in a multicultural society like the United States." He is convinced "that players suffer in some media circles. Also, non-Latino players need a deeper understanding of Latino culture so that they can be better teammates on and off the field.

There is clear leadership on issues of diversity by the commissioners of all the league offices and by the president of the NCAA. Nevertheless, while African-Americans and women have made progress, there seems to be no sense of urgency to move Latinos into the front offices of Major League Baseball or into college athletic departments. The Latino players are there while Latino decision-makers are absent.

Management Positions in College Sport

College officials took note of the 1999 *Racial and Gender Report Card* that showed how far athletic departments had to go before any form of racial and gender equality is achieved. While there had been improvement in many areas since the 1998 report, colleges got the worst grade for racial diversity in hiring practices and surpassed only the NFL in gender equity.

As in professional sports, the percentage of white and black students playing college sport is giving way to increased participation by other student-athletes of color and international student-athletes, but white men continue to dominate athletic departments. While African-Americans have achieved greater visibility in decision-making roles in professional sports, they remain in the background. Latinos, Asians, and Native Americans are rarely represented in college athletic departments.

The 1999 *Racial and Gender Report Card*'s overall grade for Division I college sport was a "C" for both racial and gender hiring practices. The colleges did well with student-athlete participation rates for minorities, which hit an all-time high of 32 percent, and for women, which grew to 39 percent. However, when compared to professional sports, colleges had the smallest percentage of people of color among head coaches (7.9 percent), athletic directors (4.6 percent), senior administrators, and administrators in general. The NCAA headquarters was well represented at the highest level by people of color and women, but showed a weaker record of hiring people of color or female midlevel managers and other professionals.

Off the playing field, the most visible positions in college sport are athletic directors, who are roughly the equivalent of the general manager of a professional sports team, and coaches. The percentage of black athletic directors in Division I decreased from an already low 3.7 percent to 3.2 percent between 1995–96 and 1997–98. The percentage continued to decrease. The 2000 NCAA report shows that a mere 2.4 percent of athletics directors are African-American, a 30 percent decline from an already embarrassing showing. However, the ratio of female athletic directors in Division I rose from 7.5 to 8.2 percent.

Dan Guerrero, athletic director at the University of California, Irvine, is one of only three Latino athletic directors in Division I. He said, "Latinos are roughly where African-Americans were a decade ago. People have finally recognized the need to make our athletic departments look more like our student bodies. With changing demographics and an anticipated increase of Latinos in higher education throughout the country, it is vital that we be represented at all levels, especially at the top. Unfortunately, as we move into the next century, Latinos, Native Americans, and Asians have failed to be included into that mix. African American representation in intercollegiate athletics is further along, but not even close to where it should be. This exacerbates the problem facing Latinos and Asians. We have a very long way to go."

For more than a decade successful black college coaches have won conference titles and even national championships in basketball. John Thompson, Nolan Richardson, and Tubby Smith all won men's titles and Carolyn Peck led Purdue to the 1999 women's title. Nevertheless, minority coaches still struggle.

The career of Grambling's Eddie Robinson provides the most telling example of the racial disparity in college football. Robinson was the winningest coach in college football history. He was the coach who sent more student-athletes to the NFL than any other coach while managing to graduate 80 percent of his players. Yet, he was never interviewed for a coaching position by a predominantly white college. The 1999 *RGRC* shows that the percentage of black head football coaches fell from 4.8 percent in 1995 to an outrageous 2.9 percent. Not only were blacks not getting the jobs, they weren't even being interviewed.

College baseball was even worse. According to the 1999 *RGRC*, Blacks held .4 percent of head coaching jobs. Granted, few African Americans play college baseball, but they do run track and field in large numbers. African American men held only 8.7 percent of track and field head coaching positions, and they were virtually shut out of coaching positions in other sports. When all Division I men's head coaches (excluding the Historically Black Colleges and Universities) were tallied, only 5.8 percent were black and 2.1 percent were other people of color—a combined total of 7.9 percent, up slightly from 6.9 percent in 1995–96. This figure was significantly smaller than that for any of the professional leagues except the NHL.

NCAA Division I institutions showed greater diversity in the coaching ranks of the sports in which student-athletes of color had the highest rate of participation. African-Americans made up 21.6 percent of Division I men's basketball coaches, but there were few chances for African American coaches in Division I football (2.9 percent).

Of the Division I women's teams, 7.8 percent were coached by people of color (3 percent women of color), up marginally from 7.6 percent in 1995–96. The percentage of women coaching women's teams was 42.1 percent, down slightly from 42.9 percent in 1995, but down significantly from the highpoint in the late 1970s when women made up 90 percent of the coaching staff for women's teams.

NCAA President Ced Dempsey has taken strong stands on issues of diversity. As he consistently advocates for more women and people of color as coaches and athletic directors. Nevertheless, white males still coach most of the college and university teams and control the athletic departments. Dempsey can't do it alone. He needs the nation's college presidents to step up to the plate.

Roberto Clemente: Latino Icon Who Paved the Way

If all of us, but especially African-Americans, owe a debt of gratitude to Jackie Robinson, then all of us, but especially Latinos, owe a similar debt to Roberto Clemente.

When the 2000 Major League Baseball season ended, MLB issued the rankings that determine compensation for teams that lose players as free agents. These rankings also determine the best players. When I wrote *Broken Promises* in 1984, blacks dominated the rankings. Latino players dominated them in 2000. According to the *New York Times*, "ranked number one in the American League were catcher Ivan Rodriguez, first baseman Carlos Delgado, second baseman Roberto Alomar, shortstop Alex Rodriguez, outfielder Manny Ramirez, designated hitters (tied) Edgar Martinez and Rafael Palmeiro, and starting pitcher Pedro Martinez. The National League ranked second baseman Edgardo Alfonzo, outfielder Vladimir Guerrero, and relief pitcher Armondo Benitez number one" The Latino domination of best-player status was disproportionate to the representation of Latinos in general in baseball.

Roberto Clemente was to Latinos what Jackie Robinson was to African-Americans. The influence of both men reached beyond players from their respective racial and ethnic backgrounds. However, although the 1997 fiftieth-anniversary celebration of Jackie Robinson's breaking into the Major Leagues attracted attention from all racial and ethnic groups, the 1997 twenty-fifth anniversary of the tragic—and heroic—death of Roberto Clemente was virtually unnoticed.

Roberto Clemente was still a star player after eighteen years in the Major Leagues when he decided to personally deliver eight tons of relief supplies to the victims of an earthquake in Nicaragua. The antiquated aircraft took off from his native Puerto Rico on December 31, 1972 and crashed off the coast of San Juan minutes later. Gone was a superstar player, a cultural hero, and a man who would not be forgotten as a committed, compassionate human being. Major League Baseball's humanitarian of the year award bears Clemente's name.

Just as Jackie Robinson displayed his own pride as an African-American, Clemente always showcased his Puerto Rican heritage. He discussed it in interviews. He requested that his wife, Vera, be in Puerto Rico for the birth of each of their three sons. During the post-game interview after he won the World Series MVP in 1971, he stopped the questions and asked for the blessing of his mother and father who lived in Puerto Rico.

Clemente was the first Latino inducted into baseball's Hall of Fame. While his career alone merited induction, his death hastened it. Yet, as of November 2000, of the 249 members of the Hall of Fame, only seven foreign-born Latinos and two American-born players of Latino heritage have been inducted.

Roberto was still playing and made his 3,000th hit in 1972. He closed that season with a .317 lifetime average. His hitting and fielding helped him make the National League All-Star team twelve times. He hit more than .300 in thirteen seasons and won four batting titles. Clemente won twelve Gold Glove awards and led the league's outfielders in assists five times. He batted a combined .362 to help the Pittsburgh Pirates capture two World Series rings. Roberto got a hit in all fourteen Series games he played in. His batting average was even better when he won the World Series MVP in 1971.

His struggles as a Latino player remind us of the problems that still exist for new Latino stars in baseball. He shared language problems with other Latino players when he came up for the first of his eighteen years playing Major League Baseball. Similar to some Latino players today, Clemente believed that he suffered in some media circles because he spoke Spanish better than English and because of his skin color. Even in 2001, more than 95 percent of American sportswriters are white men. There are only a handful of African American and Latino sportswriters who might be able to interpret the multicultural background of players more accurately. Phil Musick, who extensively covered Clemente, wrote in *Reflections on Roberto* that "there was a racial overtone to much of what was written about Clemente early in his career and, unfortunately, it precluded much reporting on his baseball skills and how they were acquired. The author of this work bears some of that responsibility."

Does this bias still exist? When Wilfredo Cordero was accused of beating his wife early in the 1997 season, several journalists and sports talk radio personalities offered the notion that Latino men tend to be more emotional and violent. They didn't bother to examine the fact that on the day that Cordero was arrested, 8,200 other American women suffered abuse from men, a fact that cuts across racial, cultural, economic, and geographic lines.

The term "natural" is frequently applied to Latino and African American players, as if they didn't need to work endlessly to acquire their skills. Such a characterization feeds a white American stereotype of Latinos and African-Americans being lazy. Latino players, including today's best, regularly play winter ball after their Major League seasons end. Another stereotype about not playing when hurt plagues Latino players today as it did Clemente 30 years ago. However, although he was public about his physical pain, Clemente played in summer and winter. Yet the press called him a hypochondriac. That for a man who averaged 135 games per season for over eighteen years.

Native American Names and Mascots in Sport

In one day, Hank Aaron did more for the campaign to ban Native American team names and mascots than has been accomplished in the thirty-plus years that the campaign has been active. As fans gathered for the 2000 All-Star Classic in Atlanta, Aaron couldn't resist the platform that throwing out the first pitch gave him. He talked to the media about race and sport. This was not new for the man who had his own personal triumph of breaking Babe Ruth's career home run record marred by innumerable death threats and a barrage of hate mail. What was new was his statement that if the team name that he had worn on his chest for decades was hurtful to many Native Americans, then it should be changed. He instantly became the most prominent athlete to take that position publicly.

Hank Aaron is a high ranking executive for the Atlanta Braves. Ted Turner, the team owner and a well-known philanthropist who has given generously for Goodwill Games designed to increase understanding between people of different nationalities, never questioned the appropriateness of his team's name. To a certain extent I can understand his blindness, because in my youth I shared it.

I played freshman basketball for the St. John's Redmen. My father coached those Redmen for twenty years, and was affectionately called "the Big Indian." He never had reason to question the nickname or the wooden Indian mascot and neither did I until an incident that happened late one evening in 1969 at Mama Leone's Restaurant near the old Madison Square Garden. Whenever we were there to eat after a game, people would come up to my father to greet him or ask for an autograph. This night was no different until an older man who appeared to be in his late sixties, like my father, asked if he could join us.

The man told my father how much he admired him as a coach and as someone who helped to integrate basketball. We smiled until he added that these things made it particularly embarrassing that my father coached a team called the Redmen and was called "the Big Indian." The man was a Native American.

That was the first time that we had ever thought about what the Redmen represented. We began to conjure up memories of headlines, "Redmen on the Warpath" and "Redmen Scalp Braves [Bradley University]." The Braves even "hung the Redmen" once. The question of the appropriateness of the team name continued to haunt the school for another twenty years until St. John's, like other universities, came to understand the offense and rid itself of a name and symbols representing Native American stereotypes.

However, in 2001, more than forty colleges and universities and five professional teams, including the Braves, retain Native American names and symbols. Would we think of calling teams the "Chicago Caucasians," the "Buffalo Blacks," or the "San Diego

Jews?''Could you imagine people mocking African-Americans in blackface at a game? Yet go to a game where there is a team with an Indian name and you will see fans with war paint on their faces. Is this not the equivalent of blackface? Although the thought of changing tradition is often painful, the sting of racism is even more painful.

Supporters of maintaining the team names and mascots that are potentially offensive to Native Americans generally claim that their use furthers our appreciation of Native American culture. They say that names are meant positively, that to be called a ''Brave'' is a compliment. There are even Native Americans who don't challenge that view. Nonetheless, most Native Americans believe that campuses where Indian names and mascots are used can be hostile learning environments not only for Native American students, but also for all students of color and for all students who care about stopping the spread of racism.

Concerned students, faculty and administrators point out that most campuses where Native American symbols prevail lack a Native American studies department and these schools do not make a serious attempt to recruit Native American students and faculty. The fact that history has ignored the incredible pain inflicted on Native Americans does not excuse colleges and universities from responding to potential pain inflicted by degrading mascots.

Along with all people of color and women who fight for their rights, more voices must be raised to make people who look like me become uncomfortable, just as that Native American man made my father and me uncomfortable in Mama Leone's in 1969. Like Hank Aaron did before the All-Star game.

In June 2000 I spoke against the continued use of Native American team names and mascots at the Sovereignty Symposium in Tulsa, Oklahoma. This symposium is an annual gathering of Native American leaders to discuss issues of their sovereignty—how to protect it where it is intact and how to reclaim it where it has been stolen. The use of Native American names and mascots for sports teams is one of the issues Native Americans believe is a breach of their sovereignty. Native Americans believe that all people live within the one circle of humanity, no matter what the color of their skin. Sports teams should honor that circle.

New Barriers Falling: Tennis and Golf Open Up

Golf and tennis have been the whitest of our sports, largely reserved for the wealthy and for those living in the suburbs. Can the play of Tiger Woods and Venus and Serena Williams change that? I have written elsewhere in this book about Tiger Woods and his impact not only on golf, but also on the entire world of sport.

It may sound incredible to most, but according to two recent studies, The ESPN-Chilton study and the Neilsen Media Research study, African-Americans are the most avid tennis fans of any racial group. There was a great deal of excitement surrounding the women in the 2000 U.S. Open. Much of it emanated from an anticipated final that was not to be between the African American Williams sisters, Serena and Venus. Not long ago having an African American man or woman in the final was incredibly unlikely. Yet in 1999, Serena won it all. The 2000 Open belonged to Venus.

I have followed the USTA for nearly thirty years. Based on my own early contact, I would never have predicted the diverse makeup of today's fans. The USTA has been transformed from an organization that stood for exclusion to one that has moved toward inclusion. Tennis' grasses have been turning into welcoming places for the masses.

With the spectacular play of the Williams sisters, tennis again has stars of color. Tennis has had some recent African American stars and role models like Zina Garrison and Mali Vai Washington, but the Williams sisters have been incredible catalysts. Their arrival peaked even more interest in tennis in the African American community. In 1999, 11 percent of African-Americans called themselves avid tennis fans, a 36 percent increase over the results of a poll taken two years earlier. This is nearly twice the 5.7 percent of whites that identified themselves as tennis fans. Tennis is the fourth most popular sport among African-Americans after the NFL (39 percent), the NBA (37.4 percent), and MLB (18.2 percent). It is the seventh most popular sport among whites after the

NFL (29 percent), MLB (18.9 percent), the NBA (15.4 percent), motor sports (12 percent), golf (9 percent), and the NHL (8 percent).

Urban youth tennis programs have been tremendously helpful in increasing tennis' popularity. By providing opportunities for children of color to learn the game, many white USTA officials, coaches, and players are showing these children that there is opportunity open to them in sport. Even more, such opportunities further diversity among athletes and support for all players irrespective of color. Targeting urban areas to spread the benefits of sport can help heal some of America's racial wounds and can help give children a vision of a better future. More will be said about urban youth sport in chapter 16.

But what does the future hold for people of color at the elite levels of tennis? Certainly the past has not projected optimism. After Gibson and Arthur Ashe won their first Grand Slam events, the pundits of the press suggested that the floodgates were opening, that the ranks of black American tennis professionals would swell. Hopes were high when Althea Gibson won at Wimbledon. But four decades separated Althea from the next African American woman champion. Despite Judy Levering's becoming the first woman president of the USTA in 2000, white males still control most of the operations on all levels of the sport. Serena and Venus Williams' successes, while so important, are but a faint knock on the door of the elite level of tennis.

I wait in part because of the reservations about the triumphs of these women. On the night after the 2000 Wimbledon semifinal match, I was the keynote speaker at the banquet of the Professional Football Players Mothers Association. Of the fifty-five moms there, fifty-three were African-American. They had some questions, mostly about the press scrutiny of Venus and Serena's father, Richard Williams. In the days leading up to the semifinal, the press aired more criticism of the athletes' father than of their performance on the tennis court.

Richard Williams surprised reporters and the public when he did not attend his daughter's semifinal confrontation. There is a great deal of discussion about what the media views as his unconventional behavior. However, from the perspective of the NFL mothers, Richard Williams had helped to raise two powerful, intelligent, self-confident young women who had achieved incredible success. Because of their father's and mother's tutelage, the sisters stay focused on their education and on their future plans, on building creative lives after sport. Unlike so many star athletes, they are not obsessed by a game as much as by vitality for life. Politically conscious Serena even stood up on the issue of the Confederate flag in South Carolina. The NFL mothers were proud of these women and of their controversial father. They wondered why the press could not see Richard Williams from their perspective. They felt, as I do, that the press scrutiny of Richard Williams would not have happened if he was a white parent of white stars.

Their questions remind me of the press coverage of Notah Begay, another young star in a sport where whites have reigned until Tiger Woods. Begay, the only Native American on the PGA Tour, was on the golf team at Stanford with Tiger. In only his second year on the Tour, he won his fourth tournament in two weeks by capturing the 2000 Canon Greater Hartford Open. However, every story I read about Begay discussed his problems with alcohol and his second driving-while-intoxicated conviction earlier this year. Again, what relevance did the negatives have at Begay's moments of victory? Most writers did not mention that Notah's honesty in revealing his prior conviction to the judge just as he was about to be released. After he served his seven nights, he was lambasted because he was allowed out during the day to play golf on the same work-release program as other low-risk prisoners in that facility. I know a lot of people in Albuquerque, including many from the reservation where he was raised, who think that Notah Begay is a hero for his people.

I cheered when I saw Tiger Woods' first television commercial in which he criticized restrictive golf courses that prohibited many people of color from playing there. However, Tiger was burned by the press for what I saw as his courage. Between 1998 and 1999 golf received a 14 percent boost in its African American fan base from Woods' play. Golf officials have taken note and have marketed Tiger with unprecedented success. He is making huge money for his sport. Maybe the same will happen for Serena,

Venus, and Notah. Maybe their collective successes will really open the floodgates, not just for more players who look like them, but also for an openness of attitude that will celebrate their individualism, creativity, courage, and honesty.

I have worked on issues of race in sport for more than three decades. Tiger, Notah, Serena, and Venus were not even twinkles in their parents' eyes when I started. For all these years I have worked to get athletes to speak out on issues of race with meager results. For the most part, athletes have been understandably afraid that the whole sports establishment, which happens to be overwhelmingly white and to use a conservative marketing game, would come crashing down on them if they spoke out. Tiger himself stopped speaking out after this commercial.

More Barriers: Black Quarterbacks and the NFL and Positional Segregation in Sports

It seemed like I couldn't read a newspaper or sports magazine for months in 1999 without seeing the faces of five great quarterbacks slotted to go high in the 1999 NFL draft. Of the five quarterbacks chosen among the first twelve picks, three—Syracuse's Donovan McNabb, Oregon's Akili Smith, and Central Florida's Daunte Culpepper—were black. I took more than twenty-five calls from writers asking me what I thought the significance of this was.

I knew that only three black quarterbacks had been drafted in the first round in the history of the NFL draft. In 1999, three black players were chosen in the first round of the draft. Will the stereotype of the smart, heroic, white quarterback leading the team be shattered forever? Does this mean that we have come a very long way on the issue of race in the NFL and in professional sports in general?

Considering how many calls I received, I smiled at several draft analysts who asserted that no one was really paying attention to color and that teams were simply selecting the best available talent. I agree with the latter part of the equation. Teams who want to win are finally picking the best players. I was happy to read that Daunte Culpepper's comment, "Luckily for me, I wasn't faced with those issues. Maybe it doesn't matter that we're black quarterbacks as much as we are good quarterbacks.'' I think Daunte is right in this case. But we must not overstate the significance of this draft. Race does matter in the NFL and in the other major professional sports.

In the 1998 season of the NFL, the positions of quarterback, wide receiver, corner back, and safety were unevenly distributed among the races. At 91 percent, whites continued to dominate the position of quarterback, considered to be football's thinking and control position. White players also accounted for 83 percent of the players at center, considered by many to be football's second control position. On the other hand, blacks made up 92 percent of wide receivers, 87 percent of running backs, 99 percent of cornerbacks, and 99 percent of safeties, positions where speed and reactive ability are considered essential. The quarterback and center positions require more brains while the others reflect more brawn. These numbers imply that the brainy positions are occupieed by whites while the brawny ones go to African Americans. Given these percentages, the significant number of black quarterbacks drafted in the first round of the 1999 draft is notable.

Positional stacking seems to exist in Major League Baseball as well. In the 1998 season only 5 percent of pitchers and 4 percent of catchers were black. These two positions are considered to be baseball's thinking and control positions. Most black players remained in the outfield, where speed and reactive ability are prized. Blacks make up only 13 percent of baseball's players, but have held more than 45 percent of the outfield posts over the last two decades.

The 1999 NFL draft could well be a sign that positional segregation will become a thing of the past in professional football. McNabb and Culpepper have had great starts in their NFL careers. I hope they will get other opportunities if their successes are temporarily derailed at some point. There have been too many cases where black athletes who don't star in the game aren't kept around as bench players. Black quarterbacks throughout NFL history have rarely joined second or third string players in waiting for another chance. Several have been asked to play other positions. I hope that McNabb, Smith, and Culpepper will enjoy a very different future and inspire further change.

Setting the Record Straight: Sam Lacy and the Racial Factor in the Media

Sam Lacy was ninety-seven years old in the year 2000 and had written about sports for seven decades. I have known of Sam Lacy, his writing, and his pioneering work to integrate baseball for more than thirty years. Sam not only wrote about the history of African-Americans in sport, he helped live it and make it. He was an eyewitness for most of the past century. He experienced segregated facilities as did many famous athletes of color such as Jackie Robinson, Jesse Owens, and Joe Louis. For much of his career, he had to cover games from the stands or from the ''coloreds only section.'' There were times he covered games from the stadium roof.

I met Sam for the first time in September 1998 when we were copanelists at the official launch of ESPN's new ''Sports Century Series.'' The panel included other veteran sportswriters Bob Ryan, Robin Roberts, and Mike Lupica. Dick Schaap was the moderator. Even in this strong company, Sam Lacy stole the show. He wasn't trying to be entertaining, but he was. He wasn't trying to upstage anyone, but he did. In spite of their collective fame, the other panelists deferred to Mr. Lacy's intelligence, wit, and experience. The audience at the Museum of Radio and Television in New York was dazzled.

I flew home to my office and couldn't wait to go tell my colleagues about the crowd's reaction. The first coworker I encountered was Robert Weathers, a six-year veteran running back for the New England Patriots. The second was Rosalyn Dunlap, a five-time All-American sprinter. Robert and Rosalyn are African American and in their forties. Neither one had any idea who Sam Lacy was.

Sam Lacy recognized the host of talent in the Negro Baseball Leagues and toiled endlessly through the 1930s and 1940s to get Major League Baseball to integrate. That Sam Lacy is not better known, even among African Americans, reflects the fact that mainstream American newspapers have failed to recognize the wealth of talent writing for the African American press. As in Sam Lacy's era, in 2001 the writers on the sports pages of the 1,600 daily newspapers printed in America are overwhelmingly white and male.

In the year 2000 there are only two African American and one Latino sports editors on newspapers in cities where there are major and minor league professional sports teams. According to the National Association of Black Journalists, in 2000 there were only nineteen African American sports columnists. Ninety percent of the 1,600 dailies did not have a single African American sports writer.

I have spoken to many editors who have told me that they couldn't find African American sports writers for their newspapers. In 1947, Branch Rickey opened the doors of the Negro Leagues by signing Jackie Robinson to the Brooklyn Dodgers. It is shocking that in 2001 we are still waiting to acknowledge the African American press for its talent. Writing now, late in their careers, are the journalistic equivalents of Josh Gibson, Satchel Paige, and Cool Papa Bell. It is yet another profound injustice of the racial dynamics in America that, like Gibson, Paige, Bell, there are many outstanding African American journalists who will never be invited into the same newsrooms as great white writers such as Bob Lipstye, Frank Deford, or the legendary Red Smith.

Sam Lacy received a singular honor in 1998 when he was inducted into the Baseball Hall of Fame. In his acceptance speech, he said that he hoped this would signal the recognition of all those who have written for the African American press. Sam Lacy wants to leave a legacy for other African American writers on the major newspapers and networks.

Like many of today's astute African American journalists who have "made it," Robin Roberts of ESPN and ABC Sports recognized that Sam Lacy paid dues for her and most others. She told the New York audience, "I would not be here if Sam Lacy had not blazed the trail for me." All of today's most successful African

American sports writers, columnists, and broadcasters will tell you that Sam Lacy's legacy thrives in their hearts and minds. Now it is time for the rest of us to discover Sam Lacy and recognize those who will follow him. Our sports pages and broadcasts will be so very much richer.

Chapter 16

Youth and High School Sports

I wrote this book during the 2000 presidential campaign in which politicians once again called for a "balanced budget." Funding for education was targeted as a budget buster. At the high school level, sports programs frequently seemed to be the first to be cut.

While students' test scores decline, drugs, gangs, and violence thrive in many secondary and even elementary schools. There is no doubt that we need new sources of revenue to pull our nation out of the educational crisis we are in today. Problems are especially acute in urban areas, although events such as the school violence in Springfield, Oregon; Pearl, Mississippi; and Jonesboro, Arkansas remind us that it is not just urban America that is suffering. Part of the answer is increased funding for education. Calls for increased allotments for mathematics, the sciences, and language arts have a compelling and clear purpose. The necessity of attracting and keeping good teachers with better economic incentives is just as indisputable.

In this context, sport is often viewed as an expensive frill, as the "toy department." However, because participating in sports can be a strong source of self-esteem, cutting or eliminating school sports programs may strike one more blow at the likelihood of kids from lower socioeconomic backgrounds breaking the cycle of historic discrimination that traps so many.

All data shows that school-age children are more likely to get into trouble between the hours of three and six P.M. If we take away the sports activities that occupy nearly twenty percent of our students during those hours, we markedly enlarge the opportunities for trouble. Many families are now headed by two working parents or by a single working parent who is not at home at 3 P.M. when students return from school. Too often a child at home alone turns to trash television. If they have escaped witnessing violence first hand, it becomes part of their viewing patterns, a normal and acceptable part of life.

There is too little for kids to do in the afternoon or on weekends in our cities. Budget cuts have already closed many recreation centers, zoos, playgrounds, and ballparks that kids used to flock to after school. The supervision provided in organized sport provides structure to children participating. It is time for corporate America to invest in youth sport as another way to provide children with a safety net. The lure of joining gangs can be offset by the benefits of joining teams. Donna Lopiano poignantly spelled it out in a 1999 article for *The Sports Business Journal:* "Kids join gangs because they want respect (applause), support (coaches who care), family (teammates), recognition (batting titles, golden glove awards, or simply a salute from another player), an identity (athlete), control (responsibility for their own performance), and the future promise of money. They want structure (the "game," the team, and the rules). Most of all they want belonging."

In 1998, Boston began Urban Youth Sports (UYS), a major grassroots effort to increase access to youth sports through a partnership between the City of Boston, Northeastern University's Center for the Study of Sport in Society, and several corporate partners including Reebok, Blue Cross / Blue Shield, Partners Health, the Harvard School of Public Health, and the Robert Wood Johnson Foundation.

The Boston Youth Sports Needs Assessment Survey, sponsored by UYS, documented the compelling needs of young people in Boston, which experts say has a typical youth sport profile. Some of their findings follow:

- Just over one third of school-age children in the City of Boston participate in organized youth sports, compared to nearly 90 percent in the suburbs.

- Only 40 percent of boys and less than 15 percent of girls play sports.

- Suburban girls have six times more opportunities to play sports than city girls do.

- City parents are only half as likely as suburban parents to attend games, due to poor public transportation and other factors.

- Most funding in the city goes to one or two sports, usually basketball or baseball, at the elite youth levels.

At the same time, many adults are increasingly wary of sports. Extraordinary salaries, unethical administrators, and unruly athletes have taken away the luster of sporting events. Suggestions to cut high school sports programs or close another recreation center do not meet the resistance they once did.

Yet according to innumerable studies and surveys, the value of sport to its youthful participants is incontrovertible. When asked, boys and girls list ''fun'' as the most important reason they play. But for African-Americans and women, there are much more compelling reasons.

According to a national survey of 865 high-school students conducted by Lou Harris, many African American student-athletes still harbor unrealistic aspirations to stardom. Fifty-one percent of African American high-school athletes believed they would make the pros (vs. 18 percent of white student-athletes).

Fourteen-year-old African Americans, recognize that the color of their skin will, in all likelihood, limit the range of their life choices. Statistically they are less likely to finish high school, to go to college, and to be employed than if they were white. They have far fewer chances of making it big in corporate America as a top administrator or of being hired as a college professor. Just turn on a television and you will not see many African Americans in such professions.

But turn on a Los Angeles Lakers game and you will see Kobe Bryant making more money per quarter than the average high school teacher does per year. The 51 percent who think they will make it are, in their terms, making a somewhat logical choice. Don't tell them that they can't beat the 10,000 to one odds.

In communities driven by despair, athletes in outreach programs realized that they could not afford to snuff out hope. So, while not throwing sand on the fires of desire, athletes have been telling young people to keep hope alive and balance it with preparation for a future that does not include a career as a professional athlete.

The Harris survey indicated that professional athletes in outreach programs have had a substantial and a sustained impact and that African American student-athletes understand that playing sports can help them attain the educational, social, and life skills that will benefit them as productive members of society. They don't have to play for the Lakers. They can be the team doctor or attorney. This study gives us hope that fantasies of a career in professional sports may not lead to shock and emotional letdown. The study highlighted three important issues that follow:

- Seventy-six percent of African American and 60 percent of white student-athletes favored a minimum "C" average for eligibility in sports, demonstrating their understanding of the need to balance athletics and academics. The student-athletes were *asking* for a higher standard. As of 1990, more than forty states did not require a "C" average to participate in high school sports. We are failing them by not asking for more.

- As drop-out rates in urban communities soared, 57 percent of African American student-athletes felt that playing sports encouraged them "a great deal" to stay in school.

- Fifty percent of African American student-athletes believed that playing sports helped them "a great deal" to become a better student.

Apparently, most student-athletes don't ignore academic preparation even if they believe they will make the pros. The Harris survey was the first conclusive evidence that concerned athletes and school administrators have finally reached these young people after a decade of messages begging them to balance academic and athletic goals.

Playing sports has even more clear social benefits for African American students. While drugs and alcohol dominate the lives of many teenagers, sport seemed to help African American student-athletes avoid such potential dangers. Sixty-five percent of African American student-athletes responded that playing sports had helped them "a great deal" to avoid drugs while 60 percent believed that playing sports had the same effect on their ability to abstain from alcohol use.

While society as a whole seems to grow increasingly fearful of urban youth, 44 percent of all African American student-athletes believed that playing sports had helped them "a great deal" to become better citizens. Lou Harris noted that "it was critical to see that at a time when racial and ethnic tensions boil over in school into serious conflicts almost every day, the survey showed that team sports create friendships that cut across racial lines." Seventy-six percent of all white and African American student-athletes reported that they became friends with someone from another racial or ethnic group through playing sports.

Americans of different races are not together as equals in many places. In our racially charged society, this may prove to be the ultimate benefit of sport, finally fulfilling part of the dream of Jackie Robinson.

What about the impact of sport on young women's lives?

- In 1998, the Women's Sports Foundation Report: Sport and Teen Pregnancy shows how playing sports reduced a teenage girl's chances of becoming pregnant.

- By participating in sport for four hours a week, a girl can reduce her chance of developing breast cancer by up to 60 percent.

- Girls who play sports have better grades and are more likely to graduate.

- Girls who play sports are more self-confident, have stronger self-images, and higher self-esteem.

- Eighty percent of female executives in Fortune 500 companies played sports as children.

How important is youth sport to girls? If a girl is not involved in sport by the age of ten, she has less than a 10-percent chance of playing a sport at age twenty-five, thus increasing the chances of a less healthy lifestyle with greater health risks. Girls and boys who play sports together as youths are more likely to work well together through childhood, and adolescence and into adulthood. As adults, they may be more inclined to become mentors, coaches, and corporate sponsors who give back to their community because their personal stake in giving back was increased by youth league and high school athletic participation. Children's chances for healthy development are markedly increased when they play sport.

Sport is not a panacea. But without it, more obstacles get in the way of the people in our nation who have had the smallest chances of reaching the top rungs in the worlds of business, academics, and, yes, even sports. In addition to other preventative programs, the nation must train coaches and establish organized athletic opportunities for urban youth, especially girls, as an integral part of promoting healthy living for young people.

Investments of money and people-power can help remove most of the obstacles to meaningful participation, but it will take the will of government and partnerships between business, the academic community, and youth sport leaders. Boston, Detroit, and the California bay area are setting the example for programs every city in the nation should imitate.

Boston has assumed leadership in the effort to support and coordinate sports programs for urban children regardless of race, gender, ethnicity, and class or family structure. In 1998, Boston's Mayor Thomas Menino emphasized his determination to raise future fiscal support for urban youth sport. ''I'd like to see every kid in the City of Boston participating,'' Menino said. ''We'll find the money for this. We always do.''

As the presidential debates continued with more and more talk of a balanced budget, I argued that America needed more, not fewer, resources for education. Every city in America needs high school sports programs, open recreation centers, and more urban youth sports leagues. Sports participation can help keep today's youth from becoming tomorrow's subjects of crime stories in the news. It can help give *all* children the chance to participate in the presidential debates of the twenty-first century when it becomes their time to lead America.

Chapter 17

Gender Equity in Sport

Women's opportunities for participation in sport became *the* issue in college, Olympic, and professional sport in the second half of the 1990s. It was long overdue. More than twenty years had elapsed since the passage of Title IX, the federal legislation that banned any discrimination against women—including discrimination in sport.

Women and girls have made some astronomical gains in those years. At the high school level, there are now nearly 2.8 million girls participating in athletics, as opposed to less than 300,000 in 1972. In 1998–99, over 145,000 women participated in college sports as compared to 74,000 in 1982. At the college level, in 2001, there is an average of slightly more than seven sports offered for women. In 1978, the year Title IX went into effect, there were fewer than six.

Some of the most noteworthy moments in sports in the 1990s involved women's teams. The University of Connecticut women's basketball team won the 1995 Women's Final Four enthusiastically supported by the New York media. The U.S. women's basketball team swept the 1996 Olympics. Women's professional sport got a big boost with the launch of the WNBA in 1997. American fans, men and women alike, probably celebrated no sport triumph more in 1999 than the U.S. team winning the Women's World Cup in soccer. Serena Williams blew away the competition to win the 1999 U.S. Open. Venus Williams dominated tennis in 2000 with triumphs at Wimbledon and at the U.S. Open. The Women's United Soccor Association (WUSA) was a new women's professional league launched in 2001.

However, college sport failed to completely implement the law as specified by Title IX. If they had done so incrementally over the past twenty-plus years, women's teams would be on equal terms with men's. Instead, colleges have had to react to a successive series of court cases starting in the late 1980s that have ruled in favor of gender equity. Men who were boys in the 1970s are now fathers with daughters to fight for. The only way left for most colleges to respond seems to involve cutting men's sport to either create resources for more opportunities for women or to scale back the opportunities for men to equal those for women.

I hear men who rarely talked about racial equality saying that the cuts in men's sports are going to hurt African Americans the most. Football, where more than 48 percent of scholarships go to African Americans, seems to be a primary target. Divide and conquer—women vs. men; African-Americans vs. women—is eating away at the heart of sport.

Some of the remaining disparities indicate why this issue is so compelling. In 1972 women directed over 90 percent of women's programs. As of 1999–2000, women make up only 9 percent of the athletic directors at Division I schools. The percentage of women coaching women's teams has declined from over 90 percent in 1972 to 48 percent in 2000. Men's athletics still outspend women's athletics two to one in scholarships, three to one in expenses, and three to one in recruiting. Finally, the average number of sports offered to men compared to the average number offered to women is almost nine to seven. Colleges are that far from complying with Title IX.

I speak to many athletic directors. They all say this issue is a difficult one. Many say they really believe in gender equity but don't see how they can pay for it without totally dividing their departments and devastating men's sports. A few simply don't believe that women's sports should be treated as seriously as men's sports.

Either way, almost all athletic directors say that dealing with the issue of gender equity is "ruining the fun" of college sport. I sympathize with them. Change invariably decreases the fun—at first. However, I believe the fun really left the building when college sport became big business.

There was a feeling that "the public," that is, the traditional white, male sports fan, wouldn't care to watch women's sports. There was a time when many in the sports industry believed that "the public" wouldn't care to watch African Americans play sports; or later that they wouldn't watch African-Americans coaching sports. But bringing African-Americans into sport simply added an entirely new fan base to the existing white fan base. As *The O-Jays* sang "money, money, money," the coffers filled faster.

Most people rarely have the opportunity to view women's sport from a marketer's perspective. It is no accident that Donna Lopiano, Director of the Women's Sports Foundation, is one of the most persistent advocates for gender equity in America. While she was director of women's athletics at the University of Texas, Austin, the women's basketball team set NCAA attendance records. Attendance soared from 23,000 in 1980 to 1981 to over 135,000 in 1988 to 1989. Lopiano knew how to market a product at that level with brilliance similar to that of NBA Commissioner David Stern (who in 1996 would help launch the WNBA).

In 1998–99, a new attendance record was set for women's college basketball. Tickets to the Women's Final Four were nearly as hard to get as those for the Men's Final Four. Marketing women's sport and attracting female viewers had created yet another fan base. Many of these new fans liked the women's games so much that they now supported men's sport as well. When male fans watch world-class female athletes they frequently become fans of women's sport. Many male fans are fed up with men's professional and college sport because of free agency, greed, poor sportsmanship, and criminal activity. The absence of those foibles in women's sport makes it even more appealing to men.

Basketball fans caught a glimpse of the future of women's basketball on January 16, 1995 after CBS televised the contest between the women's team from the University of Connecticut and the women's team from the University of Tennessee. I came into the office the next day to hear *everyone* talking about women's basketball. The incredulous new fans blared *"Did you see Lobo* [Player of the Year Rebecca Lobo] *block those shots* [she blocked 5]? *Or Jen Rizzotti steal those balls* [she stole 5]? *Or Kara Wolters dominate the inside game* [she scored a game high of eighteen points]?"

That game, which catapulted Connecticut into the number one spot in the national polls, probably did more for gender equity than all the debates at NCAA conventions combined. In March 1995 one could find some NCAA women's tournament games on ESPN and the network signed a large contract for wider coverage in 1996 and beyond. Then came the 1995 Women's Final Four on CBS.

Tennessee and Connecticut blew out the University of Georgia and Stanford, respectively, setting up a classic rematch. In a game every bit as competitive as the men's championship, Connecticut finished its season at 35-0, only the second women's team to go unbeaten and win the NCAA tournament. Connecticut's triple All-Americans—Lobo, Wolters, and Rizzotti—were the talk of the town in Seattle where the men were getting ready for their showdown.

What followed was the true measure of what happened to women's college basketball that year. CBS's telecast of the final drew an overnight Nielsen rating of 5.6, a 93 percent jump from the telecast of the 1994 Final. The Connecticut-Tennessee game had a higher rating than the three regional NBA games on NBC and nearly triple the rating of Fox's debut NHL games (which ran head-to-head with the women's game).

When the women flew back to Hartford on Monday night an estimated 5,000 fans were waiting for them at Bradley International Airport. Connecticut Governor John Roland gave all the players roses as they stepped off the plane. Entire towns turned out along the thirty-mile ride back to their Storrs campus. Townsfolk from Vernon, Manchester, and South Windsor—blacks and whites, men and boys, women and girls, octogenarians and teenagers—lined I-95 and the last 7.5 miles of the journey down Storrs Road. Just as moving as the crowds was the lone man on his mountain bike atop a steep hill, holding a sign telling the team he loved them.

Bruce Cohen, who headed University of Connecticut's Counseling Program for Intercollegiate Athletics, described the trip as a religious experience. If it was, it culminated in the church known as Gampel Pavilion where an average of 7,875 fans worshipped at each regular season *women's* game. Fire marshals must have been part of the cheering section for the homecoming—an estimated 10,000 celebrants packed Gampel, more than 1,500 above capacity. Anyone paying attention saw the financial and competitive potential for women's sport that night.

Women of Color in College and Professional Sport

Women of color face a double barrier—racism and sexism—in sport and also in society. White males control too much of the power, from the media which shapes images to the sports organizations that control them. Helping only women of color who are elite athletes is not enough. Young girls who have almost no opportunity to compete in sport and live in urban communities also need help. An African American girl in a city has one-sixth the opportunity to play youth sport compared to a white suburban girl, and even less when compared to a white boy in the suburbs. That is a big challenge.

Women of color are constantly fighting stereotypical images that impede their chances to obtain more control and influence in the world of sport. If it is hard today, imagine how hard it was twenty, thirty, or forty years ago. Luckily the history of American sport contains the stories of many trailblazing female athletes. Athletes like Wilma Rudolph, Althea Gibson, Wyomia Tyus, Flo Hyman, and Willye White, along with coaches like Tina Sloan Green and Vivian Stringer, reached great heights and created opportunities for those who would follow.

African American women are bursting onto the scene in college and professional sport. They are most visible in the WNBA where, in 2000, 63 percent of the players were African-American.

Table 17.1   Percentage of Women in Professional and College Sport

Sport	White	African American	Latina	Asian	Native American
Women's National Basketball Association (2000 Season)	34%	63%	3%	0%	0%
NCAA Basketball (1998–99)	58.5%	31.4%	1.7%	0.9%	0.6%
NCAA Track and Field	60.8%	25.3%	3.7%	0.9%	0.6%
Other NCAA Sports	83.3%	2.6%	2.9%	2.4%	0.5%
All NCAA Division I Sports (combined)	75.8%	10.7%	2.9%	1.9%	0.6%

The Williams sisters have helped further the popularity of tennis in particular and women's sports in general.

According to the most recent NCAA data, among the 312 NCAA Division I schools in 1998–99, African American women represented 10.7 percent of all female student-athletes. They were concentrated largely in basketball (31.4 percent) and track and field (25.3 percent). In all other sports combined, African American women made up a mere 2.6 percent of the total of women student-athletes, while Latinas made up 2.9 percent, Asians 1.9 percent, and Native Americans 0.6 percent. Those percentages have all been growing, albeit slowly.

The pioneering women of color in sports wanted not only chances to compete but also opportunities to manage, coach and promote the games in which they played.

Excluding the Historically Black Colleges and Universities, in 2000, not a single Division I college or university employed an African American, Latina, Asian-American, or Native American female as an athletic director. The total for Division II institutions was two African American women and one Asian-American woman. Division III institutions reported two athletic directors who were women of color. In other words, while there are more than 1,000 NCAA schools, only five have women of color as athletics directors.

Who is coming up in the ranks? At Division I schools, only 1.5 percent of all the senior athletics administrators holding the titles of associate and assistant athletics director were women of color. At the Division II and III levels, 2.8 percent and 1.8 percent, respectively, were women of color. That is not very promising in the short term.

In Division I, African American women made up only 2.6 percent of all coaches of women's teams; all women of color comprised only 3 percent. In fact, women only held 42.1 percent of the coaching positions for women's teams. Men hold the majority of the available coaching positions. Of the few women of color holding college head coaching positions, 73 percent were in basketball and track and field. Women of color have been shut out of head coaching positions in most of the remaining sports.

Most Americans think colleges offer women of color the best possibility for employment. The university is thought to be a fair and noble institution, espousing the ideals of equality. Unfortunately, the reality on our campuses is far different.

Between all the professional teams in the NBA, NFL, and Major League Baseball, there were 401 vice presidential positions. African American women held three. There were a total of four women of color vice presidents in all of the league offices combined. No African American women held such positions in the NFL, NHL, or Major League Soccer league offices. Leilani Serrechia, a Latina, was senior vice president for San Jose in the MLS. She was the only Latina vice president in all of the pro sport league offices.

The NBA, which has consistently received the highest grades from the RGRC for its inclusion of both women and people of color in leadership positions, had only one African American woman as a team vice president. The NBA and Major League Baseball had two female African American vice presidents in the league office.

Because it shares much of its staff with the NBA, it was difficult to compare the WNBA with other leagues. However, wherever there were dedicated staff, the WNBA was well represented in high posts by both women and women of color.

To increase the chances that women of color will participate as professional athletes and sports team executives in the future, more of them must compete on the playing field as youngsters. Without athletic opportunity as children, it is unlikely that they will be part of the sports world as adults. Right now those chances are severely limited by lack of opportunities for girls in urban areas to take advantage of youth sport programs.

With those opportunities come the greater possibility of making it to college by increasing the likelihood that they will remain in school and by increasing the likelihood of financial support. If they get to college, their chances for graduating skyrocket. In the graduate rates released in June 1999, 57 percent of African American female student-athletes graduated, compared to 43 percent of the general African American female student population. Latina student-athletes graduated at a rate of 57 percent, while only 49 percent of Latina students in general finished. Among female Asian-Americans, 74 percent of student-athletes graduated vs. 68 percent of Asian female students in general. Native Americans female student-athletes graduated at a whopping 16 percent higher than Native American female students as a whole (54 percent vs. 38 percent respectively).

Every day, girls and women of color confront the fact that white males control the operations in most franchises, in college and high school athletics departments, and in youth sport programs. With degrees and higher level athletic experiences, however, women of color will not give employers in the sports industry any excuse to discount them for lacking qualifications.

Putting more resources into women's sports is an opportunity, an investment in the future of sport in America. While it does cost money in the short run, I firmly believe that women's sports, well marketed and packaged, will bring enough money into athletic departments to make up the initial investment. Anyone who saw Cynthia Cooper lead Houston to its fourth WNBA title or Venus Williams' triumphs at Wimbledon and the U.S. Open knows how much fun it is to watch women's sports. Women's sport is poised to come into its own as both entertaining and profitable. That seems like a win-win situation that merits redefining the terms of the debate.

Chapter 18

Issues that Cross Racial Lines

This chapter examines issues that cross racial lines, but that may disproportionately impact athletes of color: academic standards, drugs, gun control, labor issues, league-wide community service programs and public service announcements.

Academic Standards and the Issue of Race

In 1993, basketball coaches threatened to boycott games when they became frustrated by the slowness with which the NCAA tackled a series of important issues, most noteworthy, that of academic standards for freshman athletes. Ultimately, the coaches' actions would attract the attention of some powerful forces—the White House showed interest, and the Justice Department offered to mediate between the NCAA, its Presidents Commission, and the Black Coaches Association (BCA) and its supporters in the National Association of Basketball Coaches (NABC).

The coaches' arguments painted a poignant picture of the challenges faced by black student-athletes. The coaches argued that if raising certain admission standards or reducing the number of available scholarships limited black student-athletes' access to sports, then the nation as well as the students would feel the despair, built on a heritage of racism, that pervades so much of America's young black community in the form of racial incidents, poverty, and unemployment. The coaches warned that the new academic standards, due to go into effect in 1995, would dramatically decrease access for black student-athletes at a time when they needed more support and more incentives to graduate.

The new standards would have required both a 2.5 grade point average (G.P.A.) on a standard high school academic scale with "A" valued at 4.0 and a minimum combined score of 700 on the Scholastic Aptitude Test (SAT). Many educators agreed that the SAT—a standardized test—is not a good predictor of college success for students from a lower socioeconomic background. Admissions officers offered the opinion that a high school student with a 2.5 G.P.A. and good letters of recommendation stood a good chance at succeeding in college, and believed that a 650 minimum SAT score on a sliding scale would have been appropriate admissions criteria without limiting access. The NCAA held off implementation at the next convention, but the delay quieted the controversy only temporarily.

The word boycott has never been a welcome one among traditional leaders in the world of sports. The thought of government intervention has been even less welcome. But the BCA recognized that people of color and women couldn't simply put their issues on the table and expect meaningful results. History, both in and out of sport, has shown us that something dramatic must occur to obtain real movement.

Until the 1990s, the issue of race was hardly even discussed within the NCAA or in individual campus athletic departments. John Thompson's personal boycott after the NCAA passed Proposition 42 in 1989 showed what black coaches had to do to make a point. Before Coach Thompson took his stand, the NCAA seemed content to ignore or deflect attention away from one of the most tumultuous issues of our time. When boycotts and protests were a routine part of BCA's action list, the NCAA always took note. From the BCA's point of view, a boycott was a natural and necessary way to demand action. The coaches needed to be heard.

In 1995 the BCA was a vital platform for black coaches as they fought with college administrations over the initial eligibility standards presented for discussion at the 1995 NCAA Convention. The college presidents backed Proposition 16, which required either a higher high-school grade-point average or higher standardized test scores for athletes to be eligible to play during freshman year. The coaches favored making all freshmen ineligible, regardless of their test scores or G.P.As, to give them a year to acclimate themselves to the new academic and social realities of college life.

The standards as of 2001 are shown below. They reflect changes in scoring the SAT and ACT that affected all students, not just student-athletes.

When the new academic standards went into effect, the BCA

Table 18.1

Division I Qualifier Index			*Division I Partial-Qualifier Index*		
Core G.P.A.	*ACT**	*SAT†*	*Core G.P.A.*	*ACT**	*SAT†*
2.500 & above	68	820	2.750 & above	59	720
2.475	69	830	2.725	59	730
2.450	70	840–850	2.700	60	730
2.425	70	860	2.675	61	740–750
2.400	71	860	2.650	62	760
2.375	72	870	2.625	63	770
2.350	73	880	2.600	64	780
2.325	74	890	2.575	65	790
2.300	75	900	2.550	66	800
2.275	76	910	2.525	67	810
2.250	77	920			
2.225	78	930			
2.200	79	940			
2.175	80	950			
2.150	80	960			
2.125	81	960			
2.100	82	970			
2.075	83	980			
2.050	84	990			
2.025	85	1000			
2.000	86	1010			

*Previously, ACT score was calculated by averaging four scores. New standards are based on sum of scores.

†For SAT tests taken on or after April 1.

made threats, but did not follow through with action. An internal power struggle ensued. Rudy Washington, the founding executive director, left amid controversy, and the BCA foundered without strong, visible leadership. Their conventions, once a gathering place for all the top black coaches and many white coaches as well, lost momentum. The power coaches disappeared from the meetings. The time when the Black Coaches Association struck fear in the hearts of sports administrators on college campuses and at the NCAA passed, at least for the present.

The college sports community had the opportunity to do something positive to relieve the racially charged climate in America, and it failed. Proceeding with legislation (though implementation was delayed until 1996) that many perceived as tinged with racial inequities left campus leadership open to damaging criticism. Many African American students and student-athletes, as well as leaders in the African American community, joined national leaders, both in the Congressional Black Caucus and in the civil rights community, to continue to wrestle with the NCAA over this issue. *Cureton vs. the NCAA*, a challenge to the standards brought against the NCAA by four African American college student-athletes is currently struggling through the courts where the lower courts have ruled that the NCAA is only subject to federal civil rights laws if it is receiving federal funds. The issue of using standardized tests to determine athletic participation is not going to go away.

Ever since the BCA failed to take a stand in 1995, the number of African American coaches and athletics directors has declined. Since the implementation of new academic standards, the percentage of African American student-athletes has declined after a decade of dramatic growth, dropping from 21.5 percent of all student-athletes in 1995 to 18.9 percent in 1999. In the revenue-producing sports, the percentage of African American student-athletes dropped from 47.5 to 45.3 percent. Yet the public, fueled by media images, persisted in believing that the number of African American athletes continued to spiral upward.

I believe there is a direct correlation between the BCA's failure to take a stand and the subsequent decline in the number of African American student-athletes. This situation begs for the attention of a strong, powerful, and unified Black Coaches Association. The future looks bleak unless the BCA somehow regains its influence and powerful voice. I hope that Floyd Keith, named as Executive Director in 2001, does just that.

On the other hand, I have long believed that such efforts placed on college admission requirements addressed the problem of academic standards in the wrong place.

Requiring high academic standards for admission into a Division I college athletic program does not address the needs of the majority of high school athletes. Approximately one in 100 high school student-athletes will play Division I college sport. However, if all high school athletes were required to maintain a high academic average throughout their high school athletic careers, they would better their chances of benefiting from nonathletic scholarships and other available opportunities. Proposition 16 will *never* affect the majority of student-athletes. However, if young athletes were required to meet increased academic standards at the high-school level, they would better their chances of benefiting from nonathletic scholarships and other opportunities available to students of color.

This is a problem that college presidents, faculty, and coaches can work on *together* with high school administrators. Colleges and universities must reach out off-campus to create a supportive atmosphere for the intellectual development of a new generation of African American leaders empowered to meet the challenges of the twenty-first century. As it stands now, the only urban children who stand to succeed are those who are either supremely talented athletes or those who somehow emerge as the academic *creme de la creme*. By shifting our focus away from high school's top-tier of athletes, we might do something about higher education's greatest embarrassment: as low as the graduation rate is for African American student-athletes, the rate for African American students as a whole is even lower.

Drugs You Can't Escape: The Tony Elliot Story

The number of tragic, sports-related drug abuse stories has declined due to drug testing and sanctions for violating drug policies in professional and college sport. The safeguards in place in 2001 were developed over the last 20 years, too late to save Tony Elliott. Hopefully his tragic story will serve as a deterrent for current and future athletes.

Tony Elliot was an NFL nose tackle in the 1980s. Now he has more on his mind than football. Twenty years ago, while attempting to rob a drug pusher to support his cocaine habit, Tony found himself staring down the wrong end of a .357 Magnum. Facing death, Tony finally realized he had reached rock bottom. He knew that he had to put aside his professional football career and seek help just to stay alive. As the NFL training camps opened in 2000, Tony sat in a Stanford, Connecticut, hospital, paralyzed from the waist down after being shot earlier that year in what police believe was a drug-related incident.

I have known Tony since 1985 and have followed his mercurial and often tragic life both in its depths and in its rebounds. In a nation of fractured childhoods, not many can compare to the horror of Tony's. When he was only four years old, he was found collapsed in a pool of his mother's blood after witnessing her murder at the hands of his father, Bobby. They were not only husband and wife; Bobby was Ruby Elliott's pimp.

Tony's new guardian was his Uncle Wilbert. Their relationship was always volatile, but ultimately close. Over the years, he moved between relatives, finally landing in a state home for boys. When he was 14 years old, his father was released from prison, adding to Tony's fear and confusion. By middle school, Tony was affiliated with gangs and was on his way to becoming an alcoholic. The director of the boy's home provided cocaine and marijuana. Tony's selection for the Harding High School football team staved off gang membership, but not drug use.

Harding won the Connecticut State Championship and Tony was an All-State and All-American selection. Suddenly this incredibly confused young man, his life complicated by the tragic dissolution of his family, and by his growing abuse of drugs and alcohol, was being called a role model. If Tony had a moment of glory and a glimpse of success, his peace was completely shattered when, after an argument, his father shot and killed Uncle Wilbert in Tony's senior year of high school.

The next few years were even more chaotic. Tony flunked out of the University of Wisconsin at Madison and enrolled at Pratt Junior College in Kansas. He played well enough there to get a scholarship to North Texas State. Football, cocaine, and booze were the three constants in Tony's college career. Academics were never part of the equation—he passed three classes in two years.

Tony was drafted by the New Orleans Saints in the fifth round, a move that brought him unprecedented wealth. He sought out his old friends in Bridgeport, Connecticut and went on a two-week cocaine binge and spending spree that drained $14,000 of his signing bonus. Tony had made the team, but his addiction was destroying him. By midseason the team sent him to the Timberlawn Rehabilitation Center in Dallas, Texas. Released after thirty days, he rejoined the team. Tony stayed off cocaine for the rest of the season, but continued his use of marijuana, believing it was somehow harmless.

In the off-season, Tony returned to the streets and to coke culture. When the Saints training camp opened in July, Tony was still using drugs and the Saints forced him into rehab again. This session was derailed by the news that his brother had been murdered. Tony's mounting grief and anger drove him to use drugs even more self-destructively. He emptied his $10,000 savings account, sold his car, furniture, appliances, and jewelry to purchase even more cocaine. He had been loaded on cocaine for about twenty-one straight days when he began to write bad checks at several stores.

Completely broke, his insatiable appetite for cocaine drove him to more illegal behavior. He stole his friend's income tax refund check. Then Tony decided to try robbery. When the suspicious dealer answered the door with his gun pointed at Tony's head, Tony talked his way out of the precarious situation and checked himself into the Depaul Drug Treatment Center. This time it was his own choice and he remained in treatment for eighty-five days.

Tony decided to go out into the community to help others, lecturing in schools throughout New Orleans. Depaul had taught him the importance of honesty and self-disclosure. Tony soon became one of the most sought-after speakers in the city.

The courts placed him on three years probation. Tony appealed to the NFL for reinstatement and Commissioner Pete Rozelle allowed him to rejoin the Saints. It was then that I first heard his story. We agreed to meet after the 1985 season.

For his first drug-free season, Tony started every game at nose guard. During the off-season I hired him as a speaker on drug abuse at Northeastern University's Center for the Study of Sport in Society. He gripped high school audiences in Boston with his powerful story. Teachers praised him and the impact he had. He continued to spend his off-seasons with us until his playing career ended.

After he left the NFL, he went into a series of businesses in New Orleans. He finally seemed free from the streets and drug abuse, and was showcased on *The Today Show, Good Morning America, CBS Sunday Morning*, and in many of the nation's leading newspapers as one of football's leading role models.

I wanted to believe that Tony had escaped drug culture, but ultimately it did not seem to matter whether he was personally involved with drugs prior to the shooting that paralyzed the lower half of his body. The streets caught up to Tony. It seemed incomprehensible that this huge man, all 300-plus pounds of former athlete, could be immobilized, imprisoned in a hospital bed. Tony escaped death that day in February, though his life hung in the balance for more than two months after the shooting. The hospital bills have drained his resources.

Tony's story helped many children avoid drugs. He used drugs to numb the pain in his life. That made him able to understand the pain of so many other children. They flocked to him. Now I hope his story will serve as a warning to today's college and professional athletes that, no matter how strong and invulnerable they may feel, there may be no real escape from the addictive power of drugs.

Athletes Have a Responsibility for Social Change

Athletes are in a unique position to affect social change. They are powerful role models for children. Community service programs, including those of Northeastern University's Center for the Study of Sport in Society and the National Consortium for Academics and Sport, invite athletes to speak to children and young adults on issues like race, gender, conflict resolution, men's violence against women, and drug and alcohol abuse. The young people's admiration for the athletes makes them predisposed to follow the advice given.

However, many athletes hesitate to take a stand on controversial national and international issues. They know that endorsements dry up and teams trade them when the heat goes up. But there are those rare athletes who are so famous and so respected that they would be safe from such retaliation. The two who come to mind are both African-American—Michael Jordan and Tiger Woods.

Gun Control

I wrote to Michael when he first retired from basketball and again when he became the president of the Washington Wizzards, a team that changed its name from the Bullets because of the implied violence in the name. I was presumptuous enough to speak about the tragic loss of his father. Michael was not alone in his grief; the loved ones of 15,337 others died the same year his Dad was fatally shot.

I'm sure Michael knows the statistics. Forty-seven percent of high school students say they could get a handgun if they wanted one. An estimated one million students carry a weapon to school each day, mostly, they say, to protect themselves from other kids. Nearly a quarter of all students say their fear of being attacked in or on their way to school impairs their ability to learn. It isn't paranoia. There are 2,000 attacks in our schools every hour. Some schools have grieving rooms and burial funds for their students. Parents buy life insurance for their children so they can pay for their funerals. I have heard parents thank God that their child reached the age of eighteen.

No one would make a better spokesperson for gun control than Michael Jordan. Young people need to lay down their guns. Legislators need to make it impossible for young people to get them back. I can't think of anyone else who could reach both groups, and speak so compellingly on the subject.

Thousands of kids, black and white alike, want to be like Mike. Some of them carry guns or other weapons. Imagine if Michael Jordan told them to put down those guns. Imagine if Michael Jordan told them that not only are guns not cool, but also guns threaten hope in a society consumed by despair.

Kids need an incentive. Gun buy-back campaigns have been very successful in many cities. The Bulls and the White Sox have given away tickets for guns. Imagine NIKE or Gatorade establishing a buy-back fund in Michael's name. If fewer guns appeared in school corridors, perhaps students wouldn't feel so threatened and in need of protection themselves. Real learning might resume, and education might help fuel the flames of hope, breaking the cycle of despair.

At the same time, Michael could go to Congress where he would have the ear of some legislators reluctant to confront the National Rifle Association. Michael could inspire them to dream of a less violent society.

I know his father is smiling down at Michael, proud of all that he has already done. Imagine his pride if Michael helped to turn his father's tragic death into a life-saving example for so many others. Michael would be peerless on this issue. I am confident that adopting this cause would only increase the respect we have for him, just as we now admire Muhammad Ali for taking harder stands against war and racism in more tumultuous times.

Orlando's Nick Anderson incorporated his traumatic young adult experience with violence into a platform for gun control. His first statements against gun violence were unplanned and in conjunction with missed free throws that resulted in his team losing game one of the 1995 NBA Finals against the Houston Rockets. Anderson had missed four free throws, causing many to blame him for allowing the game to go to the Rockets. After the game, Anderson stunned reporters with his perspective on whether or not the missed free throws constituted a tragedy: "This is only a basketball game. I saw my best friend in high school get shot twice in the stomach . . . I watched him die. I watched a life get taken away right in front of me . . . I've seen the gangs and the drugs."

He was referring to the death of Ben Wilson, his teammate at Chicago's Simeon High School. Wilson had been named the national high school player of the year. Now with the Sacramento Kings, Anderson might become a national spokesperson for Handgun Control, the organization started by James Brady.

Many sports figures have succeeded in turning a personal tragedy into a crusade. Lonice Bias, mother of Len Bias, the Boston Celtics number 1 draft pick in 1986, became a sought-after speaker against drug abuse after cocaine took the life of her All-American son. Upon being diagnosed with HIV and AIDS, respectively, Magic Johnson and Arthur Ashe became the most recognized spokespeople in the world in the campaign to combat the spread of this insidious disease. I have already asked a great deal of Michael Jordan. Next I turn to Tiger Woods.

Labor Issues In Question: The NIKE Campaign

The campaign by activists to get NIKE to change its labor practices in Asia is the latest and among the most important wake-up calls on critical social issues in recent times. The dust has now settled on NIKE Chairman Phil Knight's announcement that NIKE would allow independent observers to monitor the factories in Asia that produce their products, root out underage workers, and ensure enforcement of America's Occupational Safety and Health Administration (OSHA) standards.

The announcement was a response to the enormous amount of negative publicity directed at NIKE when the spotlights' glare settled on wages and working conditions in factories in Indonesia, China, and Vietnam. Labor and human rights activists welcomed Knight's message, except for NIKE's failure to address the issue of the low wages employees received for producing its product.

This was not just a NIKE problem. Reebok, Adidas, Liz Claiborne, Ann Taylor, Ralph Lauren, Disney, J. C. Penny, and Wal-Mart are just a short list of American high-and low-end brand-name companies producing apparel and sporting goods in Asia. Nearly 50 percent of all apparel sold in America is produced in low-wage countries where poverty is endemic and educational opportunities are rare. Until recently, working conditions were universally scandalous. NIKE's business practices have now caught everyone's attention. As Knight said, ''I truly believe that the American consumer does not want to buy products made in abusive conditions.''

Workers in these factories were primarily young women from rural areas with high unemployment rates and crushing poverty. These women sought jobs, a living wage, and a chance to send money back to their villages to assist their families.

What they found in too many cases were crowded dorms, twelve-hour workdays, unsafe working conditions, and wages at or below subsistence levels. Chemicals causing respiratory and fertility problems were used in many factories. Underage children were frequently allowed to work. Reports of abusive factory managers were common. Whether or not every American company knew about these working conditions is arguable. If they didn't, they could have and should have.

Americans import more that 8 billion dollars per year worth of apparel from China and Hong Kong alone. The billion garments made in China and imported to the United States are enough to give four garments to every man, woman, and child in America. This is huge business.

Some companies began to take direct action after the White House established a task force in 1994 to address sweatshop issues. Liz Claiborne, L.L. Bean, and Disney were among the first companies to adopt ''no sweatshop'' policies with corporate codes of conduct and bans on child labor. Coca-Cola, Pepsi, Gillette, and Reebok raised wages. Reebok built its own factory in Pakistan to produce soccer balls under safe conditions without the use of child labor. Most of the major American corporations now have similar codes of conduct.

The second half of the solution involves enforcement and independent monitoring. For example, Disney's Vendor Compliance Program requires random, regular spot checks. Dependent on foreign currency, many of these low-wage nations may not enforce the codes, which frequently surpass their own national standards. Without regular monitoring by independent agencies, there is a serious potential for continued abuses. Companies must take responsibility for enforcing codes of conduct if the codes are to be effective and taken seriously. Factory workers wait anxiously, hoping the monitoring process will be effective and powerful, hoping that their lives will improve, and hoping that they can finally send some money back to the families they left behind.

The issue of low wages will continue to haunt the companies, including NIKE. The average American worker has read that workers in China and Vietnam, where wages are set by the government, earn two dollars a day, while those in Indonesia make one dollar per day. NIKE's announcement did not address changing wages, but the *Washington Post* reported that NIKE had raised its wages for 27,000 workers in Indonesia. Many other companies have raised wages to three dollars per day, sufficient to achieve an adequate standard of living.

Like many Americans I was unaware of the abuses of the overseas laborforce until David Kaye, a staff member at the center, brought the issue to my attention. Public protests and NIKE's own very public announcements have made it clear that these abuses must not be tolerated. Athletes, however, have remained reluctant to speak out on this issue. Women's soccer star Julie Foudy, a Reebok endorser, was one of the few athletes to speak out.

Tiger Woods, the new millennium's Michael Jordan and NIKE endorser (for the princely sum of $100 million), would be the perfect athlete to speak out on protecting Asian labor producing American products. His mother is of Asian descent, and he is a star of such magnitude that he could take a stand up without losing his earning power. As a social activist who happens to write, I know how hard it is to get athletes to speak out on social issues. They are justifiably afraid that doing so could either cost them their jobs or their endorsements. Most who have tried have paid a very severe price.

In his first NIKE commercial after turning pro, Tiger said he could not play at many country clubs. "Are you ready for me, world?" Many of those sitting in golf's clubhouses must have been deeply threatened. How else can we explain the universally vitriolic and condemning response?

Writers responded in one of two ways. One group pointed out that Tiger Woods could play *anywhere* he wants. Of course Tiger

Woods can play anywhere he chooses, but most people of color cannot. A second faction criticized him for letting NIKE exploit his success to sell products to African-Americans. It seems to me that the African American market for golf gear was very small. Even if it increased tenfold, it would barely register on NIKE's enormous bottom line. But talking about race could hurt NIKE's sales to those who make up the majority of golf's consumers and who have persisted in ignoring golf's racial barriers.

Tiger was the first athlete I had ever seen make a strong statement about race in a commercial, and the media criticized him for it. I am sure Tiger learned a lesson, one that I wish he had not learned. We are, as always, ready to tear down sports heroes at a moment's notice. Now, with his NIKE contract renewed, I hope Tiger will take the chance and speak out against exploitation of foreign labor.

League-Wide Community Service Efforts

All the major sports leagues and many of their teams, as well as college athletics departments, run extensive community service programs. One of the most effective is the NBA's Stay in School program.

I try to attend the NBA's year-end Stay in School event for Boston as often as possible. I will always remember the 1996 program. More than 1,200 students and their parents packed an auditorium at Northeastern University. I went with a friend who was cynical about the program's effectiveness. He assumed it was mostly glitter and lacked substance. He left with a different impression.

At a time when racial hatred was tearing apart our youth, Stay in School members were taught the concept of using teamwork to bring respect for each human being back into their schools. At a time when school children faced more than 3 million assaults annually *in schools*, Stay in School members were learning conflict resolution skills. At a time when gangs lured so many teenagers out of school and onto self-destructive paths, Stay in School members won 23,533 awards for their work in communities. At a time when the dropout rate for Boston schools soared above the 30-percent mark, 497 program participants had perfect attendance records. At a time when many adults thought the only thing teenagers could write was graffiti, program participants published stories and poems, and some had their artwork displayed in art galleries. Nearly 200 students won awards for their creative endeavors.

I asked some of the winners if this NBA program really had made a difference. They all said that the encouragement they received from the Celtics players involved in the program was an edge that helped them to stay on track. Angel, a student at a Boston middle school, said that knowing that Celtics forward Dominique Wilkins cared whether or not he went to school on time every morning helped him get there. His friends all nodded. Angel went on to say how happy he was when he heard that Shaquille O'Neal and Anfernee Hardaway were heading back to school themselves after the playoffs.

Public Service Announcements: Is Anyone Listening?

David, a student at one of the "toughest" middle schools in Boston, told me he learned something "real important" when he saw Patrick Ewing's public service commercial in which Patrick walked away from a potentially violent conflict in school. "To me, I thought I had to fight to be a man. Patrick showed me it took more guts to walk away."

David's classmate pulled me aside, wanting to talk about his parents. He didn't offer his name and he didn't want his friends to hear him or see the tears in his eyes. He told me that his father had beaten him for years. The only time they ever got together was to watch NBA games on television. They never talked about much of anything except basketball. Then, while sitting together one night watching an early season NBA game, they both saw Alonzo Mourning's public service announcement about child abuse. The father and son looked into each other's eyes. Two days later the father sought help. He had not beaten the boy in more than a year since getting treatment.

Surely the NBA is a major profit-making enterprise. Most of its commercials sell products, and there are many people out there who think the NBA is entirely a commercial venture. I am not among them. Neither is Angel, David, nor David's classmate, whose Latino, African American and white racial backgrounds made them a veritable rainbow of youth.

Chapter 19

The New Racial Stereotypes

Athletes and Crime

The beginning of the twenty-first century brought the hope that many social injustices would be rectified. However, surveys taken throughout the 1990s indicated that many inaccurate perceptions persisted such as the majority of whites surveyed continuing to believe that most African-Americans are less intelligent, more prone to drug use, more violent, and more inclined towards violence against women than whites are.

Sport culture, as it is currently interpreted, now provides whites with the chance to talk about athletes in a way that reinforces these stereotypes of African-Americans. Because African-Americans dominate the most popular sports, whites tend to "think black" when they think about the major sports.

Each time any athlete gets into trouble, I receive many calls from writers and television producers seeking comments. After a fight involving a basketball or football player, the interrogation invariably includes, "What makes football or basketball players more inclined to get into fights?" I have never been asked this question of a hockey or baseball player, despite the fact that there are as many game fights in those sports.

After a reported incident of domestic violence involving a basketball or football player, the inevitable question is, "What makes football or basketball players more inclined to abuse women?" Equal numbers of hockey and baseball players are accused of domestic violence, yet I have never been asked this question about them.

Each year during the professional drafts in each sport I am asked, "What do you think about college or even high school football and basketball players jumping to the pros and missing their chance for an education?" I have never been asked that question about baseball or hockey, tennis or golf players who put higher education on hold to pursue athletic careers.

Shawn Fanning left Northeastern University early to turn pro and earn millions; he was called a genius for founding Napster. The Dean of Northeastern University's School of Engineering told me that one of his biggest problems comes from companies attempting to lure away his top students each year. They leave for the money.

I believe that at least part of the systematic coupling of athletes and crime revolves around racial stereotyping. The media has persistently and consistently suggested that basketball and football players, who happen to be overwhelmingly African-American, are more violent than athletes in other sports and people in society in general. The result is that nearly everyone, including the police, women, fans, the media, sports administrators, and athletes themselves, believes that certain athletes, especially basketball or football players, are more inclined to be violent in general and violent against women in particular.

Rosalyn Dunlap, an African American who was a five-time All-American sprinter who now works on social issues involving athletes, including gender violence prevention, said, "perpetrators are not limited to any category or occupation. The difference is that athletes who rape or batter will end up on television or in the newspapers. Such images of athletes in trouble create a false and dangerous mindset with heavy racial overtones. Most other perpetrators will be known only to the victims, their families, the police, and the courts."

Once, while speaking to a group of distinguished international fellows at an elite academic institution, I asked members of the audience to write down five words that they would use to describe

American athletes. In addition to listing positive adjectives, not one missed including one of the following words: dumb, violent, rapist or drug-user. I regularly meet with NBA and NFL players, as well as with college student-athletes on dozens of campuses. There are a lot of angry athletes who are convinced the public is stereotyping them because of the criminal acts of a few.

⌈Many American men have grown to dislike athletes. A typical man might crave the money and the fame that a pro athlete enjoys, but he recognizes that such athletic success is unattainable for him. After reading all the negative press about athletes, he doesn't want to read that Mike Tyson felt he was treated unfairly by the justice system, knowing full well that Tyson made a reported hundred million dollars in his post-release rehabilitation program. He has little sympathy for the large number of pro athletes signing contracts worth more than ten million dollars a year. He is a micro-thought away from making egregious stereotypes about the "other groups" perceived as stealing his part of the American pie.⌋

Big-time athletes fit the "other groups" category. Whether it is an African-American athlete or coach, or a white coach of African-American athletes, when something goes wrong with a player, a national reaction is likely to be immediate. Tom "Satch" Sanders, who helped the Boston Celtics win eight world championships, is now vice president for player programs for the NBA. His office encourages and guides players to finish their education, prepare for careers after basketball, and adjust to all the attention that NBA stars attract. Sanders presents a view complementary to Dunlap's. He proposes that the public has made a link between the stereotypes for athletes and African Americans: "Everyone feels that athletes have to take the good with the bad, the glory with the negative publicity. However, no one appreciates the broad-brush application that is applied in so many instances. Of the few thousand that play sports on the highest level, if four or five individuals in each sport—particularly if they are black—have problems with the law, people won't have long to wait before some media people are talking about all those athletes."

APBnews.com released two revealing studies in 2000. The first was a study of NFL players on two teams that made it to 2000 the Super Bowl.The second was a study of the sixteen NBA teams in the 2000 playoffs. In the NFL study, 11 percent of the players had a criminal history. That stood in dramatic contrast to the 35 to 46 percent lifetime arrest rate (taken from extensive studies in California and New York) for adult males under thirty, the same age group as most NFL players. Most NFL players are between 18 and 30 years old although most of those are between the ages of 21 and 30. In the study of NBA players, the arrest rate of those on the sixteen playoff teams was 18 percent, again a fraction of the national figures for their comparable age group of males.

Jeff Benedict's book *Pros and Cons* created a sensation in 1998 by saying that 21 percent of NFL players had arrest records. In an article he coauthored in 1999 for the statistics journal *Chance*, he said that the lifetime arrest rates for NFL players he documented in *Pros and Cons* was less than half the arrest rate in the general population.

Fans build stereotypes of athletes from media coverage of the athletes and the games. Fans, who are mostly white, observe sport through a media filter that is created by an overwhelming number of white men. There are 1,600 daily newspapers in America employing only nineteen African American sports columnists. There are only two African American sports editors who work on newspapers in a city that has professional sports franchises. The fact that the number of sports columnists, as reported at the 2000 conference of the National Association of Black Journalists, has almost doubled from 11 since 1998 is a positive sign. However, there are no African American sports writers on 90 percent of the 1,600 daily newspapers.

I am not suggesting, nor would I ever suggest, that most or even many of the white news writers are racist. However, they were raised in a culture in which many white people have strong beliefs about what it means to be African American. The obvious result is that their reporting provides reinforcement of white stereotypes of African American athletes. According to the National Opinion Research Center Survey, sponsored by the National Science Foundation for the University of Chicago, whites surveyed share the following attitudes:

- Fifty-six percent of whites think African Americans are more violent.

- Sixty-two percent of whites think African Americans do not work as hard as whites.

- Seventy-seven percent of whites think most African Americans live off welfare.

- Fifty-three percent think African Americans are less intelligent.

Some white writers may have picked up these stereotypes in their own upbringing. When they write about an individual African American athlete or several African American athletes who have a problem, it becomes easy to unconsciously leap to the conclusion that fits the stereotype. Sanders said, "Blacks in general have been stereotyped for having drugs in the community as well as for being more prone to violence. However, now more than ever before, young black athletes are more individualistic and they resist the 'broad brush.' They insist on being judged as individuals for everything." But even that resistance can be misinterpreted by the public and by writers as off-the-court trash talking.

The athletes of the twenty-first century come from a generation of despairing youth cut adrift from the American dream. When the Center for the Study of Sport in Society started in 1984, one of its primary missions was to help young people balance academics and athletics.Since 1990, its mission has been extended to help young people lead healthy and safe lives.

Today our colleges are recruiting athletes:

- who have witnessed violent death. If an American child under the age of sixteen is killed every two hours with a handgun, then there is a good chance that young athletes will have a fallen family member or friend.

- who are mothers and fathers when they arrive at our schools. There are boys who helped 900,000 teenage girls get pregnant each year. Some student-athletes will leave after four years of college with one or more children who are four or five years old.

- who have seen friends or family members devastated by drugs.

- who have seen battering in their homes. An estimated 3 percent of American men are batterers and an estimated 3 million women are battered each year.

- who were victims of racism in school. Seventy-five percent of all students surveyed by Lou Harris reported seeing or hearing about racially or religiously motivated confrontations with overtones of violence very or somewhat often.

- who grew up as latchkey kids. Either a single parent or two working parents head 57 percent of American families, black and white alike.

Not enough campuses or athletic departments have the right people to help guide these young men and women into their adult lives. College campuses desperately need professionals that can deal with these nightmarish factors.

Academic Issues in College Sport

The amount of media coverage devoted to student-athlete literacy problems makes such problems seem unique to athletes. The media rarely reports that 30 percent of *all* entering freshmen must take remedial English or mathematics. The same holds true for the media's portrayal of student-athlete graduation rates. Although college athletic departments should strive to increase the number of student-athletes who graduate, graduation rates for the student body as a whole have changed. Only 14 percent of entering freshmen graduated in four years. If an athlete does not graduate in four years, some call him dumb; others say the school failed him. Few note that he may be typical of college students.

Don McPherson nearly led Syracuse University to a national championship when he was their quarterback in the 1980s. After seven years in the NFL and CFL, McPherson worked until 1999 directing the Mentors in Violence Prevention (MVP) Program, the nation's largest program using athletes as leaders to address the issue of men's violence against women.

McPherson reflected on the image that associates athletes with a lack of intelligence: "When whites meet an uneducated black athlete who blew opportunities in college or high school, they think he is dumb. They don't question what kind of school he may have had to attend if he was poor, or how time pressures from sport may have affected him. If they don't make it as a pro athlete, they're through without a miracle. I met lots of 'Trust Fund Babies' at Syracuse. They blew opportunities. No one called them dumb, just rich. We knew they would not need a miracle to get a second chance. I played at Syracuse at a time when being a black quarterback had become more acceptable. But the stereotypes still remained. As a player, people still remember me as a great runner and scrambler. I had not dented their image of the physical vs. intelligent black athlete."

McPherson led the nation in passing efficiency over Troy Aikman and won many awards, including the Maxwell Award, but he was most proud of being the quarterback with the highest passing efficiency rating in the nation. "I should have shattered the image of the athletic and mobile black quarterback and replaced it with the intelligent black quarterback. Unfortunately, stereotypes of football players, mostly black, still prevail. They make me as angry as all the stereotypes of black people in general when I was growing up."

McPherson wore a suit to class and carried the *New York Times* under his arm. But McPherson said that those whites that recognized his style were "surprised and said I was 'a good black man,' as if I were different from other black men. Most students assumed I was poor and that football was going to make me rich. Like many other blacks on campus, I was middle class. My father was a detective and my mother was a nurse."

Irrespective of color or gender, student-athletes graduate at higher rate than non student-athletes, yet it is difficult to get accurate reporting of this in the press. According to the NCAA's 1999 report:

- Fifty-eight percent of white male Division I student-athletes graduated vs. 57 percent of white male nonathletes. Forty-two percent of African American male Division I student-athletes graduated vs. 33 percent of African American male nonathletes.

- Seventy-one percent of white female Division I student-athletes graduated compared to 61 percent of white female nonathletes. Fifty-seven percent of African American female Division I student-athletes graduated vs. only 43 percent of African American female nonathletes.

Some disparities do appear when we compare white student-athletes to African American student-athletes:

- Fifty-three percent of white male Division I basketball student-athletes graduated versus 37 percent of African American male Division I basketball student-athletes.

- Seventy percent of white female Division I basketball student-athletes graduated compared to only 56 percent of African American female Division I basketball student-athletes.

College sport does not own problems of illiteracy and low graduation rates. They belong to higher education in general and its inheritance of the near bankruptcy of secondary education in some communities.

The publication of graduation rates, long feared by athletic administrators, reveals scandalous rates, but it also shows poor graduation rates specifically for students of color. The predominantly white campuses of most colleges and universities are not welcoming environments for people of color. African American student-athletes arrive on most campuses and see that only 10 percent of the student body, 3 percent of the faculty, and less than 5 percent of top athletics administrators and coaches look like them. Unless there is a Martin Luther King Center or Boulevard, all of the buildings and streets are named after white people.

In many ways, the publication of graduation rates for student-athletes helped push the issue of diversity to the forefront of campus-wide discussions of issues of race, ethnicity, and gender. Educators finally recognized how they were failing students of color by not creating a conducive, welcoming educational enviornment.

Drugs and Alcohol Use Among Athletes

A common stereotype depicts athletes as abusing drugs and alcohol. Some athletes do use drugs. CNN Headline news broadcasts stories about famous athletes caught with drugs. Repeated exposure to such reports inflates the size of the problem, but the facts do not reveal widespread abuse among athletes at the professional, college or even high school level.

According to an extensive 1995 *Los Angeles Times* survey of athletes and the crimes they committed, a total of twenty-two professional and college athletes and three coaches were accused of drug use or a drug-related crime that year. On average, the media reported a story about a new sports figure with a drug problem every two weeks. Center estimates now put the number of sports figures accused of drug-related crimes at fifty per year or one media story per week on average.

Stories about athletes accused of drug use or a drug-related crime are and should be disturbing. But those stories are rarely, if ever, put in the context of the 1.9 million Americans who use cocaine each month or the 2.1 million who use heroin throughout their lives. A total of 13 million individuals (6 percent of the American population) use some illicit drug each month, and 17 percent of men in the eighteen-to-twenty-five age group are drug users. Whether it is twenty-two or fifty, athletes who use drugs make up a small fraction of a single percent of the more than 400,000 athletes who play college and professional sport in America.

The NBA's drug policy, which leaves open the possibility of a lifetime ban for any athlete who is caught using drugs, is generally recognized as a model for the sports world. The policy may have stopped a substance abuse problem that predated its inception. According to an APBnews.com report, *Crime in the NBA*, released in June 2000, forty-one players were charged, booked, or arrested in eighty-two instances of crimes more serious than traffic tickets over the course of their time on the rosters of the sixteen NBA playoff teams. The story noted that "it is perhaps a credit to the NBA's antidrug policy that none of the eighty-two incidents noted in the APBnews.com study were related to hard drugs.'' (Marijuana was cited in six cases.) The forty-one players put the NBA's arrest rate at 18 percent. APBnews.com reported that, ''By way of comparison, the lifetime arrest rate of the general population as measured in four different studies ranges from 31 to 50 percent.''

On the subject of alcohol abuse, the same 1995 *Los Angeles Times* survey of athletes and the crimes they committed, reported that twenty-eight college and professional athletes and four coaches were charged with alcohol-related infractions. None of these thirty-two cases were put in the context of the 13 million Americans who engage in binge drinking at least five times per month. Yet we read about a new athlete with an alcohol problem every eleven days. Such images can fuel an exaggerated sense of crisis in athletics when they are not viewed in full social context.

McPherson remembered being ''shocked'' when he arrived on Syracuse's campus at how much drinking went on each night among the student body. He felt compelled to call football players he knew on other campuses. ''It was the same everywhere. Now when I go to speak on college campuses I always ask. It is worse today. Athletes are part of that culture, but insist that practice and academics crowd their schedules too much to be in bars as often as other students.'' Student personnel administrators on college campuses acknowledge that abusive drinking is the number one issue on college campuses today.

Athletes and Violence

Media coverage of professional, college, and even high school athletes consistently implies that the violence of sport makes its participants more violent in society.

Are sports any more violent today than they were twenty years ago when no one would have made such an assertion? I don't think so. But streets and schools across America surely are more violent than they were twenty years ago—there are 2,000 assaults in schools across the nation every hour of every day. The number of American children killed by guns in the 1900s has exceeded the total number of soldiers who died in the Vietnam War. Gun violence obeys no boundaries of race, class, or geography. Schoo. shootings occurred in Pearl (Mississippi), Paduka (Kentucky), Jonesboro (Arkansas), and Littleton (Colorado). Violence seems part of the school day.

If one were to put together a lowlights tape of the fights in sports that the public best remembers, I guarantee that most people would list Kermit Washington hitting Rudy Tomjanovich, Latrell Sprewell choking P.J. Carlesimo, and Roberto Alomar spitting at umpire John Hirschbeck. Fear of men of color attacking whites in our society is part of the culture. There is no doubt that the treatment afforded to Washington, Sprewell and Alomar was measurably different than that given Denver Bronco Bill Romanowski, who is white, after he spit in the face of a black player in 1999.

Most of the stories written about specific athletes who are violent or gender violent are about African American athletes. Stories about them that appear without appropriate filters of what is going on in society reinforce racial stereotyping.

Athletes and Gender Violence

In the wake of the O. J. Simpson case, any incident involving an athlete assaulting a woman has received extraordinary publicity. The individual cases add up to another stereotype of the new millennium: athletes, especially basketball and football players, are more inclined to be violent towards women than nonathletes are.

Joyce Williams-Mitchell has worked extensively in this field, most recently as the executive director of the Massachusetts Coalition of Battered Women's Service Groups. As an African American woman, she abhors the image of athletes being more prone to violence against women. "It is a myth. The facts do not bear this out. All the studies of patterns of batterers defined by occupation point to men who control women through their profession. We hear about police, clergy, dentists, and judges. I only hear about athletes as batterers when I read the paper. They are in the public's eye. Men from every profession have the potential to be batterers."

There have been, of course, too many cases of athletes committing assaults on girls and women. As I wrote this section, I received a voice mail message from a reporter: ''Have you heard that Corey Dillion is the latest case of an athlete hitting a woman? I guess that depends on when you pick up the message. There may have already been another case!'' His message implied that attacks on women by athletes took place hourly.

However, there has never been a thorough, scientific study conclusively showing that athletes are more inclined to violence. Jeffrey Benedict, Todd Crossett, and Mark McDonald wrote the only study that comes close. It was based on sixty-five cases of assault against women that took place on ten Division I campuses over a three year period. Thirteen of the cases involved athletes; seven of the athletes were basketball or football players.

Despite the authors' acknowledgment of both the small number of cases revealed and the fact that the survey did not control for alcohol and tobacco use or the man's attitude toward women (the three main predictors of a male's inclination to gender violence), the press regularly quoted their study without qualification. Media reports never stated that the study came up with only thirteen abusive athletes over three years. They simply said that the study concluded that student-athletes, in particular basketball or football players, committed nearly 20 percent of all campus assaults. Rosalyn Dunlap pointed out that, ''This is a racially loaded conclusion. When I was a student-athlete at the University of Missouri, I never thought of keeping myself safe from a 260-pound football player any more than any other man on the street. In fact, male athletes on campus protected me.''

The following is a list of data usually missing in the debate about athletes and violence against women.

- In 1994, 1,400 men killed their significant others. In that year, O. J. Simpson was the only athlete accused of murder.

- In 1998, an estimated 3 million women were battered and close to one million were raped. According to various reports in the press in the five years between 1995 and 2000, between seventy and one hundred athletes and coaches were accused of assault against a woman each year.

- The 1999 *Chronicle of Higher Education*'s annual campus crime survey showed that for there were a total of 1,053 forcible sex offenses reported in 1997. Fewer than thirty-five student-athletes were arrested in conjunction with these crimes.

Gender violence is a serious problem among American men. The cost of crime to America is pegged at $500 billion per year, according to a National Institute for Justice research report for the Justice Department released in March 1996. Gender assault and child abuse accounted for $165 billion—more than one third of that total.

Rosalyn Dunlap, who worked with The National Consortium for Academics and Sport to create more awareness about the issue, said, "There are no men who should be exempted from being educated about the issue of gender violence although many believe they are. It is a problem for naval commanders, daycare providers, fraternities, guys in a bar, in corporations, in halls of higher education and, yes, on athletic teams. But no more so on athletic teams."

There have been numerous cases in which women brought suits against corporations for harassment and/or assault. The *Boston Globe* gave extensive coverage in the late 1990s to the case against Astra USA, Inc., a chemical company, where women lodged sixteen formal complaints for incidents ranging from sexual harassment to rape. Twenty-nine women brought suit against Mitsubishi for the same reasons. None of the press about Astra suggested that working in a chemical company produced a climate of sexual aggression. At Mitsubishi, no one suggested any relationship between the manufacturing process and gender assault. So why do stories about athletes imply such a linkage to athletics? Does it fit white America's racial imagery?

McPherson believes it does: "Football and basketball mean black. When the public talks about gender violence and athletes, it talks black. No one discusses the problems of golfer John Dailey or Braves manager Bobby Cox. Warren Moon was another story altogether. Problems about athletes hit the papers and people think they detect a pattern because of the seeming frequency. But no one else's problems get in the papers. How do we make legitimate comparisons? With Astra and Mitsubishi, we look at the corporate climate and don't generalize about individuals. But with athletes, especially black athletes, we look at players and look for patterns to add up.''

Some observers say athletes are trained to be violent and that we can expect that training to carry over into their homes. If this is true, then what about the training in lethal force we give to the police, the Army, the Air Force, the Navy, and the Marines? Will these men also come home and kill? McPherson adds, ''There is no logic to connect these cases, but we do fit our stereotypes of African-Americans with such images when we carry through the implication for athletes.''

With all the recent publicity about the horrors of gender violence, it would be easy to forget that it was America's big, dirty secret until the O. J. Simpson case made it a notorious subject. Before that trial, few Americans were willing to talk about gender violence. The same unwillingness to confront racism diminishes society's ability to eradicate it. But the situation will never change if it remains unconfronted.

Athletes should take a leadership role on this issue, just as they have on drug abuse and educational opportunity. The MVP Program, organized in 1992 by Northeastern University's Center for the Study of Sport in Society and now headed by Jeff O'Brien, a former football player, has worked on more than sixty-five campuses training male and female athletes to be spokespeople on the issue of gender violence. Each of those schools has become proactive on an issue that has hurt so many women and their families.

Don McPherson insists that ''we have to do more to help our youth survive by including our athletes rather than excluding them in helping our youth. The stereotyping of our athletes does not help. We need to be ready with facts to dispute the easy labels.''

McPherson and Tom Sanders both argue vigorously that America's athletes not only don't fit the emerging stereotypes about athletes and crime, but the vast majority of professional athletes are extremely positive role models. Sanders said, ''when I look at the many NBA players who have their own foundations and who are very involved with giving back to the communities where they play and where they came from, I know they are hurt by the stereotypes.'' McPherson asserts that ''most of the players in the NFL are deeply religious, family-centered men who are constantly giving back to their communities with time and money.''

Rosalyn Dunlap wonders when the public and the media will stop being cynical about athletes. ''I hear so many people say that if athletes do something in the community that they do it for publicity. Why can't we accept that athletes want to help? Sport and those who play it can help educate us and sensitize us. While we can't ignore the bad news, we should also focus on the overwhelming good news of what athletes do to make this a better world.''

I do not believe the stereotypes. However, I do believe the high profile of all professional sports makes it incumbent on those involved to call on sports institutions to demand a higher standard for athletes. Athletes, once challenged, have played a leading role in the battle to educate our children; in the life and death fight against alcohol and drug abuse; and in the attempt to resolve conflicts with reason and not with fists or weapons. Now it is time to challenge them to fight the long overdue battle against gender violence.

The challenge to athletes involved a starting point of confronting the behavior of an individual athlete. Some universities had to make star athletes academically ineligible or expel them from school to convince others that they were serious about education and would not tolerate either poor academic records or athletes violating social norms.

After the tragic death of Len Bias, the nation was forced to recognize that cocaine was not ''recreational,'' but lethal. Schools began random drug testing; the NBA promised to uphold a lifetime ban for players who ignored league drug policies. This ban was necessary to show players as well as their young fans that there could be no tolerance for the use of life-threatening drugs.

The ban will always seem unfair to the player caught with drugs. I am sure Michael Ray Richardson, who was the first NBA player banned for life, still looks in the mirror and asks, ''Why me? There were other guys.'' But the discipline had to start somewhere. What was unfortunate for Richardson was fortunate for the

NBA and for society. Action, no matter how symbolic, was critical.

Likewise, when street violence began to invade our rinks, courts, and fields, sport had to take a stand with automatic and serious sanctions that cost players money and cost teams their playing services. No commissioner or director of a players association wanted their entire league and all of its athletes branded as thugs because of those who acted out during the game.

The New England Patriots bit the bullet for all professional sports and decided not to sign draftee Christian Peter, the University of Nebraska's highly acclaimed football player, who carried numerous criminal charges on his record. It was a milestone decision. Patriot owner Robert Kraft felt compelled to take a strong stand immediately after they drafted Peter, despite the fact that he would lose dollars in the draft and could have faced lawsuits from Peter's representatives. The importance of his decision was not only that players would see clear consequences for their actions, but also that children who idolize those players would also see such consequences as relevant to their own choices in life.

Sports figures are in a unique position to affect change. Keith Lee, a six-year NFL veteran who is now the chief operating officer of the National Consortium for Academics and Sport, works to improve race relations among young people. He states, ''We need positive role models who can help young people to believe in what they cannot yet see. We need them now more than ever.''

Chapter 20

Race Stories

The press readily assumes that each incident of an athlete or a coach in trouble or causing trouble reveals sport's destructive influence on the human psyche, and implies that such occurrences characterize athletes as a whole. In the final decade of the twentieth century, stereotypes of athletes have prevailed. Low graduation rates for athletes have come to represent athletes' low IQs. The tragedy of an individual athlete's drug addiction has come to represent epidemic drug abuse among athletes. On-field violence and a notable, but not extraordinary, number of assault charges against football and basketball players has come to represent the dangerous assumption that playing those sports inclines one toward battering women.

There are few denials of these images. My point has long been that society in general is ready to stereotype athletes as being on the edge of the criminal world because black athletes have come to dominate the most popular sports. Like all stereotypes, the stereotype of the athlete as a criminal is hazardous, powerful, and extremely harmful to athletes and society.

There are athletes and coaches in America who are bad people. Some are even evil, but I have not seen anything that convinces me that there is something inherent to playing or coaching sport that made them thus. There are bad or evil policemen, but I don't believe that being a cop made them that way. I am convinced that perceptions of race are a factor here.

When it comes to racism, it is easier to be in denial than to accept the reality that many people have learned to hate on the basis of skin color or religion. When black churches are destroyed by fire, white police and fire officials frequently assume the fires are accidental. When police kill a black man, most whites are ready to accept that the lives of the officers were at risk. When Jewish people cringe after seeing anti-Semitic graffiti, some may think them to be paranoid. When an all-white jury sees incontrovertible videotape of a black man being beaten by white men, they can still be convinced that the beating was done in self-defense against a menacing black male.

However, four stories involving sports figures have made Americans rethink the state of racial justice in the 1990s.

Burning Black Churches: Reggie White

Reggie White was as admired as any player when Green Bay prepared to fight Dallas in the 1996 NFC championship. Five weeks before the game, White was scheduled to have surgery. However, on the day of the surgery, he announced that he would continue to play. He said that God gave him a miracle.

A religious man, White was copastor of the Inner City Community Church in Knoxville. On the Monday before the game, eighteen incendiary devices were placed in his church and the walls were covered with racist graffiti. The original reports in Knoxville indicated the resulting fire was an accident. There was no acknowledgement of the incendiary devices or the graffiti.

The incident received national attention only when the copastor of the church was identified as Reggie White. The three other predominantly black churches in Tennessee that were firebombed in 1995 received no national attention, nor did the three black churches in Alabama and dozens of others around the nation that were also firebombed in the months before the destruction of the Inner City Community Church. The eyes of the entire nation were forced open because a popular athlete's church was threatened and not just that of another black pastor.

Police Brutality: Ray Seals and Jonny Gammage

Many people in the north would like to believe that the church burning was a "southern thing." However, they cannot ignore and must confront the case of Ray Seals, African American defensive end for the Pittsburgh Steelers, and his cousin and business partner, Jonny Gammage. Seals lent Gammage his Jaguar with Florida plates. The Pittsburgh police stopped Gammage, handcuffed him, and forced him to the ground. The police insisted that he was a threat to them, even handcuffed and lying on his chest.

Within eight minutes after he was forced to the ground, Gammage's heart stopped beating and he died of asphyxiation from compression to his neck and upper chest. Three officers were charged with involuntary manslaughter. If the victim had been simply another black man in Pittsburgh or any other city, would the officers have been charged? Since Jonny Gammage was Ray Seals' cousin and the Steelers were on their way to the 1996 Super Bowl, more information was revealed than would normally accompany the police's denial of a brutality charge. Eventually, all three police officers were acquitted in what is still a serious controversy in Pittsburgh.

Anti-Semitism: Seth Greenberg

On January 22, 1996, the Long Beach State men's basketball team played in Las Cruces at New Mexico State University. They discovered anti-Semitic slurs written in the visiting dressing room aimed at Long Beach's head coach, Seth Greenberg, who is Jewish. Neil McCarthy, the New Mexico State coach said, "If it happened, I'm sorry." *If* it happened? His comments had the uneasy ring of those who wondered whether the Holocaust happened. The

University's president implied that Greenberg overreacted, apparently thinking that the coach should simply have ignored the incident.

Justice Denied: Michael Watson

The story of college basketball player Michael Watson presents an example of why many African-Americans have so little faith in the American judicial system. The story could easily have taken place in Mississippi in the 1960s, but actually took place in Maryland in 1995. On the Wednesday afternoon before Thanksgiving, Michael Watson sat in a state court in Frederick, Maryland, waiting for his share of American justice.

His former teammates at Mount St. Mary's were practicing for the opening game of the 1995–96 season. Seven months earlier Watson, then a graduate student, had helped lead the small school to victory as Mount St. Mary's beat Rider College to win the Northeast Conference Championship and advance to the NCAA Tournament. Watson had scored fifteen points, garnered eleven rebounds, and hit six straight free throws in the last minute to slam the door on Rider's attempt to get to the Big Dance for the third year in a row.

Those spectacular basketball moments had helped Michael forget more painful ones. Around 1:00 a.m. on October 30, 1994, Michael and his date pulled up to a Thurmont, Maryland convenience store to get some food after a college party. Inside the store, three white men assaulted Michael. The back injuries Michael suffered kept him off the basketball court for several weeks while he underwent physical therapy. The back pain recurs occasionally, but far less often than the mental agony.

About twelve hours earlier, a busload of hooded and robed members of the Ku Klux Klan had marched at the State House in Annapolis. They shouted "White power" while one carried a poster of the face of assassinated civil rights leader Dr. Martin Luther King, Jr. circled by a target. The caption read "Our dream came true." Klan members were outnumbered more than ten to one by protesters who shouted them down and tensions built in the state capitol.

Did those tensions travel across the state into Thurmont, near the home of the leader of the Maryland Klan? According to Michael, one of the three men who attacked him shouted, "You don't belong here. This is Klan country. You're a nigger, boy." At the trial, the assailants denied the remarks, but they could not deny what the store's videotape had captured. It clearly showed the three men assaulting Michael Watson, shoving and hitting him while he held up his hands only to ward off their blows.

A shocked Mount St. Mary's President, George R. Houston, Jr., wrote a letter to the college community. In it he said, "We have called on the authorities to pursue prosecution of this matter with all available resources, and we expect a fair, thorough, and prompt investigation."

In an uncelebrated version of the earlier Rodney King case in Los Angeles, the investigation produced the videotape and witnesses who only testified for Michael Watson. While no one could verify the racist remarks, witnesses corroborated Watson's version that seemed indisputable given the videotape.

Through the help of various local friends, counselors, and nationally prominent activists, Michael Watson began to recover from the emotional scars of the attack. He did not seek publicity. There were no television cameras in the court, no Chris Dardens or Marcia Clarks for the prosecution, and no F. Lee Baileys or Johnny Cochrans for the defense. There were no Mark Fuhrmans or Stacey Koons on the Thurmont Police. The case was an easy one for him to win from all possible perspectives.

While waiting for the tediously slow wheels of justice to turn, Michael focused on basketball as his source of emotional rehabilitation. "There was no sense of race on our team. We were all so focused on winning. We worked together with a special solidarity. Our team was a safe haven for me and while we were together, I was able to forget what had happened outside the walls of Mount St. Mary's. My white teammates gave me the perspective that those three attackers did not represent all white people. However, when I was away from my teammates, the pain always came back" Watching his attackers go to prison was going to be his final step toward recovery. Michael Watson was poised to cele-brate with a heartfelt Thanksgiving.

Dino Flores, the prosecutor, was confident that the case would be a cut-and-dried victory for the prosecution. When jury selec-tion began on Monday the first ominous portent appeared. An all white jury was chosen. Still confident, prosecutor Flores took his case to them.

The witnesses in the store verified what was seen on the video-tape. A defense lawyer called Michael a racist and claimed that he provoked the attack against the three white men. Raised to respect everyone regardless of color, Watson cringed in disbelief at what he was hearing.

Nevertheless, when the jury went out on Wednesday, Michael and prosecutor Flores felt good. Michael said, "I was 90 percent certain of a favorable outcome. The evidence was clear and the judge had ruled favorably on most of Flores' motions. The 10 per-cent of doubt came only from what I knew about the fate of blacks in the justice system. But I was sure." Two hours later the jury returned with "not guilty" verdicts on the charges of assault and on the charge of committing a hate crime.

The verdict, read to an incredulous Michael Watson, lent a hol-low ring to the end of Mount St. Mary President Houston's letter to the community. "It is imperative that all government officials, community, and church leaders join us in making it inescapably clear that this county has 'zero tolerance' for racist actions such as these."

Michael Watson told me, "I just sat there for several minutes. The accused were gone before I totally realized what happened. There is nothing I can do but carry the scars throughout my life while these guys went out, free to celebrate or do whatever they pleased."

Thurmont, Maryland is seven miles from Camp David where President Clinton prepared for Thanksgiving. Without any na-tional publicity, the president, like most Americans, did not know who Michael Watson was or why he could not join his fellow countrymen in their Thanksgiving celebrations.

I was sickened when I watched the videotape of the attack. Surely the verdict should have been just as clear as it should have been in the first Rodney King trial. I wrote a column for *The Sporting News* to bring this case to national attention and begin the healing process for Michael Watson. Though the national media picked up the article, Michael never got another day in court. I was inundated with more hate mail than at any time since the end of the apartheid era, and even received two telephone death threats after the article was published. The one good thing we both got was the beginning of a rich friendship that I treasure.

These cases unfortunately demonstrated the depth of racism in America and how hard it is for blacks to obtain justice without status and public attention to force a second look. Once again, sport teaches us lessons life.

Chapter 21

Stories of Transformation

This final chapter is about stories of transformation, including those of such famous sports figures as Muhammad Ali and O. J. Simpson, and lesser-known people like Clifford Moller, a student-athlete who returned to get his undergraduate degree thirty-three years after beginning college. It describes an entire community, LaGrange, Georgia, that went from Klan country to an open community after a group of African athletes lived there. The final story is about an elderly man in South Florida who gave me hope and reminded me that change is always possible.

Different Kinds of Power: From O. J. to Ali

America's obsession with O. J. Simpson may finally have faded, while Muhammad Ali's resurgence, which began with his lighting the torch at the opening ceremonies of the 1996 Olympics, remains bright on the sports horizon. It is ironic that Americans have felt so strongly and so differently about two of our nation's greatest African American athletes.

I have accompanied Muhammad Ali and his wife, Lonnie, on many public occasions. We are blessed to call them friends. They have gone from city to city to talk about racial healing. In most cases, Lonnie talks to the students assembled at each school. Gyms are packed with young people from elementary school through high school. They have all been made to understand what Ali had done to make their principals and teachers so excited that Ali could actually be coming to *their* school.

I was informed that students were drilled about his artistic boxing career, his stand against the Vietnam War, and his work for the civil rights of African-Americans. Each time Muhammad Ali entered a gym, pandemonium broke out. Children who didn't remember their history lessons were simply swept away by the stature and charisma of this man. Though slowed by Parkinson's syndrome, his mind is as sharp as ever.

The energy and enthusiasm were greater than anything most students or their teachers had ever experienced before. The students of one school had gifts for Ali, and one fifth grader had written a poem that the student was ''the greatest and not Ali.'' Ali asked the student to approach him and communicated through an ''Ali Shuffle''—an eloquent means of expression without words.

My eleven-year-old daughter Emily met Ali when she was a very shy five-year-old. She was standing with my wife, Ann, when Ali caught her eye from the other side of a table. This girl, who takes fifteen to twenty minutes to warm up to friends she hasn't seen for a week, flew across the room and jumped into his open arms. That was 1995.

Emily is still a little shy. She, Ann, and I went to dinner with the Ali family on the second night of his stay in Boston in 1997. We joined Muhammad, Lonnie, their son Assad, noted photographer Howard Bingham, and Henry Louis Gates of Harvard's Afro-American Studies Department. We were guests of the LoConte family at the great Italian eatery in Boston's North End, know simply as LoConte's.

The dinner took place early in the evening on what happened to be the night of President Clinton's State of the Union Address, though the evening was so special that no one thought of trying to hear the president. Then a waiter came to our table and informed us that the jury was coming back with the O. J. Simpson verdict in the civil case. Professor Gates asked if there was a television on which we could watch the verdict. An old black and white set was promptly brought to the table.

I observed Ali as he watched intently, but giving no clue as to what he hoped for as a verdict. Everything went against O. J. this time. We turned the television off and resumed the conversations around the table. Ali drew a picture for Emily. She made him a valentine. Emily and Assad sent notes to each other. It was one of those nights that I know I will always remember.

I listened to the news on the way home. Commentators speculated that this new verdict would further divide the races in America, just as they had described the impact of the verdict in the criminal case. I wondered how commentators could remain so blind to the enormity of the racial divide in America, with or without the O. J. Simpson case.

I thought long and hard that night about Ali and O. J. These two African American men had incredible athletic careers. O.J. seemed to transcend race and was one of the first black athletes to be a very successful endorser of product, to make it in Hollywood, and as a network broadcaster. Ali stood up as a proud black man, emphasizing boldly that race does matter as no other athlete has so forcefully before or since.

It seems ironic that one of these men now roams free but lives in disgrace in the eyes of the majority of Americans, accused of dividing the races. The other, who once was accused of dividing the races because he spoke out as a black American, now brings people of all racial groups together by preaching ''healing'' and appealing to everyone, irrespective of their race, religion, or age.

Nearly four decades after he won his Olympic gold medal, Muhammad Ali is still ''the greatest.'' Their respective stories show how the American public can come to truly embrace a hero of any race because he stands by his principles.

Graduating Just Right: The Clifford Moller Story

Each spring generates thousands of heart-warming stories as thousands of college students graduate. One in particular stands out—a journey started by Clifford Moller in 1967 that was finally completed thirty-three years later when Moller was awarded his bachelor's degree from the University of Nebraska, 1500 miles from his Harlem home. I was lucky enough to be, at least in a small way, involved in the story.

I was part of a program on the black athlete that HBO Sports hosted in New York City in the mid-1990s. Among the speakers were Reverend Jesse Jackson, Spike Lee, and myself. At a reception for the large audience before the program, I was introduced to an African American man in his mid-forties. Clifford Moller was in the real estate business in New York. Dressed for success, he was eloquently discussing many of the issues that would be addressed during the program. When he mentioned how difficult it was for a black athlete from a place like Harlem to attend a predominantly white college, I was sure he was talking from his own experience.

When I asked him where he went to college, Clifford laid out his story for me. His namesake father was a serious gambler who lived the high life in Harlem clubs in the 1980s. He finally left his wife, Bernice, and young Clifford to fend for themselves. As a child, basketball was his escape and his identity.

Clifford, who was a lightning-fast guard, was a player to watch in a city full of basketball legends. He was an outstanding guard for William Howard Taft High School in the Bronx. By his senior year, he was devoted entirely to basketball. He was sure that he would play in college, and might even make it to the NBA. It was during that year that his father was shot and killed while he was shooting dice. Clifford knew then that he would not allow himself to fail in life as his own father had.

When Glen Potter, the coach at the University of Nebraska, offered him a scholarship, Clifford was ready to leave New York, but was unprepared for what he found when he got to Lincoln, Nebraska in the fall of 1967. He had left an almost all-black world in Harlem and had arrived in an almost all-white world in Lincoln.

"Even basketball couldn't keep me going. I felt so isolated and could not study. I missed New York too much. I was lost and came home." Clifford left the university in his first year. But the drive to succeed kept him off the street and he worked hard to support himself. Before becoming a successful real estate agent, he drove a cab and worked in a school-based anti-drug program. He rented a comfortable apartment, got married, and had a son also named Clifford. When he and his wife separated, he became even closer to the boy. He drove him to school every day and took a second job to pay for the private school's tuition.

"My son is a great student. The only thing missing is that I can't show him my degree. I want to get it." Clifford was aware that I was the Director of the National Consortium for Academics and Sport, which has a degree completion program, based at more than 190 colleges and universities. Nebraska was one of the schools and Clifford had come to the HBO event to tell me that he was going back to Nebraska to get his degree. I was happy, but also knew how hard that would be for someone his age used to the lifestyle of a successful businessman. I never heard from Clifford again.

In the winter of 1998 I was the keynote speaker for a meeting of the National Association of Athletic Academic Advisors in Lincoln. I have many friends in the Athletics Department and in the university's central administration. Therefore, I was surprised when an African American man who I did not recognize got up to introduce me—"I met Richard Lapchick at an HBO program in New York a few years ago." Suddenly I realized it was Clifford. Looking me in the eye, he went on, "Meeting Dr. Lapchick that night helped get me back to Nebraska. I am here with my son, Clifford. I will graduate in the spring of 2000."

I looked over at his son, who was beaming. I had tears in my eyes.

Clifford called me in May of 2000. "I want you to know that I graduated. My son was there. So was my Mom. I felt so proud because I knew Clifford junior now had a Dad who had a college degree. I love to learn and I want to go to law school here. I was admitted to graduate school, but not to the law school. Maybe I will go to grad school for a year and reapply for the law school next year." He continued, "The only thing I hate about this is that my son is in New York while I am here. I miss him so much. All of this is for him. He loves to learn and so do I. When I move back to New York, I want to be a dealmaker and developer of major real estate deals. Having the law degree will help that. I wish I didn't have to wait a year to start.''

I got a card from Clifford a month later. It read, ''Shortly after talking with you I received a telephone call from the Dean of Admissions of the University of Nebraska Law School. She informed me that my file had been reopened and the admissions committee granted me admission to the Law School. All I could do was thank God.'' At this time, Clifford is a full-time law student at Nebraska. The Consortium has had more than 19,000 former student-athletes come back to their campuses, but when you see the results up close, it takes on another meaning. It is never too late to complete a dream.

Changing Klan Country: The Story of LaGrange, Georgia

I was doing a favor for some very good friends driving to the airport at 4:45 a.m. to fly to LaGrange, Georgia for a ''civic luncheon.'' Driving back from the airport that night, I knew that they had done a favor for me.

Logan Airport had been closed almost all day the day before by a storm that pushed Boston past its all-time snowfall record. I hadn't counted on the twenty minutes it took to scrape the ice off the car and I barely made the 6:15 a.m. flight. Skimming along on the icy roads, I felt I should be going to the office to catch up. But I wanted to do this for Ron Davis and Bobby Reardon, two friends.

The luncheon was being held to commemorate the ''I Train in LaGrange'' athletic facility that had grown out of discussions nearly a decade ago between Davis, Reardon, and Andrew Young, the former Ambassador to the United Nations. If Atlanta was awarded the 1996 Summer Olympic Games, then these three men were committed to trying to establish a unique training facility. It would be for athletes from developing nations, especially African athletes, to train somewhere in the United States.

Ron Davis, an Olympian from Harlem, knew both the power of dreams and the sting of racism after he sympathized with other black athletes in the now-celebrated 1968 protest in Mexico City.

At first forced to coach track in various African nations, he learned to love doing it. But bringing some of those athletes to train in America and coming home for good would be special. He wanted to be near his elderly mother and father.

Bobby Reardon, is a white, prosperous Georgia native who helped bring the Summer Olympics to Atlanta. Bobby had a mother in LaGrange. I can't think of any other reason why the Center is there. LaGrange is about sixty-five miles south of Atlanta, a small city with a population of 26,000 people. About 60 percent of the residents are white; the rest are black. LaGrange was known as an unsafe stopping point for civil rights workers in the 1960s. Some of the black leaders at the luncheon told me that they would not have gone to LaGrange during their youth.

Before Andrew Young got up to begin his presentation, I realized I was in the middle of a social transformation. So did he. Every community near Atlanta wanted a part of the global buzz that surrounded the Olympics, including LaGrange, but it was considered too far from Atlanta to be an official venue. Instead, it accepted this seemingly strange role of welcoming mainly African athletes to the United States. This was a community where not long ago it was not easy for blacks and whites to appear together in public.

Two years and fifty athletes from fifteen countries later, the day had come to show America what had happened. I sat next to Ambassador Young on the head table, gazing out in wonderment at what we saw. There were about eight hundred people at the luncheon, including Olympic celebrities who collectively had won some eighteen medals at the 1996 Olympics and five athletes from the 1968 team, including Bob Beamon who demolished the world record in the long jump. No one mentioned the symbolism. It gently settled on the audience. These were the risk-taking athletic troops who stood up for what was right thirty years earlier. I can only imagine what the attitudes of whites in LaGrange would have been toward them in 1968. Now the whites in the audience joined fellow black residents in a tumultuous standing ovation.

By the day's end it was the people of LaGrange who were the celebrities. More than one hundred local school children marched to Olympic anthems while carrying the flags of nations from every corner of the globe. A high-school choir belted out the *Star Spangled Banner*. The locals didn't need this luncheon to know what had happened in this town. The fanfare was for outsiders from as far away as Boston and a close by as Atlanta.

It was a time when children were growing up with hate implanted in their hearts. It was a time when the global community seemed more fractured than ever. Peaceful nations became killing field as neighbors fought neighbors. But in LaGrange, residents opened their community and their homes to strangers.

Andrew Young quoted an old religious saying about the spirit of God settling in to transform a people. He said he felt it there in LaGrange. I have frequently talked with audiences about the only three totally integrated events I had ever attended where I knew that people wanted, even needed, to be together. The first was when Nelson Mandela spoke on the banks of the Charles River in Boston; the second was Arthur Ashe's funeral; and the third was Reggie Lewis' funeral. After the luncheon, I told Bobby and Ron that I would be adding a fourth.

As people filtered out, a Dr. Nye approached Ron. "God bless you, Ron. I have been in LaGrange for twenty-two years and I never thought I would see this day. It is a new community where love can flourish."

I remembered Jackie Robinson and knew that he must have been watching part of his dream for sport come true in LaGrange, transformed from a segregated town to a community embracing all people irrespective of race or nationality.

Hate and Redemption: John Rocker and Hurricane Carter

I would love to see John Rocker and Hurricane Carter in a room together where the discussion focused on diversity. That may seem like a strange combination, but the chasm between Rocker's hate and Carter's heart may reveal to them and to others in American sport some answers to the problem of racism.

Anger management is a hot topic and professional psychological counseling seems to be the primary consequence for professional athletes who commit violent acts. In cases of violence against others, counseling is certainly an approach worth pursuing as long as the athlete knows that serious consequences may also be part of the punishment.

Many writers interpreted Major League Baseball's decision to have Atlanta Braves' pitcher John Rocker undergo psychological testing as a sign that MLB thought Rocker's racist and homophobic remarks in a December 1999 *Sports Illustrated* interview were an indication of mental problems. I think this belated first step by Commissioner Bud Selig was intended primarily to address an underlying problem with Rocker. It seems clear from the *Sports Illustrated* article on Rocker that his problems went beyond hating "other" people. But it was Rocker's virulent hate that the sports community focused on. He went far beyond the offensive rhetoric of Al Campanis, Marge Schott, and Reggie White.

For Rocker, whose Braves were a very integrated team, his consistently racist remarks showed that increasing the number of players, coaches, and administrators of color alone was not enough. Sport needs to change attitudes. All racial groups hold stereotypes about one another. Fortunately, these attitudes don't necessarily convert into actions or overt expressions of hate. Many whites that hold stereotypical beliefs are able to change their views when confronted with a more realistic picture of African-Americans and Latinos as equals.

Diversity management training is one way of replacing stereotypes with real images that people in front offices and on teams can openly discuss in a safe environment. One of the most pernicious problems with racism in our country is the American people's unwillingness to talk frankly about it until they can no longer avoid the discussion.. Rocker made such a discussion unavoidable. Now it is time to talk.

Fear is generally the operative factor in converting hateful attitudes into courageius actions, and this is where the life of Hurricane Carter enters the equation. Hurricane Carter was an angry young person. Imprisoned for nearly two decades for a crime he did not commit, Carter was another African American man discarded by the justice system. But because he was famous, people kept looking to help him until the truth finally prevailed. Over the course of those decades, Carter had plenty of time to focus on his anger.

South African Bishop Desmond Tutu, who led the Truth and Reconciliation Commission in South Africa, speaks eloquently of the need for reconciliation and for the victim to forgive the oppressor. Carter is a perfect example.

Carter now speaks of America and whites with a sincerity that his own life experiences would seem to defy. He was amazed that he watched *Hurricane,* the film about his ordeal, with President Clinton in the White House and that he addressed the United Nations General Assembly. People want to hear from Carter not only because he was denied justice for so long, but also because he has embraced the notion of reconciliation. Like Nelson Mandela in Bishop Tutu's homeland, Carter emerged from injustice and hatred with the intent to heal both himself and his society of the wounds caused by racism.

I hope John Rocker can see that racist attitudes like his put people like Hurricane Carter in prison. I hope he can also see that attitudes of people like Carter give racists the chance for redemption.

One Man's Ripple: It Is Never Too Late

In 1998, I spoke about racism at the University of Southern Florida. While I described the attack on me for my anti-apartheid work, I watched three young college students writhing in their seats. They were scribbling something in their notebooks. At one point in my speech they simultaneously turned those notebooks toward me. The scribbling spelled out "KKK."

I did not leave that night with the memory of their hate uppermost in my mind, but with the words of an elderly man in the audience. At the end of the presentation, a large line of people formed who wished to speak with me. One man stood in the back, waiting for all the others to leave. I could see he was shaken and took him aside so that his back was to anyone left in the auditorium.

He told me that he was from a mining town in Pennsylvania and that when he was young, he would have beaten me for my beliefs. Tears flowing uncontrollably, he told me that after hearing me, he knew he would now be the one to fend off anyone who attacked me. As a young man, he no doubt could have inflicted great harm on me. As an old man, he probably couldn't have done much physically, but what he said made my heart swell with happiness and hope.

Don't ever doubt that a single person can make a difference. One person alone may not change the world but if that person can change one heart, just think of what a ripple that may have throughout humanity. One person does have the power to bring about change, to give hope. Imagine that man telling his grandchildren and perhaps even his great-grandchildren that he had been wrong for all those years when he told them hateful things about ''other'' people.

Conclusion

I started my life in the sportsworld as a starry-eyed player and fan; I then became a serious cynic about the value of sport. Now, after working more than 30 years in sport as an activist and an academic, I have gained a new perspective.

My new perspective began in 1982 when I spent two weeks in Angola with an American basketball team, experiencing some of the best that sport has to offer. The basketball tour was designed to to pave the way for better diplomatic relations between the two countries after a lapse in diplomatic relations and five years of vitriol.

The American team, coached by Lou Carnesecca, was chosen from the Big East Conference. The players—eight blacks and three whites—did not know what kind of reception they would receive from the Angolans in light of the country's prevailing hostility toward America. Their concerns melted away as they walked onto the big court of the Citadella Arena in Luanda. Fifteen thousand Angolans cheered wildly for the team as it marched out behind the American flag, never before flown in Angola. It was a stirring moment for everyone. A total of 75,000 people came out to see the games, as much for their political as for their athletic importance. Our players learned about Africa and Angola, and the Angolan players learned about life in America. Both teams transmitted their eye-opening experiences to their own people through the tremendous press coverage the tour received.

This event tempered my cynical feelings about sport and reminded me what a positive force it can be. The revelation was reinforced in 1994 when I was asked by the National Olympic Committee of South Africa and the newly emerging government in South Africa to bring Project TEAMWORK to South Africa. I asked NBA Commissioner David Stern and NBA Players Association Director Charlie Grantham to help. As a result, we brought NBA players and coaches to South Africa for two consecutive years. Among the players were Patrick Ewing, Dikembe Mutombo, and Alonzo Mourning. Coaches included Wes Unseld, Lenny Wilkins, and Alvin Gentry.

Basketball was barely played by black Africans and only marginally by white Africans. In South Africa, whites played rugby and cricket, blacks played soccer, and neither played with each other. As the popularity of basketball soared since these trips, it is now a sport that black and white South Africans play together. Sport was, once again, a crucible for change.

Summary of Progress Thus Far

College sport, is finally aware of the academic problems not only of black athletes, but of all athletes. There are more black head coaches in college; positional segregation has nearly disappeared; and a quota system dictating that a certain number of whites need to be on the team is no longer widespread. Black athletes have occasionally spoken out on political issues without facing repercussions on campus and the black athlete seems to face less overt discrimination on campus (unlike regular black students).

In professional sports, progress includes increased numbers of blacks playing basketball and football (although there was a slight decline at the end of the 1990s); increased endorsement possibilities for black stars; and near parity in salaries between blacks and whites. Professional sports has also progressed to an apparent end to racial quotas for teams and a diminishing of positional segregation in football at quarterback and center and in baseball at shortstop and second and third bases. Jackie Robinson's dream of integrating the executive levels of professional sport is somewhat closer with dramatically increasing numbers of black coaches and general managers in the NBA; smaller but significant breakthroughs for black and latino managers in baseball, and the first modern-day black head coaches lead the NFL. There are also many more women and people of color in the front offices and league offices of professional sports teams as well as black minority ownership in the NBA; and better representation of blacks in the respective halls of fame.

All of this progress, it must be noted, is relative. At the college level, black athletes still graduate at significantly lower rates than whites and are overrepresented in basketball and football. They are academically and sometimes physically separated from black students; have few black mentors on campus; have absolutely unrealistic expectations of making the pros; and still have a hard fall if they neither make the pros nor get a degree. In professional sports, those in the front offices of the NFL and Major League Baseball are still predominantly white.

Changes have also emanated from contemporary social concerns. In the late 1960s, campus-wide protests provoked athletic protests under the inspiration of the likes of Harry Edwards and Jack Scott. In the 1970s, the feminist movement inspired the passage of Title IX to promote gender equity in sport. In the 1980s and 1990s, the Reverend Jesse Jackson orgainized protests against racial and gender hiring practices in sport and Native Americans protested the use of mascots and names depicting their people in derogatory ways. In the latter half of the 1990s, vigorous student protests arose against the production of athletic goods in sweatshop conditions, especially in Asia. The media, as watchdog and informer, has been a catalyst for some change.

While the racial environment in sport may be improving, it seems like it is worsening in society at large. Difficult economic times usually signal a rise in racism, and the first half of the 1990s proved to be no exception. The Center for the Study of Sport in Society and the Reebok Foundation's survey of youth attitudes toward racism showed frightening results. A majority (57 percent) of high school students had seen or heard racial confrontations with violent overtones, significantly more than had been previously believed. These incidents were not isolated to any particular area and were commonplace in high schools nationwide.

One in four students reported that they had been the target of an incident of racial or religious bias. Almost half (46 percent) of the blacks surveyed said they had been targets. When confronted with a racial incident, 47 percent of students volunteered that they would either join in (30 percent) or feel that the group being attacked deserved what it was getting (17 percent). Only one in four students would tell a school authority. On the positive side, a core of 30 percent of high school students was prepared to intervene to stop or condemn the incident.

Four in ten students reported that when they saw someone from another race or religion doing something they did not like, they were tempted to respond, ''What else can you expect from those types of people?'' Teenagers, adopting age-old insensitivities, are ready to blame victims for their problems.

By 2000, colleges and universities were the third most common site for hate crimes. More than one million bias incidents took place on American campuses.

The foremost condition for meaningful change is to recognize the need for change. Teenagers are aware that discrimination and racism are serious problems in society. America is beginning to face up to racial problems in sports. Since sport free of racism can only exist in a society free of racism, it is more realistic to suggest changes that would ease the problem of racism in sport by giving the young athlete a better understanding of, and thus more control over, his own destiny. For me, education is crucial to this process.

Increased Academic Standards in High School

Changes must come about at all levels to have the desired effects. At each level, the role of education is the key. Everything that happens to athletes after their careers end depends on what knowledge and skills they obtained while playing on the field or court. We can't realistically expect that individual and institutional racism will change quickly. Therefore, the emphasis must first be on exposing it, and second on teaching young athletes to deal with it. Preparing them for the nonathletic job market is most crucial.

The NCAA's academic standards have helped focus attention on the education of high school athletes. Academic standards for high school athletes are probably the least rigorous of all education levels. The academic future of these athletes is in serious jeopardy unless they are required to devote themselves more fully to a balance between academics and athletics.

Prior to the passage of Proposition 48 by the NCAA in 1983, fewer than 100 of 16,000 high school districts had a "C" average as the requirement for participation in extracurricular events. In Massachusetts, the home of the Center for the Study of Sport in Society, not having a "C" average as the requirement for participation in extracurricular events means that a high school basketball player can be eligible to play all four years without ever receiving a "C" in any course. My question is: What have we prepared that young person to do in life?

Coaches were the largest group opposed to implementing "no-pass, no-play" legislation. They said that ineligibility would lead to student-athletes dropping out, perhaps turning to a life of crime and drugs. Now there are ten states and hundreds of localities with such higher standards. Coaches are running 7:00 a.m. study halls. Players see them involved in the educational process for the first time. Best of all, the student-athletes themselves have met the challenge and raised their grades.

Without higher academic standards, the lack of a mental challenge feeds on and fuels lenient admissions standards in self-fulfilling prophecies of academic failure. Athletes who love the game are a captive audience. Raise their educational standards by making a "C" average a condition for playing, and raise moral standards by demanding social responsibility from student-athletes. A Sports Ethics Corps of college student-athletes can enter high schools and challenge their younger brothers and sisters to stay in school, to stay off drugs and alcohol, and to treat each other with respect, no matter what the color of their skin or their ethnic origin.

Northeastern University's Center for the Study of Sport in Society, together with AmeriCorps, launched Athletes in Service to

America in 1995. Since then, more than 400 corps members have performed 400,000 hours of community service in Boston, Buffalo, Philadelphia, Kentucky, Orlando, Tampa, Reno, and Chicago. President Clinton said "Athletics play an important role in shaping our character and values. I commend the staff and supporters of Sport in Society for their commitment to expanding the positive role of sports in our society, to curbing violence, and to promoting academic excellence through programs such as Athletes in Service to America."

Nearly 20,000 athletes have returned to finish their college degrees through institutions of higher education in the National Consortium for Academics in Sport (NCAS). Those athletes work in school outreach programs counseling young people about academic balance, drug and alcohol abuse, men's violence against women, and race relations. They also teach conflict resolution skills. As executive director of the NCAS, I am proud to say that by 2001 they had worked with more than 8 million high school and middle school students in the outreach program.

Institutions of higher education must work with high schools to raise levels of academic expectations. If increased standards force high school athletes to take their studies more seriously, they will not only help those who actually continue to play in college, but also those who aspire to do so but never make it beyond high school. An average of one out of every 3,400 male high school basketball players will be drafted by the NBA, while 1 in 5,000 female high school players will be drafted by the WNBA. For most, their athletic careers end in high school. If they don't acquire nonathletic career skills by their senior year, they almost certainly face a menial job or, worse, a place among unemployed youth.

The Student-Athlete and College

While I do not support Proposition 16, I now believe that Proposition 48 has had a positive effect. However, it attacks the problem only at the high school level and does not address the student-athlete after he or she gains admission to college. By the time most scholarship athletes begin college, more than half of the black athletes are sure that becoming part of a professional sports team is a reasonable possibility and that academics are even less important than they were in high school. Universities are obligated to ensure that every athlete obtains a real education.

Increased minimum academic standards in high school will help prepare the student-athlete in high school. But selecting a college is very difficult. How can the athlete recognize the type of coach who might want him to help his team so badly that he would bend the truth about the school?

Publishing Graduation Rates

The Student-Athlete Right to Know Act was introduced in Congress by Congressmen Tom McMillen and William Townds and Senator Bill Bradley. The legislation required that prospective student-athletes be presented with a school's graduation rates, and that the rates be sport, race, and sex specific. I had the opportunity to testify in both the House and Senate in favor of this legislation and noted that while a single total graduation rate of all the athletes on each campus would be helpful, the most helpful totals would be figures broken down by race, sex, and sport as was ultimately required by this legislation. The prospect of federal legislation in this area forced the NCAA to adopt its own legislation similar to the Student-Athlete Right to Know Act at its 1990 convention. These records have proven invaluable to high school athletes and their parents as they try to choose the right school to attend. In spite of the NCAA legislation, Congress passed a more broad Student Right to Know and Campus Security Act in 1990. It required publication of graduation rates for all students.

Just as students deserve an unbiased evaluation of a prospective college, coaches deserve a fair analysis of a potential student's academic ability. Concern with academic achievement begins even before the college admissions process. However, once a student-athlete applies for admission to a college, the coach must consult with the admissions office to see if the athlete can make it academically. If the recruit is borderline, the coach must be able to assure the student that sufficient academic assistance will be available. If the recruit is below borderline, the recruiting process should stop.

Campus Support

The 1991 NCAA Convention in Nashville proved to be a bench mark for college sport with more than 230 college presidents taking control and working cooperatively with athletic departments and conference officials. While many of the reform proposals focused on cutting costs (such as the reducing the number of athletic scholarships offered as well as reducing the number of coaches the college employs), other reform proposals were designed to help student-athletes stay on track academically. The legislation affected the Division I schools the most.

The legislation eliminated residence halls made up exclusively of athletes, allowing athletes to be integrated into the student population. Athletes can spend no more than twenty hours a week on their sport. The legislation also required that academic counseling and tutoring services be made available for all student-athletes. A sampling of athletes must be given exit interviews when leaving the institution through graduation, expulsion, or decision to transfer to another institution, to help keep the institution knowledgeable about the needs of its student-athletes. Student-athletes must fulfill more than half of their degree requirements prior to the commencement of their fourth year to remain eligible to play.

I agree with those who say that athletes deserve special treatment. Part of their enrollment is an obligation to give the school literally thousands of hours of their time during their four years of eligibility. Their time brings the school entertainment, prestige, and, frequently, handsome revenues. However, what I mean by special treatment is the assurance that athletes will get the help they need to maintain academic preparedness and not exemption from such preparedness.

The overall message has to be that the school will provide special attention to its student-athletes to ensure that they are academically prepared. In exchange for this, student-athletes will be expected to fulfill the same academic requirements as all students. Philosophically, the school must emphasize the student in student-athlete—not only their class attendance and graduation rates, but also the quality of their educational experience. Student-athletes must be encouraged to value learning, not simply eligibility.

I divide the special on-campus responsibilities of the school into two areas: creating the best possible academic environment and the best possible social environment. Several issues fall under both categories.

Freshman Eligibility

For any ordinary student, the transition from high school to college is difficult. It is more difficult for athletes, due to the time demands imposed on them. It is even more difficult for black athletes who quite possibly have arrived in a culturally different atmosphere, with less-developed academic skills, the result of star treatment and institutional academic neglect in high school.

One way to reduce the controversy surrounding Proposition 16 over the use of standardized tests, would be to eliminate freshman eligibility altogether so that all athletes can make a better transition to the academic demands of college. Given the proper guidance and adequate time to grow into their new environments, athletes would begin the second year on a more equal footing with other students. This proposal is not meant to suggest a return to freshman basketball, football, and baseball teams. The freshmen would have no athletic obligations in their first year although they would receive full financial support. This would increase the university's costs since it would be forced to carry more scholarship athletes on the varsity. However, athletes could be given an additional year of eligibility if they would be able to graduate in that year. This would reduce the financial burden.

The elimination of freshman eligibility would also end the practice known as redshirting, in which coaches decide that a student-athlete is not officially on the team and thus gains a year of eligibility after his or her fourth year in school. The goal of all athletes and athletic administrations should be identical: every student should try to graduate in four years and no one should be deliberately delayed because of sports. Making freshmen ineligible would go a long way to taking care of this problem.

University Hiring Practices

More people of color should be hired as coaches, assistant coaches, sports administrators, and academic advisors. As demonstrated, too little has been done to increase these numbers beyond a handful of head coaches and a few more assistant coaches.

For that to happen, more people of color must become college presidents and athletic directors at schools that have major sports programs. Head coaches of color need to be hired in all sports, not just sports in which blacks compete most (basketball, football, and track and field). Second, athletic departments should begin each academic year with an in-depth seminar for all athletes and coaches. Experts and former athletes should be brought in to discuss the range of issues that today's student-athletes face, including keeping up with their studies, staying away from drugs, and facing the reality of future careers choices: professional athlete or ordinary citizen. In terms of race, such sessions should face all the issues honestly and directly. Black former athletes should meet with players and coaches. These discussions should deal with all racial issues, both related and unrelated to sports.

The Transfer Rule

The transfer rule should be eliminated. As the rule stands today, very few athletes consider transferring to another school because they would have to sit out from sports competition for one year. This rule unfairly punishes athletes who wish to transfer to other colleges because they find themselves in uncomfortable social environments or faced with a coaching staff they can't deal with adequately and want to transfer to other colleges. Under the present system, the athlete who leaves pays a high price in terms of competition. While the average college student can and does transfer easily, the athlete is trapped. To be at all fair to the athlete and his future, the transfer rule should go.

The Academic Environment

Certainly not all athletes need help. However, athletic scholarship recipients who are defined as being ''at risk'' academically should be required to attend orientation programs, including academic counseling, evaluation of the student-athlete's educational needs, and intensive workshops at their schools prior to their freshman year. These workshops should deal with study skills, reading and writing skills, the use of the library, and basic computer skills. A year-round freshman adjustment program should be available for all freshman student-athletes.

Academic support services must be made available, including academic advising, tutors, and counseling. These services should work toward integrating student-athletes into the academic life of the university rather than furthering their isolation as a subculture outside the mainstream of the university. Such an integrated system of services should encompass both the resources available to all students and a set of services based in the athletic department designed to supplement those resources. Better career counseling must be offered so that student-athletes take majors that will prepare them for the job market.

The coach should be part of the student-athlete's academic life. If problems develop, such as waning class attendance, the coach has the most powerful tool—the suspension of game participation. The coach should be in regular contact with the school's academic advisors in monitoring the scholarship athlete's academic progress. Reasonable progress should be maintained—progress beyond NCAA requirements—so that student-athletes will be as close as possible to graduation when their eligibility expires.

The question of financial support of athletes in general and black athletes in particular is a major one. Any serious reforms for athletic financial support must guarantee athletes the chance to complete their education within a reasonable period. They should include a minimum five-year guarantee, with extensions available if academic problems developed directly as a consequence of sports participation. Thus, the athlete would be certain that, if he is sufficiently motivated, additional tuition and fees would never stand in the way of obtaining a degree.

Additionally, athletes who attend a school on scholarship but fail to obtain their degree within their eligibility period may need help. This is especially true in the revenue sports where academic problems are magnified. Athletes should be able to return to complete their education at the expense of the university in exchange for community service. Such a policy should only apply to athletes who have already left school, so as not to be a disincentive for current student-athletes needing to complete their education as soon as possible.

This, of course, raises the question of whether or not athletes are motivated academically or are simply using college as a training ground for a professional sports career. The results of the programs of the National Consortium for Academics and Sport, initiated by Northeastern University's Center for the Study of Sport in Society in 1985, go a long way toward proving that athletes do want an education. Between 1985 and 2001, at the 214 institutions in the Consortium, more than 12,400 college athletes who didn't make the pros and had lost eligibility either returned to school or continued on aid; 7,757of these returnees graduated. Another 7,600 current professional athletes and 171 Olympians returned to college, either by paying their own way or at the expense of teams or the U.S. Olympic Foundation.

These athletes returned to campus without the glory of their sports careers and under much more difficult circumstances. They obviously wanted an education and were looking for the support and self-confidence to obtain it. The fact that 214 colleges paid the tuition and fees for 12,400 athletes, at an estimated cost of $147 million and without the students performing in the arena, showed the institutions' commitment to providing their former student-athletes with a sound education.

The NCAA has also established its own degree completion program offering aid in a sixth year. As of 2000, approximately 1,100 former student-athletes have been helped by this program.

The Social Environment

The student-athlete needs better representation on campus. A regular cast of individuals meets on campuses around the country to discuss the plight of the student-athlete in general, or the black student-athlete in particular. Of the two hundred or so programs I have attended since the Center opened in 1984, less than ten had student-athlete participation. The establishment of campus-by-campus student-athlete advisory councils has been an important initiative.

One of the most poignant moments I have ever experienced took place on the campus of Loyola Marymount University in February 1990. I was the keynote speaker on the issue of ''Ethics in College Sport.'' Members of Loyola's highly regarded basketball team shared the platform. After I gave a presentation about the problems in college sport, a student asked, ''Who is to blame?'' This question is always asked, and I usually sense that the questioner is looking for a quick answer like ''the coach'' or ''the athletic director.'' I try to explain the root and development of the problem, going all the way back to the childhood home where parents go to games, but not to parent-teacher conferences, or talk about their son's jump shot, but not about his grades.

Mark Armstrong, a graduate and former Loyola basketball player who was then working for the university, shared the platform with me. He stood up, gently looked at the student, and said, ''You're to blame. The only thing you ever asked me about was how I played the last game or what I thought about the next game. You never asked me about the economy or events in Eastern Europe or South Africa. To you, I was just a basketball player.'' Mark stunned the students in the audience with what struck them as a profound thought. It was profound, but I know from speaking to athletes in our degree completion program that what Mark said should have been obvious—and would have been if student-athletes were given a more direct voice on campus. They should be counted among the valued advisors to presidents and athletic directors in the creation, administration, and evaluation of programs. The collective voice of student-athletes should be racially and sexually diverse.

In addition to student-athlete representation, coaches should be models to the community and to players in hiring practices and social relations. If black players see their coaches hiring and socializing only with whites, they will feel more isolated. All associations with exclusive social clubs and country clubs should be terminated.

Team housing, road trips, and meals should be integrated to avoid white student-athletes and black student-athletes from living separate lives. Student-athletes of color should be encouraged to join in university-wide social and academic student activities and be given the opportunity to take responsibility for their own affairs, both academic and social. The development of life skills programs has been extremely helpful.

Off campus, student-athletes should be encouraged to participate in summer corporate internship programs to gain real world experience. This would be especially valuable to the black student-athlete, who may have had less opportunity for meaningful work experience.

Finally, an ombudsman in the president's office should be appointed to objectively hear the grievances of all athletes toward their coaches or athletic administrators. Hopefully, this person would operate preventively and diminish tensions rather than increase them. The ombudsman would need the respect of key athletic department people without being so close to them as to lose objectivity.

Accreditation

So far I have listed basic proposals, realistically adoptable by universities, designed to give the student-athlete a fighting chance to succeed academically. However, being realistically adoptable by universities does not mean they will be adopted. The NCAA has not had great leverage in enforcing academic standards. The interest shown by college presidents in changing this is encouraging, but there must be a better way of inducing universities to act.

The best suggestion I have heard came from Jack Scott, the late sports activist, more than twenty years ago. He proposed that the academic progress of athletes should be part of a university's acquisition and maintenance of accreditation. With the institution's overall academic integrity on the line, the university or college would have no choice but to establish the necessary programs that would ultimately give all athletes, including athletes of color, the chance to obtain a useful education off the playing field. When their sports careers end, athletes would be more prepared to control their fates in the job market. In turn, this would help diminish the effects of racism.

The fact that the original work of the Knight Commission cited accreditation as one of its main pillars for reform should give this proposal additional credibility. The NCAA's Certification Program, which requires institutional standards for NCAA certification, is similar to accreditation but does not have the same institution-wide clout.

One final and very important point: athletic departments should require their student-athletes to give something back to young people by participating in educational outreach programs in area schools. This will help prepare future generations of student-athletes and reinforce educational values in the athletes involved in outreach. It will also put the athletes in touch with racially diverse groups of people.

Project TEAMWORK

In 1978, I was a victim of racial violence. It was a time when police and others said "these things don't happen anymore." I discovered that "these things" had never stopped happening. Other victims of assault taught me not to use anger as a flash point, but to try to heal things. Backed by a $750,000, three-year grant from the Reebok Foundation, the Center for the Study of Sport in Society created Project TEAMWORK. It is the Center's most ambitious undertaking and I see in it our greatest hope to use a multiracial group of athletes to reach all children—black, white, Asian, Latino, Native American, boy and girl, athlete and non-athlete.

I know that athletes can reach children because they have been the basis of the Center's School Outreach Program. In 1984 the

Center had no money, no athletes, and nothing but hope when Scott Black, a local business leader and head of Delphi Management, stepped forward out of concern for the future of the nation's children, especially children of color. Since 1984, Scott has allowed the Center to grow by donating $1 million to grow the outreach program; by 2000 the program had reached more than 500,000 Boston-area young people with messages about academic balance, drug abuse, teenage pregnancy, conflict resolution, and the prevention of men's violence against women. All our survey instruments and the responses from students, teachers, and parents convinced us that athletes do make a difference with young people. That is why we decided to launch a direct campaign on the pernicious problems of racial discrimination with a similar model.

The Northeastern University/Reebok Foundation survey referred to earlier shows that children learn to hate and that racial and religious violence and harassment among young people are the rule rather than the exception. The wounds in our society are very deep indeed. Yet the survey shows that youths have an underlying goodness and sensitivity. They are aware of discrimination; while nearly half might join in attacks or bear silent witness, half would work to stop attacks.

Young people need role models, and the survey shows that athletes are clearly among the role models most often cited by young people. Project TEAMWORK is designed to enable teams of athletes to help young people convert what they feel into what they can do, to contemplate contribution and not destruction, to shed a sense of helplessness for one of empowerment. The team was made up of two blacks, two whites, and one Latino, and included well-known athetes like Luis Tiant, a Major League Baseball star for nineteen years; Norm Van Lier, four-time NBA All-Star during his ten-year NBA career; Robert Weathers, whose runs helped the Patriots make it to the 1986 Super Bowl; and Holly Metcalf, world champion and gold medal winner in rowing in the 1984 Olympics. Keith Lee, a six-year NFL veteran, was the team's captain. The Center originally thought the athletes had to be famous. However, we soon realized that even high school student-athletes can have a positive impact on middle-school-age children.

Integration was originally no more welcome in professional

sports than it was in neighborhoods in Boston. By working together on teams, athletes learned the principles of TEAMWORK. By becoming interdependent instead of exclusionary, athletes of different racial groups learned to respect one another, learned that they shared the same values and hopes for their families, and learned that they actually enjoyed living and working together.

Racial harmony is the message that the Center's group of athletes brings into schools. When my father was coach of the Knicks, he brought Nat "Sweetwater" Clifton to the Knicks to help break the color barrier in the NBA. As one of the NBA's first black players, Clifton, like Chuck Cooper with the Celtics, became a master teacher of race relations for his teammates. Bob Douglas, the owner of the Rens, was my father's master teacher. Now the Center's team of athletes is a master teacher for children. Young people must understand the principles of TEAMWORK and incorporate them into their daily lives if they want to improve racial and ethnic sensitivity.

TEAMWORK is a national and international program. Northeastern University's President Emeritus, Jack Curry, called upon his fellow presidents at the National Consortium for Academics and Sport to join us in spreading the TEAMWORK message in their regions. Their response was overwhelmingly positive. TEAMWORK then sought cosponsors from the worlds of education, sport, and civil rights. The list includes a variety of supporters from the NAACP to the NCAA.

In Boston, TEAMWORK has created a living legacy in many schools called the Human Rights Squad. Modeled on the highly successful group Students Against Drunk Driving (SADD), the Squads meet monthly with the following purposes: to learn more about civil and human rights issues, to build group respect, to work toward improved racial and ethnic relations in the schools, and, most importantly, to create a core of activists in the schools and in their surrounding communities. The Northeastern University/Reebok Foundation survey showed that students would be willing to help in adult literacy programs, work with the homeless, join programs to help disadvantaged young people and their families, and participate in voter registration campaigns. These are the sorts of activities on which the Human Rights Squads focus. Each squad agrees to manage five projects per year.

The hope I have for TEAMWORK springs from several sources. First, from the lessons I learned from my father, especially about how competing with the Rens in segregated cities showed that some people accepted integrated sports before other forms of integration. This showed me the positive powers of sports and teamwork. My own limited playing career reinforced this lesson, as many of my earliest black friends were athletes.

Second, when we hired public opinion analyst Lou Harris to evaluate TEAMWORK in 1993, he called it "America's most successful violence prevention program." It won the Peter Drucker Foundation Award in 1994 for being the nation's most innovative program in the social sector. In 1995 the Clinton Adminsitration named it a national model for conflict resolution. When the Harris Research Group reassessed it in May 2000, the results were even better than had been reported in their 1993 survey.

A related source of hope comes from having worked in Norfolk, Virginia, in the 1970s. Norfolk was a major Navy port and I became familiar with a series of diversity training programs that Naval personnel had to attend under the direction of Admiral Elmo "Bud" Zumwalt. In discussions with participants I saw three different reactions. The hostility of racist whites remained unchanged. Those whites who had little contact with or knowledge of people of color, but did not bear hostility toward them, were the most affected. They began to understand the origins of racial stereotypes and to grapple with them. Blacks saw clearly what they were up against with the racists in the group, but also saw hope with the other whites. Most importantly, they clearly comprehended where they stood in a primarily white institution and gained knowledge about what they had to do to successfully cope with the obstacles they would face. I believe the same type of program can help students in high schools, where so much hate has built up.

The Center and the National Consortium partnered to create the Teamwork Leadership Institute (TLI), which has provided diversity management training for more than sixty college athletic departments, the entire National Basketball Association league office, and all of Major League Soccer, including the players. In the 1970s the Navy viewed diversity training as a moral imperative. Those who contract with the TLI in the new millennium view it as a business imperative. Business leaders finally recognize that they cannot grow their businesses without successfully managing a diverse workforce and serving a diverse customer base.

In sport or in society, no rational person wants to be thought of as a racist. My own experience with the police and their accusations is a modest example. I have tried to show how irrational the arguments of the police and medical examiner were in that instance as representative of similar instances that occur daily. Regardless, the local press ran with their point of view and I believe that the vast majority of white people from the area still believed the press when I left. Isn't that more comfortable than thinking that violence can be directed at a college professor, even an outspoken one? Or that South Africa was involved in so small a matter?

The nation must recognize that in some substantive ways blacks are actually worse off in society today than they were forty years ago. In the 1960s it took blood and death to wake America up to effectively challenging racism. It took the courage of Tommie Smith and John Carlos in the 1968 Mexico City Olympics to force the United States to examine racism in sport. Without such acts of resistance and rebellion, apathy is easy.

Racial violence reemerged in the 1990s. Racially motivated hate acts increased throughout the 1990s as did anti-Semitic acts. All of this is exacerbated by the fact that black Americans had their expectations raised by civil rights victories in the 1960s only to have them dashed in the 1980s and 1990s. The frustration, disappointment, and anger of young blacks are reaching new peaks. This is also true of the black athlete carried by educational institutions for his or her athletic prowess until eligibility expires. It is equally true of the many black students socially promoted through American public schools. The result is the same—a lack of learned skills forces some blacks to become part of the vast sea of unemployed youth or to take up unskilled and low-paying jobs in the secondary labor market.

Eighty years ago, my father was thought of as a ''nigger-lover'' when he and his teammates played against black teams. Fifty years ago he was considered even more of a ''nigger-lover'' when he brought Nat Clifton up to the Knicks. Forty years ago I was called a ''nigger-lover'' when I brought my black friends into our almost all-white neighborhood. For most of my adult life I have been a ''nigger-lover'' to some because of my work in the civil rights and antiapartheid movements. In his teenage years my son Joe was a ''nigger-lover'' to others who hated his father or hated him because he had so many black friends. Where will it end? Will it end?

I am frequently asked how a family man can stay in the struggle and take the risks I have been subjected to. It is precisely because I am a family man that I continue. In my fifty-six years, I have never once felt totally free. No matter how good my personal and professional life might have been, no matter what short-term accomplishments I might have achieved, I have never been and can never feel totally free myself as long as others are not. I want my children Joe, Chamy, and Emily and their children to know freedom, so I continue to join the thousands of others working for freedom.

When I joined the civil rights movement in the 1960s I was somewhat of an oddity as a white person. When I joined the antiapartheid movement in the late 1960s, I was an oddity as a white American working on an international racial issue. I worked for two and a half years for the World Conference of the United Nations Decade for Women on the issue of South African women. The woman who hired me, Rasil Basu, became a lifelong friend. When I was hired for that position, she informed me that except for my race, sex, and nationality, I was perfect for the job.

However, problems of race relations are not only problems for blacks and other minorities, women's issues aren't issues only for women, and restrictions on Africans affect people other than Africans. All such issues are ultimately human rights issues that must be solved collectively by blacks and whites, men and women, Africans and non-Africans.

What greater sign of hope, of the black community's forgiveness for all the wrongs done to them over the centuries, than the attitude of Darryl Williams, the black Boston high school football player wounded by a sniper in 1979. After the near-fatal attack that left him without the use of his arms and legs, after countless broken promises of medical and financial support after the shooting, Darryl had this to say to the *Boston Globe*, "A lot of people perceive me as a white-person hater, because my injury was at the hands of a white person. I can't fault the whole race for that because there are bad people in the white race; there are bad people in the black race as well. You don't hate a whole race of people for one other person."

I have chosen sports as the vehicle through which I can best challenge racism. This vicious form of hatred has poisoned people and artificially divided the human family for far too long. White America needs to take a profound look at itself, understand what it has allowed itself to become, and work collectively as well as individually to initiate the transformation.

What is the power of sport? In 1996 President Clinton invited the Center for the Study of Sport in Society to bring National Student-Athlete Day Giant Steps Award winners to the White House for the first time. The ceremony was to take place on April 5. Commerce Secretary Ron Brown died on April 3. All events except the Center's were canceled. I expressed our deep gratitude that President Clinton would meet us at that terrible time, just as he was leaving to fly to Oklahoma City for the first anniversary of the bombing of the A. P. Murrah Federal Building. He said to me, "Richard, I really needed this."

Even for a president facing distressing times, sports can bring good news that can lift the weight of the world. That is a powerful gift to possess, one we all share when we use it in the most noble way we can—to lift the spiritual poverty that hovers over the world's children. The noble spirit of sport can be the antidote to the loneliness and the feeling of being unwanted that so many are burdened with. Sport can give them the richness of spirit that comes with being part of a real team, being interdependent, and being able to count on a brother or sister in a time of need. The people of the world must make the right choices for their children.

A close examination of sport helps confront broader societal problems. If, however, the people of the world choose to ignore the signs around them, they may be doomed to perpetuating the current self-consuming fears of one another. Society doesn't get many second chances. This may well be its last chance. This time, promises must be kept. This time, the barriers must be smashed forever.

In 1963, I watched the televised news and, tears flowing down my cheeks, I saw the back of Nelson Mandela as he was being led away to prison. That night, I dreamt that he would not only someday be freed but that he would also lead his people as South Africa's president. On May 10, 1994, I stood on the steps of the Union Building in Pretoria, directly facing Nelson Mandela as he was sworn in as president. There as a guest along with other antiapartheid leaders as well as heads of state, I witnessed the reigns of power being passed from a racist regime to a democratically elected president. Instead of going to any of the diplomatic parties, the new president went back to Johannesburg to witness the Zambia-vs.-South Africa soccer game in recognition of the role that sports had played in ending apartheid. I sat in the box with the new president and knew at that glorious moment that anything and everything is possible, and that sports, at its most noble, can help create miracles.

Epilogue

Sports has exploded and has become big business. In too many instances, those managing sports have not been able to keep up with the speed of the changes.

Our society has also changed so that today's children are growing up in a world where too much hate flows, too many children live in fear, and those managing programs for our youth, including educational programs, are often at a loss.

I believe that many of the leaders in the business of sport want to bring about change and make this a better world for their children. This is why I have decided to accept the position of the DeVos Eminent Scholar Chair and the Director of Sports Business Management Program at the University of Central Florida. The program was endowed by RDV Sports, which is the parent company of the NBAs Orlando Magic and the WNBAs Miracle.

I believe that the University of Central Florida will make the DeVos Program into one producing graduates who will not only be caught up but also be ahead of the game of sports management. At the same time, they can develop a sense of business conscience that can effectively use the platform sports now possesses to address the needs of the community in a unique and powerful way.

After I was approached by Dean Tom Keon of the College of Business Administration, I did some research and found that there were 11 Ph.D. programs in sports management, 33 full M.A.s, and 20 M.B.A.'s with a concentration in sports management. There were 167 undergraduate schools offering a sports management major.

After meeting Tom Keon, I couldn't stop asking myself, "What could be done to make the DeVos Sports Business Management Program unique?" I have known the UCF President, John Hitt, for nearly 10 years and recognize him as a leader in higher education committed to diversity and having institutions of higher education serve the community. UCF and John Hitt remind me of Jack Curry and Richard Freeland, my Presidents at Northeastern. I knew President Hitt supports creative new ideas and programs that make a difference. The more I got to know Tom Keon, the more I realized the same about him. We had provided RDV with diversity management training services and I had witnessed their commitment to community service. I knew they would be an outstanding partner.

I got more and more excited about the potential for the program. I like to create vision and saw the opportunity for a cutting edge program that would immediately distinguish itself from the other sports management programs across the nation. First, few of the 64 graduate programs in sports management were in a school of business.

With all that has changed in past 10 years with TV, media revenue and corporate sponsorship dollars becoming the leading factors in driving the business of sports, a business school is where a sports management program should be.

Of great importance to me, I saw that the DeVos Program could deliver cutting edge, innovative and progressive programs to its students, and as a fundamental value, would be committed to its director, faculty and students providing meaningful service in the community.

I was the Director of Northeastern University's Center for the Study of Sport in Society for more than 17 years and of for the National Consortium for Academics and Sport for 16 years. I loved that work and many years ago decided that I would end my career in those two positions.

I had been offered several very interesting opportunities in professional and college sport as well as in higher education. While they were all great opportunities, I felt I could make a more meaningful contribution to society at the Center and with the Consortium. I still will be very much involved with the Center as Director Emeritus and with the Consortium as Director.

I did not accept my new position because of any lack of passion for what I had been doing. In fact, I told the UCF people that I wanted to stay involved in a significant way with both the Center and the Consortium. When they enthusiastically agreed, I accepted the position because I see the potential of the mission of the DeVos Sports Business Management Program to do great things in the years ahead so that sports business operates with a sports business conscience. And, like the successes of the Center, I believe that in 10 years most sports business management programs will be emphasizing diversity as a business imperative, leadership as a key to success, an ethical grounding as the mode of operation and the involvement of the sports organization in community service and community philanthropy as a fundamental value.

I see the program's mission as being able to develop future leaders in the world of sports who will use their knowledge and skills not only to build their businesses financially but also to use the platform of sport to improve their communities and their nation. In effect, the principles driving the Center and the Consortium will be directly applied to the graduates of masters' degree programs who will be running our sports businesses.

The program will be known as the source for a student body which is diverse in terms of race, gender and ethnicity and is prepared to work in one of America's most integrated workplaces.

Students will graduate with a set of ethical values that will emphasize both their business standards and their desire to make community service and philanthropy cornerstones of their business organization.

The curriculum will draw on the College of Business Administration's foundational and professional core courses whose content can be applied in sports as well as sports management courses. All students will be required to take courses that cover Sports Leadership, Diversity Issues in Sport, Sport and Social Issues, Sports and the Community, Ethics in Sport and Research Methods in Sport.

In the future, sports businesses will know that the DeVos Program is the one to turn to when seeking sports business leaders who possess not only an understanding of the contemporary sports world but who will also have a sports business conscience driving them in their professional careers.

A visiting scholars program will draw on the top names in the sports industry including commissioners, senior Olympic committee officials, athletes, sports agents, executives from broadcast and print media, professional and college coaches and university presidents.

The same will be true about a regular speakers series that will bring the top names in the sports industry to speak to our students about their own work.

A wide-ranging internship program will place interns not only in Central Florida with RDV Sports but also in the WNBA, NBA, NFL, MLB, MLS, NHL, NCAA, athletic departments of the top college programs, the US Olympic Committee and its national governing bodies, TV networks, major newspapers, and in the sporting goods industry.

Every student in the program would have a personal mentor who is a leader in the business of sport. The students will have their own sports business management student association that will meet regularly, advise the faculty on certain issues and also organize special community service programs.

The program will co-sponsor a major national conference with other key organizations that would become the conference for people who are concerned about not doing business as usual would come to.

I believe that my work at the Center and the Consortium have helped me to develop some unique skills that will serve me well in the creation of this singular, cutting edge, premier program at the University of Central Florida.

Why do I believe that the DeVos Program can be successful? The history of the Center and the Consortium convince me that the DeVos Program will help change the way we view and teach sports business management in the future.

Project TEAMWORK was called "America's most successful violence prevention program" by public opinion analyst Lou Harris after he evaluated the program in 1993. In 1995, the Clinton Administration declared Project TEAMWORK a model for conflict resolution. It was also honored with the 1994 Peter F. Drucker Award as the most innovative non-profit program in the social sector. A new Harris evaluation in May 2000 concluded that TEAMWORK was even more effective now than when it was originally called "America's most successful violence prevention program."

Since 1993, the MVP program has motivated more than 24,000 male and female student leaders in 72 high schools and middle schools in Massachusetts and at 70 plus colleges and universities to work together to solve problems that have been historically considered "women's issues" such as rape, battering and sexual assault. As of the year 1999–2000, there has not been a single act of a male student-athlete committing an act of violence against a female on any of those 70 plus campuses since MVP trained there. Since 1998, MVP has annually trained the New England Patriots coaches and rookies. Due to its success, the United States Marine Corps contracted with the Center for the Study of Sport in Society to provide MVP to its non-commissioned officers worldwide.

In five years, Athletes in Service to America, which combines Project TEAMWORK and MVP at five sites around the nation, has enrolled over 400 corps members and provided over 400,000 hours of community service.

AmeriCorps CEO Harris Wofford said, "Athletes in Service is a star program that needs to be spread." Eli Segal, former AmeriCorps CEO and founder, has said, "Athletes in Service to America is the best of the best of AmeriCorps programs."

Social and economic barriers prevent urban youth from participating in 85% of youth sports programs as compared to youth in suburban communities. The focus of Urban Youth Sport is to create both non-traditional and traditional sports opportunities for children in Boston while teaching life-skills to participants to help insure their success in the classroom and in life as adults. UYS has become a national model.

On the same national scale, when we started the Consortium in

1985, there were five colleges that we knew of that allowed their student-athletes to get aid for a fifth year after their eligibility had expired. It was against NCAA rules to grant a sixth year of aid.

Now almost all Division I colleges give 5th year aid. The NCAA made 6th year aid permissible if the school is in the NCAS. More than 20,000 former student-athletes have continued in NCAS programs alone. The schools have put up more than $147 million in tuition support. The NCAA started its own degree completion program which has assisted another 1,500 students to complete their education.

When we started there were two colleges that we knew of that had their student-athletes doing community service. We started that very idea through the NCAS. Now almost every college in the land has some form of community service. More than 8.1 million young people have been reached and have received 8.3 million hours of service in NCAS member programs.

As college and high school sport became more about business and entertainment, the student-athlete was becoming more and more of a commodity and simply an athlete. The media regularly said the term "student-athlete" was an oxymoron. We started National Student-Athlete Day in April of 1987 to counter this trend with 30 events around the country. In April 2001, 311,000 high school student-athletes were acknowledged for academic achievement and community involvement! The NCAA and its high school equivalent, the National Federation of State High School Associations, now cosponsor NSAD.

Not one US college had done diversity training in athletics before we brought our Teamwork Leadership Institute to the University of Maryland in 1990. Now we have done it on 75 plus campuses and the NCAA offers diversity training as part of its outreach programs.

No one was assessing how athletic departments fit in with the overall mission of the university until the College Student-Athlete Project did that with 23 campuses in three years under a United States Department of Education grant. Shortly after the launch of the CSAP, the NCAA announced its certification program which has proven so valuable to our campuses over the last decade.

No sports organization banned athletes involved in violence

against a woman until the Center formed such a policy adopted by the NCAS in 1997.

Northeastern University put together the first group of colleges that took a stand against sweat-shop labor, which became the vanguard among colleges pressuring companies like NIKE to stop such sweat-shop practices.The Racial and Gender Report Card is, of course, unique. The disparities it documented and publicized has led to many leagues, teams and athletic departments embracing diversity management training in response while making their hiring practices more inclusive.

I am so proud to have worked with so many great leaders at the Center and the Consortium for 17 years. I will still be part of both organizations in addition to my new role with the DeVos Program.

These experiences leave me with no doubt that I have no doubt that we can create a nationally and internationally acclaimed Sports Business Management Program in the College of Business Administration at the University of Central Florida. I am convinced that it will attract the nation's top students and produce our nation's new leaders in sports management. It is a challenge that I have accepted and look forward to with great anticipation.

175 04/05 42
43059
BUI